Jordan's Journey

barn shoot, Sep 2011

JORDAN's JOURNEY
an ILLUSTRATED history
of my family ancestry

by Jordan M. Scoggins

bd
nyc

this book is dedicated
to all those who came before me,
both living and dead

and

to my mother
your love for the family tree
built a bridge
and saved our own family

bd
nyc

a luke kurtis/bd-studios.com production
Published by bd-studios.com in New York City
Heirloom Edition (original hardcover), 2012
This paperback edition, 2017

Copyright © 2012 by Jordan M. Scoggins
Some Rights Reserved
Jordan's Journey is licensed under a
Creative Commons Attribution-NonCommercial-
ShareAlike 3.0 Unported License
http://creativecommons.org/licenses/by-nc-sa/3.0/

Design by luke kurtis

ISBN 978-0-6155817-9-8 (hardcover, full color)
ISBN 978-0-9890266-9-7 (paperback, black & white)

"Trans" (and the accompanying map) was contributed
by Emily Clement Payne.

"Caney Fork" was previously published as "Caney Fork
Township in the 19th Century: Pioneers from Georgia
and Beyond Settle the Arkansas Wilderness" in *The
Gems of Pike County* and co-written with Joyce Wood

barn, Sep 2011

JORDAN's JOURNEY
CONTENTS

PREFACE 7 • ACKNOWLEDGEMENTS 9 • PROLOGUE 11

POPE
Pope Pedigree 16 • William, Henry, and John Pope 18 • Micajah Pope 20 • Micajah Felton Pope 26 • Villanow 32 • Goodson and Visinand/Whisenant families 36 • Benjamin Hill Pope 43 • Clement, Love, and Robbs families (and Shahan too) 58 • Trans 69 • Mary Evelyn Pope 73

JORDAN
Jordan Generations 86 • William Jordan 88 • Burrell Jordan 90 • James William Jordan 92 • William Brownlow Jordan 94 • Anderson family 100 • Earl Felix Jordan 104

SCOGGINS
Scoggins Saga 125 • Alexander and Gresham Scoggins 126 • Scoggins Soldiers 128 • William Delaney Scoggins 130 • James Harvey Scoggins 134 • Green Bush 139 • Chapman and Lawrence families (and Grigsby, Richardson, Ramsey, and Maloney too) 142 • Lawrence Chapman Scoggins 150 • Rambo and Peck families 156 • Subligna 171 • Harold Wallace Scoggins 175

HOLCOMB
Holcomb Heritage 188 • William Holcomb 190 • Francis Marion Holcomb 192 • Caney Fork 198 • William Jackson Holcomb 202 • Zenas Eugene Holcomb 206 • Hawkins, Ward, Keown, and Cavender families (and Puryear, Hunt, Clements, and Park too) 213 • Ethel Dorthelia Holcomb 228

EPILOGUE 235 • BIBLIOGRAPHY 236 • INDEX 238

more at bd-studios.com/journey

Grandpa, tell me 'bout the good old days
Sometimes it feels like this world's gone crazy
And Grandpa, take me back to yesterday
When the line between right and wrong didn't seem so hazy

    —from "Grandpa (Tell Me 'bout The Good Old Days)"
       by The Judds

The past is not dead. It isn't even past.

    —William Faulkner (1897-1962)

We are all connected to each other biologically, to the earth chemically and to the rest of the universe atomically.

    —Neil deGrasse Tyson (b.1958)

Human beings look separate because you see them walking about separately. But then we are so made that we can see only the present moment. If we could see the past, then of course it would look different. For there was a time when every man was part of his mother, and (earlier still) part of his father as well, and when they were part of his grandparents. If you could see humanity spread out in time, as God sees it, it would look like one single growing thing—rather like a very complicated tree. Every individual would appear connected with every other.

    —C.S. Lewis (1898-1963)

We die. That may be the meaning of life. But we do language. That may be the measure of our lives.

    —Toni Morrison (b.1931)

PREFACE

This book is my attempt to relate the epic tale that is my family history. Like the quilts my ancestors pieced together with such care, so too family history is formed from the pieces and scraps left to us. This story is a part of me. We are all connected in an intricate web so this story is part of you as well.

The cornerstone of this book is the material I have curated to illustrate the story. I have gathered many interesting stories, photos, and other information to form this book. But our history was scattered far and wide and I am certain there are tales and images that I have not yet discovered. If you have anything to contribute, please get in touch with me. I would love to hear your stories or pore through your photos. This book is not the end of the journey!

Other aspects of this book are rooted in genealogical research. While I have made every effort to document facts as thoroughly as possible, I have not searched out the original records to trace the most distant ancestors. This is partly because the time, effort, and expense required to locate this information exceeded the time frame in which I sought to publish this book. But beyond that, the primary purpose of this book is to illustrate, both visually and through stories, my family heritage. I, therefore, did not let myself get overly bogged down in the details and instead aimed to present a general overview of the most far reaching generations. The information I have presented about those earliest ancestors is intended to provide introduction and context for the more recent generations.

History is dynamic. The process of discovery means that through examination and analysis we learn more over time. It can even mean what we once thought to be true might become disproved through new evidence. Technology is changing all aspects of our lives—even genealogy and family history. But as soon as it is printed it is likely to become outdated. Inevitably errors will be found. If you find any such errors please let me know. This project is ongoing and I am always looking to further my research. I will publish any corrections to the material in this book on the *Jordan's Journey* web site at http://bd-studios.com/journey. From there you can also link to my tree on Ancestry.com if you want to get into the really nitty-gritty.

A brief word on some of the conventions used in this book: A few abbreviations are used throughout the text. b. = born, m. = married, d. = died. Additionally [I], [II], [III] are used to differentiate between people in the same family line with the same name. The numeral is not part of the actual/documented name but is added here for ease of identification. Women are generally referred to by their birth/maiden name to eliminate confusion and maintain consistency when talking about someone at different stages in her life (exceptions are made where appropriate, i.e., when I refer to work published under a married name).

Without further adieu, I invite you to curl up with this book and take a trip into the past. Pull off your shoes and feel the grass under your feet, smell the freshly plowed fields, listen to the song of the wind, and join me on *Jordan's Journey*.

With much love and light,

Jordan M. Scoggins
jordan@bd-studios.com
69 West 9th Street, 5J
New York, NY 10011, USA

self-portrait, Sep 2011

ACKNOWLEDGEMENTS

This book would not have been possible without the assistance of many different people. I would like to express my heartfelt gratitude to…

Julie Hinds Griggs, for introducing me to Ancestry.com and kindling my interest in genealogy. You set me on the path that led me to write this book.

Mom & Dad, for your endless research assistance; visits to cemeteries, courthouses, libraries, and more; the countless hours you spent scanning masses of photos and information; and for being my presence in my homeland when I could not physically be there.

My sister, Julie Scoggins Cook, for putting up with all those cemetery visits, for picking me up at the airport, and for getting me where I need to be.

Andrew Jones, for always looking over my shoulder when I need a second set of eyes.

Joel Garcia, for supporting this project and putting up with me when it's all I want to talk about.

Louis Hunt, for helping me gain access to some hard-to-find graves and for your enthusiastic encouragement of my efforts for this book. And to your mother Georgia Ward Hunt—an icon of the East Armuchee Valley—who I am certain would have been a great friend had I been given the opportunity to know her.

Evelyn Morgan Shahan, for your valiant effort at documenting your family story—if only everyone would label the back of photographs the way you did! And to your daughter, Judy Blackstock, for providing access to your archive.

Nelda Scoggin Reynolds, though I have never met you in person you are a splendid virtual research companion. Without your generous assistance the early chapters of the Scoggins section would not have been possible. You helped me sort out numerous details in the Scoggins line that surely would have taken me ten times as long to uncover alone.

For those who shared photos and stories with me: Mary Jordan Manis, Charlotte Jordan Griggs, Glynn Griggs, Dorthelia Scoggins, Frances Scoggins (who knows Elvis is King), Becky Holcomb, Joey Holcomb, Martha Delle Richardson, David & Delores Grigsby, Charles Clements, Jodie Hunt Bell, Jim Pope, Guy Pope, Robert Paul Maloney, and Joyce Wood.

An extra special thanks goes to Emily Clement Payne for going above-and-beyond.

And to everyone, known and unknown, who shares family information on Ancestry.com. There are so many things I would never know about my family without this invaluable service.

Christmas always brings a smile to my face, Dec 1985.
(Collection of Michael & Rhonda Scoggins)

PROLOGUE

At home on the farm, East Armuchee, Georgia
Christmas Eve, mid 1980's

Presents are piled under the tree with tags that tease, "Don't Open 'Til Xmas." I shake all the ones with my name more than a few times, trying to figure out what's inside. After weeks of anticipation Christmas is finally almost here.

"Jordan, start gathering all the presents to take to Grandmother's. We need to leave soon," says Mom.

I'm pleased with any excuse to rummage about beneath the tree. And it takes a while to sift through them all anyway—don't want to leave anybody's present behind.

"This one's for Julie, and this one's for me. Those stay," I say. "This one says it's for Papa Jordan... who's that Mama?"

"Papa Jordan. You know, Grannie and Papa," Mom says.

"Ok, that stays here. I'll look for the ones for Papa Julie then."

"What, Jordan?" Mom asks.

"Well you said that present is for Papa Jordan. If he has my name, then the other Papa must have Julie's name. So I'm looking for Papa Julie's presents."

Mom, Dad, and Julie laugh.

"The things kids say sometimes," Mom says to Dad. "In some weird way it just makes sense doesn't it?"

Mom takes a pen and relabels all of Papa's presents, "To: Papa Julie."

POPE

GOODSON • WHISENANT
CLEMENT • LOVE • ROBBS

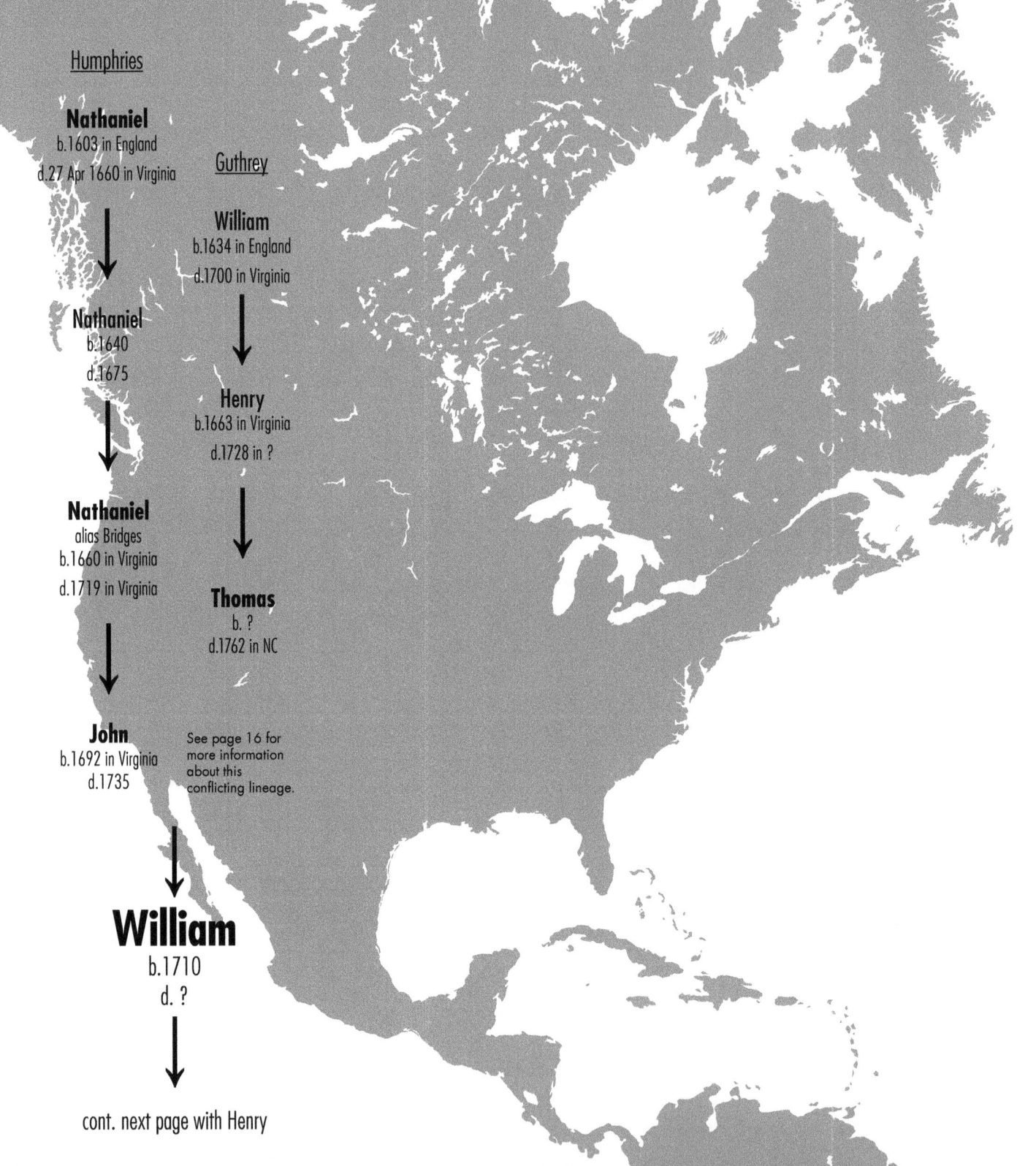

Henry
b.1747 in North Carolina
d.1810 in North Carolina

John
b.30 Dec 1778 in North Carolina
d.1849 in Georgia

Micajah
b.21 Nov 1808 in North Carolina
d.15 Aug 1867 in Georgia

Micajah Felton
b.4 Jul 1849 in Georgia
d.5 Nov 1925 in Georgia

Benjamin
b.5 May 1883 in Georgia
d.3 May 1966 in Georgia

my grandmother Mary Pope, my mother Rhonda Jordan, and me

There is controversy over which Pope lineage is correct. I can neither confirm or deny either lineage and therefore present both options here. Either way it is safe to say the Pope family came from England in Colonial times and were involved in the formation of this country from the beginning.

Pope Pedigree
The Pope Family Origins

The Pope family has its origins—as far as I have been able to trace—in Colonial America. However, the exact line of descendancy is a bit of a mystery.

John D. Humphries published a book titled *Georgia Descendants of Nathaniel Pope of Virginia, John Humphries of South Carolina, and Allen Gay of North Carolina*. His work traces the descendants of Nathaniel Pope, who came from England to Virginia. This portion of Humphries's work is largely based on articles originally published in the *William and Mary College Quarterly Historical Magazine*. The other part of Humphries's work focused on the descendants of John Pope (b.1778) and is presumably his original research.

Many years later, William Guthrey published his much more extensive study of the Pope family, *Genealogical Chart of the Known Descendants of Micajah Pope 1808-1867, with an Outline of His American Ancestors, 1634-1844*. Where the central figure of Humphries's work is John Pope, the nexus of Guthrey's research revolves around John's son Micajah. In the introduction he writes:

> "There is considerable controversy about the correct connections in pre-Revolutionary days. I have tried to determine the correct ancestry of Micajah Pope" (1).

Guthrey continues, referencing Humphries work:

> "A booklet by the late John D. Humphries ... ties his grandfather, John Huell Pope and my great grandfather Micajah Pope [brothers] to the Nathaniel Pope line of Westmoreland Co., VA. Mr Hugh Johnson, Jr. of Wilson, NC informed Mr. John R. Malone of Homer, LA, that in his opinion Judge Humphries was in error in showing his great-grandfather, William Pope, as the son of John & Elizabeth (Pope) Pope of the Nathaniel Pope line. This William Pope appears to be the son of Thomas & Constantine Pope. Thomas was in turn the grandson of William & Marie Pope (Generation 1) of Isle of Wight Co, VA. Evidence indicates that this is correct and that Micajah Pope is a seventh generation descendant of William Pope 1st rather than an eighth generation descendant of Nathaniel Pope" (1).

Unfortunately Guthrey does not proceed to explain or cite the evidence that leads him to defer from the line as published by Humphries, nor have I uncovered such evidence (in favor of either line) myself. It is therefore with great hesitation that I adhere to neither specific lineage and have chosen to present both options here (see previous page for an illustration of how the lineages deviate).

However, it is interesting to note that *The Nance Register* (one of Guthrey's primary sources which I have also consulted directly) states William Pope (b.1634) and Nathaniel Pope (b.1603) are probably brothers. If this is true it means only the details of the generations between William and Nathan's father and William Pope (b.1710) are unclear. Either way it is safe to say the Pope family came from England in Colonial times and were involved in the formation of this country from the beginning.

Right: I reviewed the Guthrey book while researching in the Milstein Division, NYPL, Jun 2011.
(Photo by Andrew P. Jones)

Page 12: Trees cover the grave site of Micajah Pope, Villanow, GA, May 2010.
(Photo by Jordan M. Scoggins)

William Pope
b.1710 d.?
father of

Henry Pope
b.1 Jan 1747/8 d.1810
father of

John Pope
b.30 Dec 1778 d.1845

The earliest generations of the Colonial Popes were born and died in Virginia. Henry's (b.1663) location at the time of his death is unclear but it was probably in Virginia. Likewise, Thomas's (b.?) location at the time of his birth is unclear but, again, likely Virginia. However, Thomas did die in North Carolina. His son William (b.1710 in Virginia) relocated to northeast North Carolina, probably Choan County, as a young man. There he lived out his life, as did his son Henry (Guthrey; Humphries).

Henry served in the American Revolution as Ensign in the First North Carolina regiment in 1775. In 1776 he became Captain in the Eighth North Carolina Regiment. He retired from his military service on 1 Jun 1778, the war still in its infancy (Hay 44)

Henry's son John and family relocated to Georgia around 1815 (Humphries 11).

Above: Lee's Mill Road in Clayton County, GA. This spot, just minutes from the Atlanta airport, s approximately two miles south of Hapeville, matching the description in Humphries's book of the old Pope burial ground. Deed research has not yet been performed to determine the exact location.

While residing in Putnam County, John drew a lot in the 1821 Georgia Land Lottery (1821 GA Land Lottery). Humphries describes this as follows:

> "John Pope drew land lot thirteen (13) in the fourteenth (14) district of originally Henry, then DeKalb, now Fulton County, containing 202 1/2 acres, now lying within the City of Atlanta. It was on that land lot that a portion of the battle of Atlanta was fought in July, 1864" (11).

Humphries then describes how land lot 109, also within present day Atlanta, was drawn by a man named Thomas Sanford and later sold—for $100—to John's son Micajah Pope on 4 Oct 1831. Three years later on 19 May 1834, Micajah "conveyed the West half of that land to his father ... for $150, who on June 6, 1849, conveyed the same for love and affection to his youngest son, John H. Pope" (Humphries 11).

John and Susan were members of Utoy Primitive Baptist Church, Fulton County's oldest church (Humphries 12). I don't know anything about the circumstances of their deaths but presumably they were still living in this area. The location of their graves is unknown. Micajah already had moved to Villanow by the time his father died in Atlanta in 1849 (the city having been incorporated only in 1849). It was in that small community where Micajah settled that the Pope family would build its legacy as prominent Villanowian citizens. While many of Micajah Pope's descendants have spread from coast to coast, other Pope descendants remain in Villanow even to this day. It is where I was raised and the next chapters will trace those Pope generations.

This is an image of an 1821 Georgia Land Lottery grant. This specific grant is for Samuel Kollock and is not related to my family. John, however, would have received a paper like this for the land he was granted in the same lottery. (Shared on an eBay.com auction)

Micajah Pope
b.21 Nov 1808 d.15 Aug 1867
and his wife

Harriet Ann Bruce
b.10 Mar 1810 d.30 Aug 1874

Micajah and Harriet had eleven children:

1. William Henry (b.11 Sep 1828, m. 1st Lucy Ann Anderson, 2nd Margaret M. Hulsey, d.1 Feb 1883)
2. Sarah (b. abt.1830, m.Smith Haynes, d.6 May 1868)
3. Jefferson Austin (b. abt.1832, m.Elizabeth Ann Bomar, d.9 Oct 1915)
4. Daniel Walter (b. abt 1834, m. 1st Jane Worthy, 2nd Maryann Isabella Keown, d. abt 1868)
5. Henry Morris (b. 28 Dec 1835, m.Mary Elizabeth Rhea, d. 21 Dec 1902)
6. John D. (b. 17 Feb 1838, m.Grace A. Sims, d.25 Dec 1913)
7. David Huell (b.12 Mar 1840, m.Martha Hodgus, d.7 Jun 1904)
8. Susan Frances (b. abt 1842, m.George Simmons, d. abt 1867)
9. Harriet Ann (b.Mar 1845, m.Flavius Joseph Fricks, d.1 Dec 1907)
10. Mary Elizabeth (b. 30 Mar 1847, m.William Bowden Wells, d.30 May 1912)
11. Micajah Felton (b.4 Jul 1849, m. 1st Martha Ann Goodson, 2nd Josephine Love, d.5 Nov 1925)

Micajah Pope was born 21 Nov 1808 in North Carolina. In 1815 his family moved to Putnam County, GA. They resided there for several years before moving to Fulton County (originally Henry, then DeKalb), GA in 1821. Micajah married Harriet Ann Bruce about 1827. Around 1834 he and Harriet moved to Cobb County. They lived there until 1848, when they moved to Walker County and settled in Villanow. He was apparently very successful (Walker Heritage 329).

The above photo, taken from *Walker County Georgia Heritage*, is the only known photo of Micajah. I would like to find whoever has the original so I can make a digital copy for preservation. There are no known images of Harriet Ann Bruce. Micajah's brother David also married a Bruce, Harriet's sister (Humphries 19).

Micajah and Harriet's home in Villanow was located about a half mile north of Concord Church. I don't know if the house was built by Micajah himself or if it existed before he moved there in 1848. I would venture to guess he built it himself since he would have been among the early settlers of the area. After his death his son Micajah

Felton lived in the house for a time (see a possible photo on page 29) before it burned in 1929. Micajah and Harriet are buried near where the house stood. The small graveyard is still there, surrounded by an iron fence overgrown in thick brush.

Micajah was a slave owner, counted with four slaves to his name on the 1850 slave schedule. By 1860 this increased to ten slaves (Ancestry.com, 1850 Slave; 1860 Slave). He also owned and operated a store in Villanow. During the Civil War his store was only "torn up" (see letter on next page) by the Yankees. No one knows for

I visited the graves of Micajah and Harriet, my 3rd great grandparents, in May 2010. My father and I had to use a machete to cut our way through the overgrown brush. Luckily the graves are somewhat protected being surrounded by an iron fence.
(Photo by Michael Scoggins)

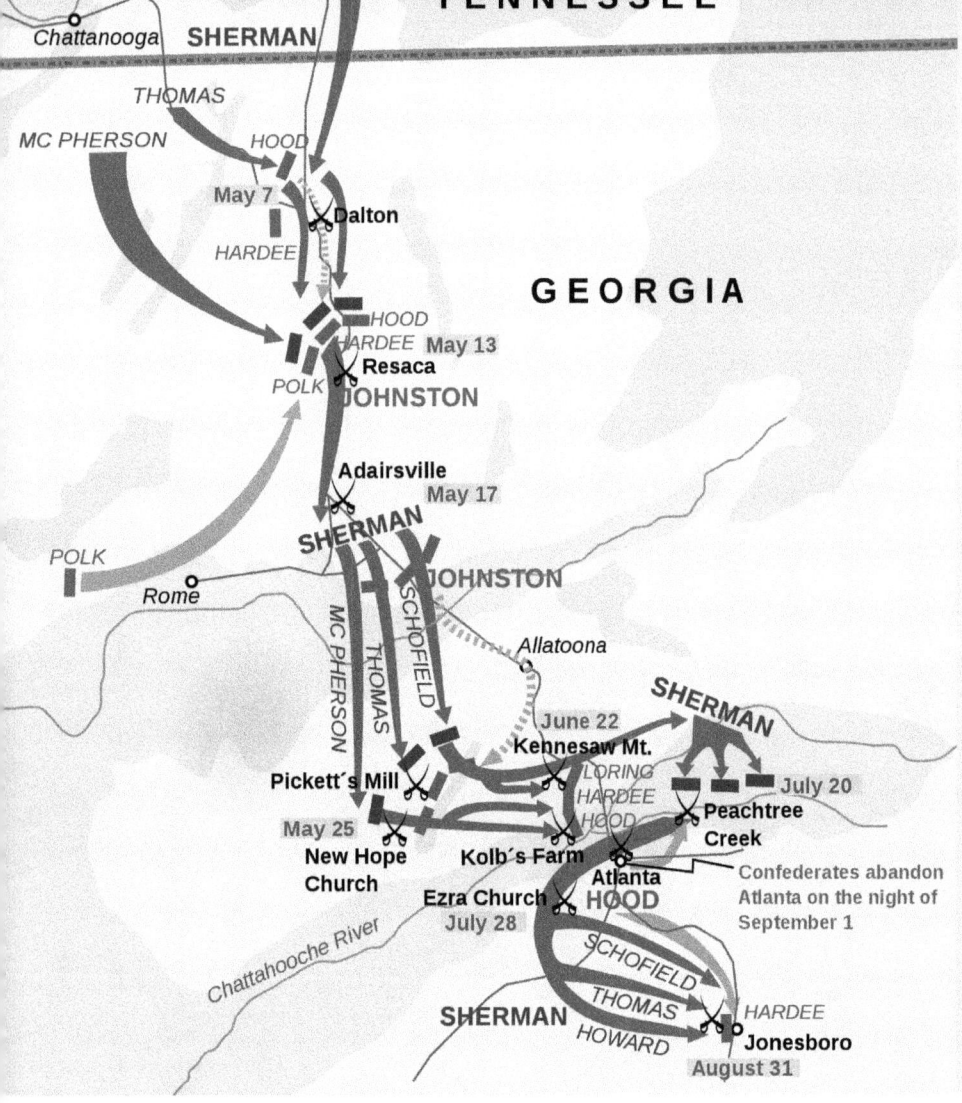

December 16, 1865

My Dear Son [Jefferson]:

Yours of the 26th Sept. has just been received. It has been delayed so long I suppose you will hardly look for any now from me but I have concluded to write you a few lines anyway. Perhaps you may get it. I suppose that the first thing you would like to know would be to know how the Yanks treated us. I cannot write you a full history of the affair. It would take too much paper to hold it to put in any one letter. It will, I suppose, satisfy you until I see you to know that they took everything we had in the way of stock but two cows and six sheep. The cows we put in the smoke house. The sheep ran off so they could not find them. Never left us a pig much more a hog. No corn, no potatoes of any kind, no fodder, no hay nor oats, no cabbage or turnips. Left us about 30 bushels of wheat by our carrying it in the house and keeping it there until they left. In fact we have been buying all the corn we have used since last May was a year ago. The Yanks has taken 15 head of horses and mules, one hundred and 25 or 30 bbls. corn, wheat, flour, meat, all our chickens and about 1500 dollars of merchandise, burnt the houses at Villanow, tore up my store and burnt about fifty thousand sacks (?), left but few on my place. We are as poor as people gets to be. I have never received one dime from the Yanks for anything they have taken from me and I don't expect ever to get anything. They burnt and wasted 1000 lbs of my cotton. I will not write anymore on that subject. You may guess the balance. You wish to know how a man can live in a country where everything has been taken out of it. That is a plain case. He could not without bringing something to live upon. Corn is selling for $1.25 to $1.50 per bushel. pork 10 to 12 CtS, grass(?) beef 10 cents. pound(?), wheat $3.00 per bushel. Too

Above: Map of the Atlanta Campaign (*Wikipedia*)

Opposite page, top: Kurz & Alliosn's *Battle of Resaca*, c1889. Lithograph. (Library of Congress Prints and Photographs Division)

Opposite page, bottom: front page of *Southern Confederacy*, 29 May 1864 (*Georgia Historic Newspapers: Atlanta*)

sure but "it stands to reason that the store would not burn because it was a brick structure," so it's possible he ran his store in the old store building still at Villanow today (Williams).

Walker County Georgia Heritage outlines Micajah's involvement with Union troops in the Civil war:

> "Although there were no major battles fought in the Villanow vicinity during the Civil War, Micajah's family came in direct contact with the Union troops as they moved through this area. Many Union troops, apparently the Second Cavalry Division under the command of Brigadier General Garrard, encamped on Micajah's farm for several days. Micajah's house was used as the unit's headquarters and billets for the generals" (329).

From Sugar Valley on 11 May 1864 at 3:40pm, McPherson wrote to Garrard:

> "Keep out your patrols to the south and west toward Rome and La Fayette, and advise the major general commanding fully of all movements of the enemy in either direction, covering our flanks and protecting the trains. Remain at Villanow until further orders" (Procter 141).

many people coming back unless provisions were not so scarce. As regards the price of land in this country I know of none so cheap as has been reported to you by your N,W. friend. As regards my own lands I have not fully determined what I will do but I think I shall make a will soon and give your Ma for her life time 99, 100 and 101 land lots as my health is entirely gone. I have been sick over one year, not able to do anything at all. I do not expect to live long, hardly able to set up today. I never knew what it was to suffer before.

I will sell the Graves Miller place for ($500) five hundred dollars in greenbacks if I could get the money now and give possession next fall as the place is rented for next year and I might perhaps sell the other half of 117 but I have no price on it at present.

I want you to come to see me if possible if you ever expect to see me again. I would be glad to see you all once more in this life but I know I never shall before I close. I must say that I am truly sorry that there is such a bad feeling seething(?) between you and Henry. The family is all well but myself and Ma. Fannie and George are here staying with us. (They) have nothing left in the way of stock. Dan is at Villanow. Write often. Give my love to Liz and the children and bid the same yourself.

Your Father, affectionately,

Micajah Pope

P.S. You can further say to Lou that it would be unreasonable for me to pay his expenses back if I had the money. Henry has got back since the above was written and says the negros had plenty to eat while at his house. Do not let them deceive you. I tell you there is no dependence in negros in this region.

(Source: Guthrey, research files)

On 14 May, W.T. Sherman wrote to McPherson:

"I will send Garrard from Villanow by Dirt Town and Dry Creek to cross the Oostenaula above Rome" (Procter 184).

It would have been over this small span of days, 11 to 14 of May, that Garrard's cavalry occupied Villanow and Micajah's farm while farther east troops engaged in the Battle of Resaca. This was during the early days of the Atlanta Campaign (7 May to 2 Sep 1864).

When I was growing up the older generation in my family often told the story about a Union soldier's gun being fired in Micajah's home:

"Only two shots were known to have been fired on Micajah's farm. One general accidentally fired his gun in Micajah's house and shot a hole in the floor. One of the Union soldiers fired a warning shot at Micajah Felton, apparently thinking he was an intruder. An old letter written by Micajah indicated the Yankees confiscated most of his vital possessions to help supply their unit's needs; otherwise they treated Micajah's family respectfully. The Yankees left behind an artillery short sword and many blacksmith tools on Micajah's farm" (Walker Heritage 329).

On the nearby Puryear homestead, the Union army left "a large chain, evidently used for drawing artillery

23

… [and] it was placed over and around a high limb on a white oak tree standing in the [Puryear] yard." It was used as a swing for the children for many years and became "imbedded in the limb." The swing was still

there in 1932 when Sartain wrote of it (245).

I wonder if these remnants of a military invasion still exist today? Have they survived the generations?

A daughter of John Puryear who lived through this time remembered "how she saw the yards and fields literally blue with Yankees" (Sartain 245). It is surreal to imagine what it must have been like. McPherson's army alone numbered about 24,500 troops when he marched to Snake Creek Gap (Oake 191). It must have seemed like a swarm of locusts descending upon the valley. And as Garrard's men marched from Villanow towards Rome they would have passed through the familiar landscape of my childhood, having been raised about 2 miles south of Villanow in the East Armuchee Valley.

There are many other mentions in *War of the Rebellion* of Union troops in or near Villanow during this time. For such a tiny place on the map by today's standards it seems to have been quite the Civil War crossroads. The campaign for Atlanta was not the last time the Union army would pass through the area though. Later that same year in Oct 1864—after Atlanta had been defeated—Union forces again came through Villanow during the Franklin-Nashville Campaign (18 Sep to 27 Dec 1864). There are numerous correspondences concerning Villanow. Even Sherman himself came up from Atlanta and passed through Villanow before returning south and embarking on the Savannah Campaign (15 Nov to 21 Dec 1864), more commonly known as his March to the Sea.

An unnamed correspondent for the *Southern Confederecy* newspaper wrote in the 29 May 1864 issue:

> "It is, indeed, lamentable that the enemy should possess North Georgia, with its beautiful hills clad in the green foliage of spring—its bold streams, bright springs, and its fertile valleys, teeming with harvests, which was already bowing its head as if attempting to anticipate the stroke of the reaper. Blow calmly, ye winds of Cherokee, Georgia, for soon will thy breezes invigorate thine own sons, thy luxuriant soil will yet bring forth fruit for thine own children, and thy plains again delight those who survive the fierce conflict for thy disenthrallment" (Letter from the Front)

The Civil War would haunt the psyche of the southern soul for decades to come. An article about East Armuchee in the 6 Apr 1893 *Walker County Messenger* mentions H.Y. Puryear "who never tires of hearing or telling of stories of the late war." Indeed, here I am over 150 years after that horrible conflict recounting the war experiences of my own family.

Opposite: Mary Pope Jordan and J.C. Pope took Ed Pope—a distant cousin from Oklahoma—to visit Micajah's grave (this was some time in the 1970's). Ed shared this image with me after we met on Ancestry.com in 2010.
(Collection of Ed Pope)

Left: My father works to uncover the same graves when we visited in May 2010.
(Photo by Jordan M. Scoggins)

Micajah Felton Pope
b. 4 Jul 1849 d. 5 Nov 1925
married

Martha Ann Goodson
b. 3 Mar 1850 d. 24 Mar 1919

Above: This crayon portrait of Felton is one of the only known surviving images of my 2nd great grandfather.
(This reproduction: collection of Rhonda Scoggins; original crayon portrait: collection of Jim Pope)

Below: Taken from where Concord Rd intersects E Armuchee Rd, this was part of Felton's farm. The antebellum barn stood during the Civil War—before Felton owned it—and is still in use today. A small store once stood just behind where I was standing when I took this photo—possibly run by Felton himself. May 2010. (Photo by Jordan M. Scoggins)

Micajah Felton Pope was the son of Micajah Pope and Harriet Ann Bruce. He was born 4 Jul 1849 in Villanow, GA. Commonly called just "Felton" by friends or "Pap" by his grandchildren, he was the youngest of eleven children and the only child of those eleven to be born in and remain in East Armuchee for the rest of his life. In 1890 he was called "the heaviest man in Walker County" at 5'8" and 285 lbs (Griffith 66)!

Felton farmed with his father until he married Martha Ann Goodson on 22 Jun 1867. They purchased a farm from the Puryear family located about two miles south of Villanow. The house where they lived was on Concord Road. While it no longer stands it was located in the yard where Guy Pope's house is located. Still today Guy Pope (Felton's grandson) owns this land.

Guy, along with Hill Pope, Jr. and James C. Pope, wrote in *Walker County Georgia Heritage*:

> "[Felton's family] farmed their section as a family, plus other families who farmed for a share. They operated a store and a cotton gin. The cotton gin was powered by two horse power. Two bales was a good day's work" (330).

Fred Pope, who was about 10 when Felton died, remembers him well:

> "When he died he still had all his teeth. He'd brag about his teeth. And he wore a long tail coat, winter and summer. I said, 'How'd that old man stand that old hot coat?' He'd be out on the porch and watching the field, people working in the field for him, to see if their work had stopped" (F. Pope).

L.F. Coker, writing in the *Walker County Messenger*, described Felton's sharp wit, saying he "just can't be beat for cleverness" (Grigsby, transcriptions). I can see this wit passed down through the generations in my present day Pope relatives.

Felton was a Mason. The pin on his lapel in the portrait to the left is the Masonic symbol. His tombstone also bears this symbol. He and Martha are buried at Concord Methodist Church. They had four children:

1. John D. (b.26 Jun 1869, m. 1st Etta Nola Ramsey, 2nd Minnie D. Strickland, 3rd Eula Brown, d.25 Nov 1937)
2. Mary Elizabeth (b.14 Aug 1872, m.Thomas Chelsey Jackson Childs, d.20 Sep 1900)
3. David Felton (b.25 May 1875, m. 1st Laura B. Coker, 2nd Ella Agnes Kiker, 3rd Katherine Louise Sims, d.27 Jan 1955)
4. Benjamin Hill (b.5 May 1883, m.Nannie Elizabeth Clement, d.3 May 1966)

Ben Hill, the youngest child, followed in his father's footsteps, inheriting his father's farm and building the Pope legacy in the East Armuchee valley.

Above left: A tintype of Josephine Love Goodson. (Shared by Nita Henry [bnh711] on Ancestry.com)

Above right: An original crayon portrait of Martha Ann Goodson. (Collection of Rhonda Jordan Scoggins, passed down by her mother Mary Pope Jordan)

Right: Felton and Martha (both seated in the middle) in front of an unknown home. Jim Pope believes this is the house where Micajah Pope, Felton's father, lived. Guy Pope, however, believes it could be Felton's home before being added on to/renovated at a later date (see next page). If you compare the two photos they look incredibly similar. Micajah's house burned down in 1929 and Felton's was demolished in the late 1960's. Either theory is plausible as we know the latter home was originally in the dogtrot style (as seen here) and later closed in. (Collection of Jim Pope)

In Mar 1919 Martha fell ill with pneumonia. She was sick for about a week and died "in the still hours of the night" on 24 Mar. Funeral services were conducted by The Rev. B.F. Hunt at Concord Church "in the presence of a large concourse of sorrowing relatives and friends." She is buried in the Concord cemetery (Austin 132, 154).

Later that same year, Felton married Martha's sister-in-law, Josephine Love. The marriage was in Rossville on 4 Aug (Austin 152). Josephine was the widow of Jesse Marsh Goodson, Martha Ann's brother. Jesse had died in 1903. Felton and Josephine did not have children together (though Josephine had borne 14[!] children to Jesse). To make this web even more confusing, Josephine Love is Emily Love's sister. Emily is my second great grandmother in a different line from the Pope's. Of course these relationships are all through marriage and not blood, but it's enough to make your head spin trying to figure it all out. This makes Josephine my step 2nd great grandmother as well as my 2nd great grand aunt. Certainly at first it seems so abnormal to have such intermingling among families. But when you stop to consider the time and place where this occurred it's not so far fetched. Relatively speaking there weren't that many people and families around at the time. Unlike today, your social circle for meeting potential mates or even just friends was exponentially smaller. Today there's almost no such thing as geographic boundaries when it comes to relationships. But even just 100 years ago that was not the case.

Felton and Josephine must have found a special comfort together, each having survived their spouse and finding new hope in life together. They were married just over six years before Felton died on 5 Nov 1925. He was buried with Martha Ann at Concord. Josephine lived for another decade, outliving not only two husbands but several of her children. She is buried at Macedonia in Villanow.

Left: Felton's home as it appeared in later years.
(Collection of Rhonda Jordan Scoggins)

Above: In use since before the Civil War, this shed—a wheat house—was built with pegs and square nails. It is only paces away from where Felton's house stood.
(Photo by Jordan M. Scoggins)

VILLANOW

Originally known as Sunset, Villanow is a small antebellum community located in the northern end of East Armuchee Valley in southeastern Walker County, Georgia. Some say it got its name "when a Post Office was to be established … and Capt. J.Y. Wood's mother said, 'It is no longer a Hamlet but now a village,' so they decided to call it Villanow" (Walker Heritage 38). Yet the historical marker located there says the name was "taken from Jane Porter's novel: *Thaddeus of Warsaw*." The crossroads community is located along "the Indian trail known as the Chickamauga Path which came down from the north through Rock Springs, across Taylors Ridge past Villanow and on to Calhoun and New Echota" (Walker Heritage 39). Today it can be found nestled at the crossroads where East Armuchee Road and Highway 201 meet Highway 136. In the old days, Highway 201 and East Armuchee Road would have been referred to as the Dalton-Rome Road.

The identifying landmark of Villanow is the brick country store. Much like the community's namesake, the history of the store—once referred to as "The Brick" due to the uncommon nature of brick buildings at the time—is subject to disagreement. Some people claim The Brick was built before the Civil War while others believe it was built slightly later. The original builder/proprietor of the store is also unclear because of this but J.W. Cavender—a veteran of Cos F and B in Phillips' Legion of the Confederate Army (National Park Service)—is known to have operated it for the longest period of time and is therefore most closely associated with its early history.

The post office operated in Villanow from 1840 to 1934, "sometimes being in the store and sometimes being elsewhere" (Williams 6A). The first postmaster was Roland Kinsey, serving from 16 Oct 1840 to 18 Mar 1843. About a decade later, William D. Underwood was the postmaster from 1853 to 1856. Other postmasters include Ewing M. Reed and J.A. Clements. Some speculation, based on the writings of J.W. Clements, suggests Underwood could have operated the brick store during his time as postmaster. Similar speculation, as I discussed in the chapter on Micajah Pope, suggests it could have been operated by Pope during the Civil War. The fact remains that the early history of the brick store is all but lost to history and all claims about this time can only be considered a best guess at this point. Underwood and Pope certainly did operate stores—but Villanow was once a place more populous than the city of LaFayette and sustained at various times a number of small country stores, cotton gins, a grist mill, a blacksmith, a harness/saddle store, a notary public, a watch/clock/jewelry shop, and a doctor (Williams 6A). Other small stores littered the area around Villanow, too, including a store run by George Hames at the Hames place 0.4 miles south of East Armuchee church as well as a store at the old Bowman place about half a mile north of the same church. There was even a small store (it may have been run by Felton Pope, see pg 26, though no one recalls for sure) at the corner where Concord Rd meets E Armuchee Rd. From my mother's time, she remembers a store just across the road from The Brick that was operated by Jack Stansell. His wife even ran a beauty shop for the local women. Spat Eakers was another local business woman who ran a store just behind The Brick. By the time I was growing up you only had the store in The Brick and a modern Favorite Market on the other side of Highway 136 (originally operated by Jack Stansell). Today it is a Mapco and is the only operating store of the crossroads community.

But The Brick is the one that gets all the attention—and rightfully so for all the years of business it sustained. The earliest person who we know for certain was associated with the store is J.W. Cavender (see more about the Cavender family on pg 224). Counted on the 1870 census as a merchant, he had many business partners over the years, among them John A. Clements (his brother-in-law), James Harvey Shahan, David Shahan, and Julius Ward. In 1903 James moved to Oklahoma

Left: An antique photo of "The Brick" (shared anonymously online).

Below: Another antique image of the store from a later time. (Collection of Delores Grigsby)

See a present day image of the store on pg 223.

and no longer held his share. After operating the store for at least 50 years, J.W. Cavender died in 1919. The store was sold to a group of men: Roy Morgan, Claude Clements, J.A. Shields, M. Gordon Keown, J.C. Phillips, and Otto Morgan. Tom Cantrell, Basil Corey, and Ben White worked in the store and are associated with its history—but none of them ever owned it though the shares did change hands several times over the years (Williams).

During the late 1930's, Villanow and the East Armuchee area got electricity. In 1942 Ottis Porch purchased the brick store at Villanow and ran it for the next 29 years. He expanded the building by adding living quarters in the 1950's. He even operated "rolling stores" operated for him by Ed Sweatman and later Mitchell Manning [Mary Pope refers to these rolling stores in my interview with her on pg 76] (Williams). These rolling stores were especially useful as the roads in East Armuchee were dirt until the late 1950's or early 1960's (R. & M. Scoggins, correspondence).

On 21 Oct 1971, Porch sold the brick store to O.H. "Doc" Penland and, finally, on 1 Sep 1987 Penland sold the store to Rodney and Ebeth Edwards who ran the store for many years (Williams). The Edwards sold it to Marty Vess, the last person to operate the store until it closed in about 2009 (R. & M. Scoggins, correspondence).

During the Civil War, Villanow was a stop along the way for the Union army. A letter from Micajah Pope to one of his sons survives to tell us first hand what the people of Villanow endured (read this letter on page 22). Sherman's "scorched earth" policy meant that "all animals, grain, and fodder were taken or destroyed." No actual battle took place. Villanow only served as "a convenient place for the troops to gather before they went south" (Williams 6A).

Above: This photo of the Villanow post office, which appears also to be a store, was originally owned by Charles Love, passed down to J.C & Helen Pope, and then to Jim Pope. Charles is on the steps and Milton McClure stands by the horse. There's also an unidentified person in the window. Charles Love is the nephew of Emily & Josephine Love. (Collection of Jim Pope)

Following pages: Concord Church at dusk, Nov 2010. (Photo by Jordan M. Scoggins)

East Armuchee Baptist Church as it appeared before 1941 when the front porch was added. This probably was taken at a homecoming celebration. (Collection of Mary Pope Jordan)

A Terrible Tornado
The Rome Commercial
2 Oct 1872

Walker County has been the scene of probably the severest tornado that ever swept through Georgia.

On last Sunday evening, it was possibly on Saturday evening, a densely heavy cloud come up and lowered over East Armuchee between Subligna and Villanow. The cloud was broidered and fretted with incessant flashes of lightning, that leaped and lingered in livid play on its dark body. Suddenly and without any premonition a howling wind storm swept over the country, shrieking like a thousand fiends, buffeting grown trees on its burly bosom as if they were cathers, and sweeping houses from their foundation with a single breath.

It extended over a space about a half a mile wide, and destroyed everything in its course. Where it swept through a forest its track can be followed as plainly as if a corps of engineers had with their axes leveled the trees. Not a tree is left standing in its track. Several dwelling houses were blown down and utterly destroyed. Among others our informants knew positively of Mr. Jones Richardson, Mr. Pinckney Tate, Mr. Toney Hart and Mr. Moore's. Mr Moore's wife was standing in the door when the wind come and was blown out of the house, out of the yard and into the public road, where fortunately behind the shelter of a point of a hill she recovered herself. Mr. Geo. Eepey's house was also destroyed. Mr. Bomar had a fine orchard of apple trees which were twisted from their places and sent whirling the Lord only knows where. The cotton fields that lay in the zone over which the cyclone swept are rendered absolutely worthless, and the loss occasioned by it may be estimated at thousands. Where it came from and where it went no one knows and no one cares. It utterly devastated one of the fairest valleys in Georgia. It is reported that Sugar Valley had a visit from this terrible fiend. We sympathize with our friends who have suffered. Messrs. J.W. Davis and Wardlaw were our informants, and they were direct from the scene of the disaster.

The Villanow store was always a gathering place for locals too. Even during my childhood the farmers of the area gathered at the store and courteously waved, like any good southern man, when you drove by. In the old days court was even held on the front porch of the store. William Jasper Love (see pg 62) was Justice of the Peace for some time, as was E.F. Bowman.

But Villanow extends beyond the country crossroads where the store stands. Churches and schools played a vital role in the life of the community.

The first churches in the Villanow area were Concord Methodist and Macedonia Baptist, both established in 1844. Bethlehem Baptist was founded in 1847, Friendship Baptist in 1854, and East Armuchee Baptist in 1886 (Walker Heritage 37).

Concord Methodist is well known for the camp meetings that were held every Sep beginning in the late 1840's (Orr 2). These camp meetings lasted a whole week and were said to draw from 1,500 to 2,000 from all around the region:

> "The meetings were held in a brush arbor because of the size of the crowd and houses and tents were erected for the families to stay in. Cooking and eating was done together outside with the food being prepared in large pots. These meetings were held in the summer and fall and would last a complete week with many bringing their animals along with them. The entire week was devoted to Bible study, worship, singing and just good fellowship. There were three sermons a day, morning, afternoon and night, with singing in between in the grove of trees around the camp. These meetings continued until around 1893" (Walker Heritage 37).

While my 2nd great grandparents in the Pope line (see pg 43) are buried at Concord and attended church there, and other family members are buried at Macedonia and Friendship, my family history is most closely aligned with East Armuchee Baptist Church. Several of my ancestors were charter members, including James Constantine Clement/Emily Love (see pg 58) on my mother's side and Nathan Alexander Keown/Julia Ann Cavender (see pg 218) on my father's side, among others who are related but not in my direct line. According to early church minutes, the first East Armuchee homecoming appears to have been the third Sunday in Jun 1922 (East Armuchee). Homecoming is a yearly tradition that continues to this day. At one homecoming my great grandmother Lizzie spoke at the gathering and welcomed all the friends and family, "for those of us who have been so fortunate to still claim East Armuchee Valley as our home—this is a day we through the year look forward to with great pleasure for many of you we only see at our annual homecoming day" (L. Pope).

There were numerous schools in the area,

including Pocket, Furnace, and Concord. These schools gradually disappeared and were consolidated into larger schools. Concord closed in 1930. The Villanow school operated longer. Established some time in the 1880's, it operated until 1952. As these small "one room" school houses began to fade, larger schools served the area. Many of the students that had previously gone to Villanow and other area schools went to high school at Subligna in Chattooga County. Many of its students still get together at reunions. Armuchee Valley, the last of these local schools, opened about 1952 (though it did not teach high school grades like Subligna). Both my mother and father graduated from 8th grade there. I, too, went to Armuchee Valley and became the last graduating class when the school burned in Jan 1992 and was never reopened (Father; Grigsby, transcriptions; Walker Heritage 37-38).

Many of the families in this book are from or associated with Villanow and the broader East Armuchee Valley, including Pope, Goodson, Love, Shahan, Ward, Keown, Cavender, and more. Read about each of these families in their respective chapters.

Today Villanow is a shadow of its former self. The old country store closed around 2009 and only the old Favorite Market (now Mapco) remains across the way. However a few businesses do remain, including Hatchet Equipment and Paradise Arabians. A National Forest building stands where the Villanow School was once located and just down the road towards the old Armuchee Valley School the Armuchee Valley Community Center opened in 2010.

David Williams summed up the fate of Villanow best:

> "Villanow gives the appearance of having been a prosperous town with several businesses and other services available. As time went on the same thing happened to Villanow that happened to many towns like it as the 20th century progressed. With no industry other than farming and not being on a river or railroad, it gradually closed, many young people moved away" (6B)

And it is too true. I sit here in my apartment in Greenwich Village—a very different village from Villanow—writing away the night about that small hamlet of my childhood. I return there often in my mind, and I see Cavender and Shahan and all the rest. I sit with them in the shade of that brick store—the Georgia sun can be intense—and dream of those "good ole days." The past may be a fading memory but Villanow you will always be my home.

GOODSON and VISINAND/WHISENANT families

Jacob
b.14 Feb 1805 in North Carolina
d.9 Jun 1882 in Georgia

↓

Martha Ann
b.3 Mar 1850 in Georgia
d.24 Mar 1919 in Georgia

↓

my great grandfather Ben,
my grandmother Mary, my mother
Rhonda, and then me

Opposite: Page from a Goodson family Bible. (Shared by LundieDyer27 on *Ancestry.com*)

Above: quilt made by Martha Ann Goodson. (Collection of Charlotte Jordan Griggs, handed down by her mother Mary Pope Jordan)

Next page: detail of above quilt

GOODSON

Felton's wife Martha Ann connects my line to the Goodson family. Martha Ann was the youngest of 12 children of Jacob Goodson.

Jacob was born in North Carolina, the son of Nancy Goodson (her maiden name is not known). He was married to Barbara Sarah Whisenant. At some point the Goodson family relocated to Habersham County, GA (Walker Heritage 189). Jacob was living in Smith's District in that county when he was awarded land in the 1832 Cherokee Land Lottery (Ancestry.com Cherokee). Unfortunately, this land lottery is what ultimately drove many tribes from their native lands, culminating with the Trail of Tears.

Jacob was granted land lot 187 in the 9th district, 4th section of Cherokee land (Ancestry.com Cherokee). This land was in Walker County, north of Chickamauga. According to Viola Smith and R. Conlee:

> "[Jacob] came into Walker County about 1834 and settled on his land. By 1840, Jacob had sold this land and moved to what was later known as Gordon Spring. Some time after, he sold this to Rev. Zachariah Gordon, and moved North of Villanow where he had bought another farm" (Walker Heritage 189)

Census records show Jacob and Barbara lived out the rest of their days on that Villanow farm. In 1850 he is counted with two slaves (Ancestry.com 1850 Slave). He and Barbara are buried in a small family plot on their farm that today is maintained

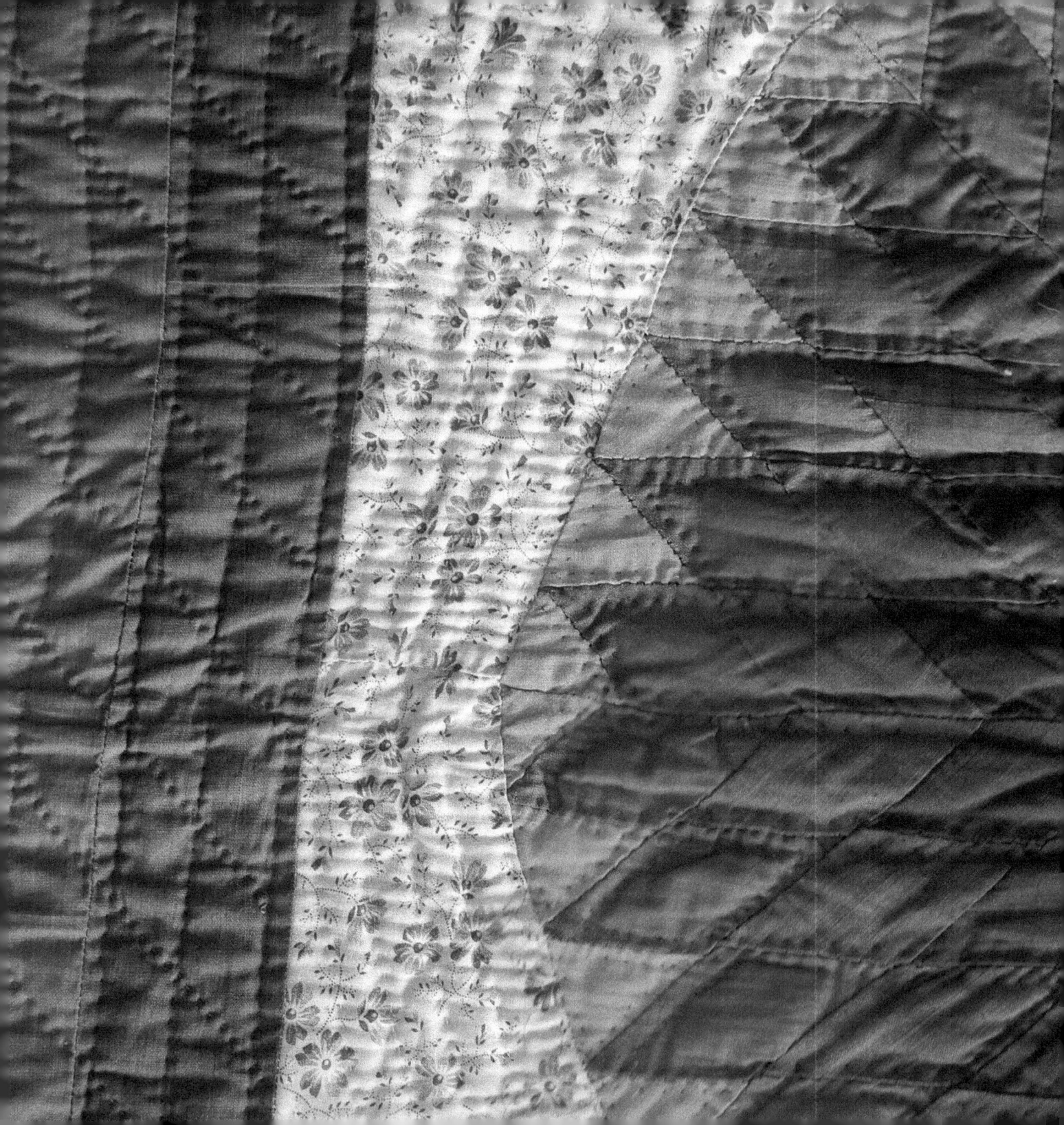

Above, L to R:

Me, my mom, and sister at Jacob Goodson's grave.
(Photo by Michael Scoggins)

A view of chickens roaming the Goodson Cemetery.
(Photo by Jordan M. Scoggins)

Tombstone of Jacob Goodson.
(Photo by Jordan M. Scoggins)

All taken May 2010.

with love and respect by the current owners.

Jacob and Barbara had 12 children in total. I descend through their youngest daughter Martha Ann, my 2nd great grandmother.

Four of Martha Ann's brothers served in the Civil War. Williamson Byrum (b.1831) and Nicholas (b.1843) both enlisted on 31 Aug 1861 as Privates in Co H, 23rd GA Volunteer Infantry, CSA. Nicholas was killed at Petersburg, VA in 1864. Petersburg is known for its use of trench warfare that would become widely used in Europe in World War I. Williamson was still with the Company when they surrendered on 26 Apr 1865 at Greensboro, NC. James (b.1839) enlisted as a Private on 10 May 1862 in Co B, 5th GA Infantry Regiment. His record states

that he deserted from the same company on 15 Nov 1864. Family information states that John Thomas (b.1837) also served though I have not been able to confirm a service record for him (Goodson; Historical, Soldiers & U.S.; National Park Service; Walker Heritage 189).

Martha Ann and her brothers Jacob (b.1852) and Jesse (b.1854) were the youngest of the Goodson children.

Jacob was an admired Villanowian citizen. According to L.F. Coker writing in the *Walker County Messenger*, he was "a model farmer in this section and … ha[d] some of the finest brood mares to be found any where. He [was] also engaged in sheep and [kept] generally some spare horses just for the sake of accommodating those who wish[ed] to trade" (Grigsby, transcriptions).

In 1893, Jacob was charged with the murder of Wesley Short. The conflict took place at Villanow. Portions of the testimony from the trial are described in the 9 Mar 1893 *Walker County Messenger*. The witnesses do not paint Wesley Short in a flattering light. He seems to have been a bully and made numerous threats against Jacob. Ultimately Wesley confronted Jacob, drew his knife and threatened to cut Jacob's throat "from ear to ear." Like a scene from an old western, Jacob pulled his gun and fired five shots as fast as he could. Clearly only defending himself—and having made every effort to avoid his antagonizer—Jacob was found not guilty (Grigsby, transcriptions).

Martha Ann's other younger brother, Jesse, had been present the day of the murder in Villanow and was among the witnesses at the court trial.

Coker wrote of Jesse, "happy Jesse, who can turn around oftener in a given number of seconds than any other man and who is agent for the world renowned McCormick mower."

Jesse Marsh Goodson and Josephine Love. I'm not sure which of their children is pictured. (Shared by LundieDyer27 on *Ancestry.com*)

He was also a deputy U.S. Marshall (Grigsby, transcriptions).

Like his brother, Jesse also fell victim to the underside of life in East Armuchee. On 27 Dec 1880, a six horse engine used to run his mill and gin was vandalized:

> "...some cowardly scoundrel placed dynamite in the fire box and attaching a fuse exploded it. At the time of the explosion, which occurred about 10 O'clock, Mr. Goodson had just gone to bed. A few moments before he retired he went out in the yard and down near where the engine stands. The force from the explosion threw a piece of the boiler on the house. Mr. Goodson left his bed, called his oldest son, and armed himself, went out to see what the trouble was, but could not locate it til next mourning (sic). The damage to the engine will amount to about 150.00. This is undoubtedly the work of some one bent on murder."

The writer went on to say that "the attack was made upon one of our best citizens" (Grigsby, transcriptions). From these brief sketches it seems someone had a bone to pick with Jacob and Jesse. If we can learn one thing from this it's that drama and danger are nothing new but rather a core ingredient of the human experience.

About a decade later in 1902, Jesse decided to leave his homeland of Villanow and moved his family to Texas. He sold his farm and he and Josephine, along with eleven of their children (the two oldest remained in Georgia), moved to Pittsburg, Texas. The youngest daughter, Carrie, wrote memories of her father's farm in Texas where he "owned seven hundred acres of land" and "raised horses and cattle." Unfortunately, Jesse died after living in Texas for only a few years. Josephine brought her family back to "her beloved Georgia" and eventually married my 2nd great grandfather M. Felton Pope (also a widower, see pg 31). This makes Josephine my step 2nd great grandmother by marriage. However she is also my 2nd great grand aunt by blood, being the sister of Emily Love (my 2nd great grandmother through the Clement/Love line, see page 58) (Dyer).

VISINAND/WHISENANT

The connection to the Visinand/Whisenant family comes in through Martha Ann's mother, Barbara Sarah Whisenant, as follows:

Guillaume Visinand is my 11th great grandfather who was born between 1555 and 1570 in the town of Lausanne (an ancient Roman town) in Vaud, Switzerland. His great grand son, my 8th great grandfather, was Francois Visinand (1647-1700). Francois began what would become a generations long migration, taking his family to Germany. His son, Philip Peter Visinand (1684-1744), my 7th great grandfather, made the journey to the new world. Philip and his family sailed from Rotterdam by way of Dover on the *Snow Lowther*. They arrived in Philadelphia 14 Oct 1731 and ended up in Lancaster County, PA. From there, Philip's son John Adam Whisenant (1719-1784) came to Lincoln, NC. Notice how the name changed in John Adam's generation. His son John Nicholas Whisenant (1743-1831) came to South Carolina. And his son John Nicholas [II] (my 4th great grandfather if you have been keeping up!) was the first generation to end up in Georgia. Finally, John's daughter Barbara Sarah Whisenant (1813-1893) married Jacob Goodson (1805-1882), connecting the Visinand/Whisenant line to the Goodson family and ultimately the Pope family and me (Burgert 368-70; Whisnant).

Benjamin Hill Pope
b. 5 May 1883 d. 3 May 1966
married

Nannie Elizabeth Clement
b. Oct 1886 d. 11 Jan 1966

Born 5 May 1883, Benjamin Hill Pope—the youngest son of Felton Pope and Martha Ann Goodson—represents the third generation of the Pope family to live in the Villanow area of the East Armuchee Valley.

On 20 Jan 1907 he married Nannie Elizabeth Clement (commonly called Lizzie), a daughter of J.C. Clement and Emily Love (see pg 58 for more about J.C. & Emily's families). Together they had eight children (though one lived only three days):

1. Luther Hill (b.12 Feb 1909, m.Beulah Belle Huggins 16 Oct 1927, d.1 Aug 1968)
2. Burke Hall (b.23 Jul 1911, m.Georgia Mae Richardson 10 May 1930, d.19 Jul 1981)
3. Mary Evelyn (b.13 May 1913, m.Earl Felix Jordan 4 May 1930, d.6 Sep 2004)
4. James Constantine Micajah (b.24 Sep 1915, m. Helen Elizabeth Grigsby 6 Mar 1938, d.27 Sep 1988)
5. Little Brother (b.5 Mar 1918, d. 8 Mar 1918)
6. Santa Orville (b.25 Dec 1920, m.Battie Lee Smith 21 Dec 1940, d.28 Jan 1965)
7. Martha Emily (b.16 Dec 1923, m. James A. Wary 11 Mar 1943, d.28 Apr 2002)
8. Guy Adam (b.27 Jun 1932, m.Marjorie Dorothy Grogan 5 Jul 1959)

Ben & Lizzie in their front yard. In the background to the right you can see Ben's bee hive.
(Collection of Rhonda Jordan Scoggins)

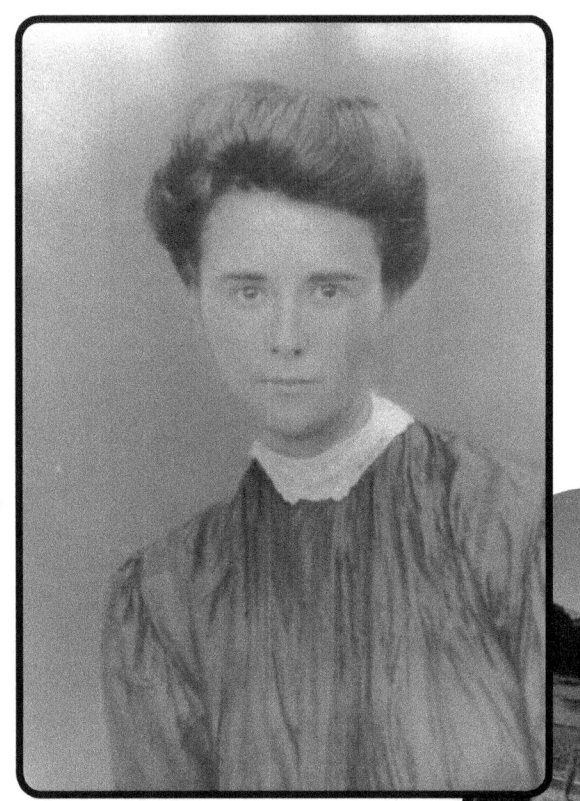

Ben — Lizzie

- **Luther** m. Beulah Belle Higgins
- **Burke** m. Georgia Mae Richardson
- **Orville** m. Battie Lee Smith
- **Martha** m. James Wary
- **Mary** m. Earl Felix Jordan
- **Guy** m. Marjorie Grogan
- **J.C.** m. Helen Elizabeth Grigsby

Opposite page: portraits of Ben and Lizzie. Lower left, Lizzie with her first child, Luther. Spanning the pages, a view of the bottom land of the Pope farm.

This page: Burke and friend/brother-in-law Charlie Richardson; sisters Martha and Mary; and the three youngest brothers J.C., Guy, and Orville.

(Collection of Mary Pope Jordan)

For the first few years of their marriage, Ben and Lizzie lived with Ben's parents. Some time between 1910 and 1913 they moved to their own house. It was just a short walk from where they had lived on Concord Road with Felton. Built in 1893, it still stands today on parcel number 0563 005 and is the first house just after crossing the bridge (and navigating two sharp turns) on East Armuchee Road (Walker Tax). My Grannie, Mary, was born in this house and spent the earliest years of her life there.

When Ben's parents died he inherited their home (pictured on pg 30) and moved his family there, where Ben and Lizzie lived out the rest of their days. Although the house was torn down in the late 1960's, I have heard stories about the home my entire life. My mother remembers the house well, as do her siblings. Ben and Lizzie's home served as a gathering place for family far and wide. It seems like it was practically the social nexus of the valley. I imagine if you knew Ben and Lizzie and happened to be passing through you would always stop by for a visit, sit on the porch and sip a glass of sweet tea.

Ben carried on the farming tradition of the Pope family. A "master farmer" of the region, cotton was his main crop (Walker Heritage 328). He also grew many other things, from corn to hegari (informally called hi-gear), and raised cows and bees. All the household worked hard to help make the farm a success, providing sustenance for the family. The story goes that Lizzie could pick 300 lbs of cotton a day, more than pulling her weight as she was a tiny woman!

Guy, recalling a memory about the wheat house (see page 31) that still stands on his farm, remembers "daddy used to combine hi-gear and we'd have to throw the sacks up in them little ole windows and pour it out in them bins in there. Then when you got it out it was the same thing and you had to sack it up" (G. Pope)!

A well-rounded man, beyond the cotton and corn fields Ben was:

"very active in the growth of his community, county, and state. He was often called on as a 'grand juror' and 'traverse juror.' He was elected a Justice of the Peace and served some thirty years in this capacity. He served as a member of the Democratic Executive Committee for many years. He remained active in this regards until he retired about the age of 78." (Walker Heritage 328)

Lizzie was also active beyond her farm duties. Guy remembers "mama quilting all in the winter time. The women would come down here and they'd quilt. When they got through, I don't know how they done it but they just pull it up and leave it you know, get it up over your head and leave it there" (G. Pope). Unfortunately, I do not know of any surviving quilts made by Lizzie.

Guy also remembers Lizzie's first electric iron:

"I never will forget when we got electricity, they just wired it with that little old twisted

wire for your lights you know. And she [Lizzie] finally bought her an electric iron. She went in there and hooked that electric iron up to a little old socket and screwed that thing in and that wire just went to smoking" (G. Pope).

The advent of electricity and the endless innovations to follow would come to change our world forever. Ben and Lizzie witnessed so much change during their life that it can be hard to visualize what it would have been like for them in their early years.

Although I never had the opportunity to know him, from the stories I have heard Ben was quite the character. He knew how to turn a phrase in that grand southern tradition and had a sharp wit to boot. Affectionately he gave many in his family nick names:

Burke Pope was "Bear"
Mary Pope was "Rub"
J. C. was "C" Pope
Orville was "Buckle"
Martha was "Peal"
Guy was "Buggar"
Earl Jordan was "Bog"
Battie Lee was "Tinnie Bell"
Georgia Mae was "Peaches"
Hill, Jr. was "Bud"
Bennie Pope was "Franklin"

Guy remembers some of the things his dad used to say, "Peaches and her sister don't do nothing but ride up and down the road" and "Helen's [wife of J.C.] singing is like a bumble bee in a jug" (G. Pope). And while pointing out a certain area in his yard Ben would tell a story, "A Yankee soldier is buried right there." To this day Guy Pope and his cousin Fred Pope still joke they are going to dig that soldier up one day (F. Pope).

Guy is the last remaining child of Ben & Lizzie and I imagine "like father, like son" rings true. Guy has a knack for storytelling that few others possess. When Guy tells a story it's not that hard for me to close my eyes and imagine Ben in his place. He has a way of telling outrageous things that

Opposite page: Ben snoozing at home after a hard day's work on the farm, c.1950. Lizzie posing with flowers in her yard, 1962.

This page: Ben & Lizzie's family poses for a family portrait at their home, c.1957. L to R: Standing: Hill, Burke, J.C., Orville, and Guy. Sitting: Martha, Lizzie, Ben, and Mary.

(Collection of Mary Pope Jordan)

Above: Relaxing at the swimming hole c.1938.
L to R: Guy Pope, Robert Jordan, Martha, Mary Earl, Charlotte, Lizzie. (Collection of Mary Pope Jordan)

Left: Lizzie gives Rhonda a Christmas present c.1952.
(Collection of Mary Pope Jordan)

Opposite page:

A candy dish that belonged to Lizzie.
(Collection of Rhonda Jordan Scoggins)

Top photo: Mary with her father Ben, 1958.
(Collection of Mary Pope Jordan)

Bottom: Lizzie & Ben visit Martha & Jim in Louisville.
L to R: Jim Wary, Lizzie, Ben, J.C., Helen, Mary Earl.
circa early 1950's.
(Collection of Mary Pope Jordan)

could have easily been made up—but you can't help but believe when it comes from his lips. It's the oral tradition, alive and well. This is how humans have handed down stories for centuries.

One such story is the time a tornado came through East Armuchee (see pgs 34 and 174 for more about severe weather in the valley) and hit Ben and Lizzie's house. They had a dog leashed to the house and the wind was so strong that it blew the dog to about where Brian Hart now lives (just past the bridge back towards Villanow). The dog survived but the chain was wrapped around a tree. The same storm blew the roof off the house. This was before Guy's time but is a story told to him—no doubt by Ben—and Guy still passes it on today.

In Nov 2010 I interviewed Guy about Ben & Lizzie's home (the house where he grew up). He showed me where the house sat and described what it was like. Originally the house was two main rooms with a hallway down the middle. Each end of the hallway was open to the outside to allow the breeze to blow through and cool things down. This dogtrot style was a common way to build houses when this home was originally built before the Civil War. Later on the house was expanded. The central hallway was closed in with French doors and three rooms were added to the back.

The original kitchen was a separate building. When the house was torn down J.C. Pope moved the kitchen to his back yard about a mile down the road. J.C. remembered, "I guess you would say I drug it up

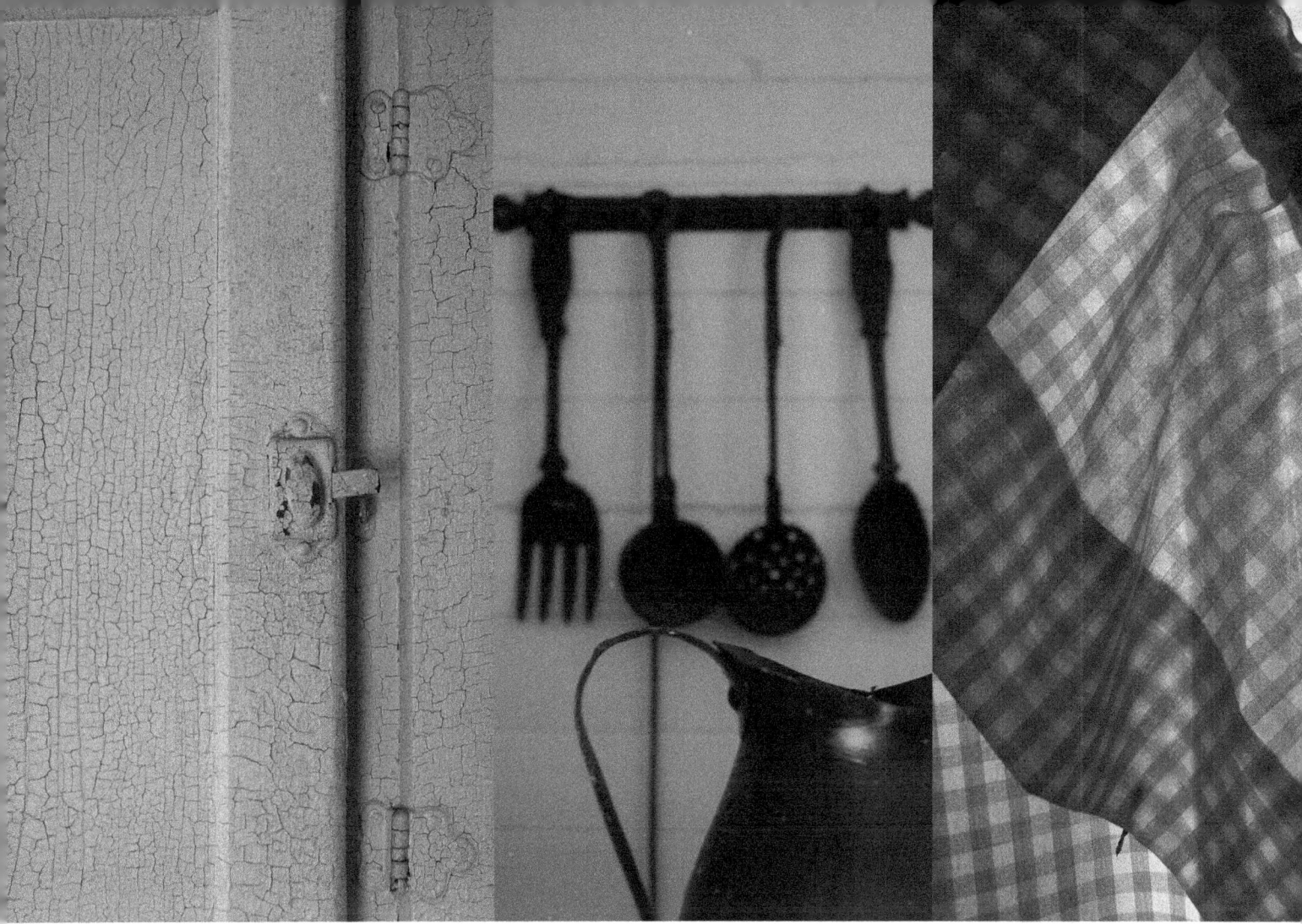

here. I put it on two big telephone poles behind a big tractor." There he and his wife Helen preserved it as a relic of family and local history. Inside the kitchen you'll find an old stove, ice box, pie safe, and numerous other items from the era. Some are actually from Ben and Lizzie but most of the items are simply antiques of the era, collected to represent a time and place of the past (Pope's Kitchen).

But the kitchen is not a relic to be looked at from afar. While speaking of the kitchen, Helen said, "It's a good place to come for that second cup of coffee" (Pope's Kitchen). Indeed, I remember Helen serving my cousin Jamila and I lunch in that kitchen when we stayed at her house. It was always a special place to me, capturing my imagination and sparking an interest in the past that, as an adult, carries through to the writing of this book.

The kitchen is still there today, looked after by J.C.'s son Jim. It preserves both the memory of Ben and Lizzie as well as a general history of what life in the country used to be like.

The above series of photos are of the old Pope kitchen that is kept by Jim Pope, Nov 2010. (Photos by Jordan M. Scoggins)

Pope Home

I asked my father, a draftsman and CAD artist, if he could draw a plan of the old Pope home. Based on my mother's memories and preliminary sketch (pictured in the background), he made these CAD drawings, detailing the floor plan, furniture placement, and major exterior features. The drawing, of course, is not to scale since the structure no longer exists. But this is a good approximation based on memories. When I look at these drawings it helps me feel what it was like to be there.

The original house (which had the same footprint as the second story shown to the right) was built in the dogtrot style, a common rural southern style characterized by "a covered open space between two closed spaces, providing a sheltered, breezy area to gather during the hot summers" (Spencer).

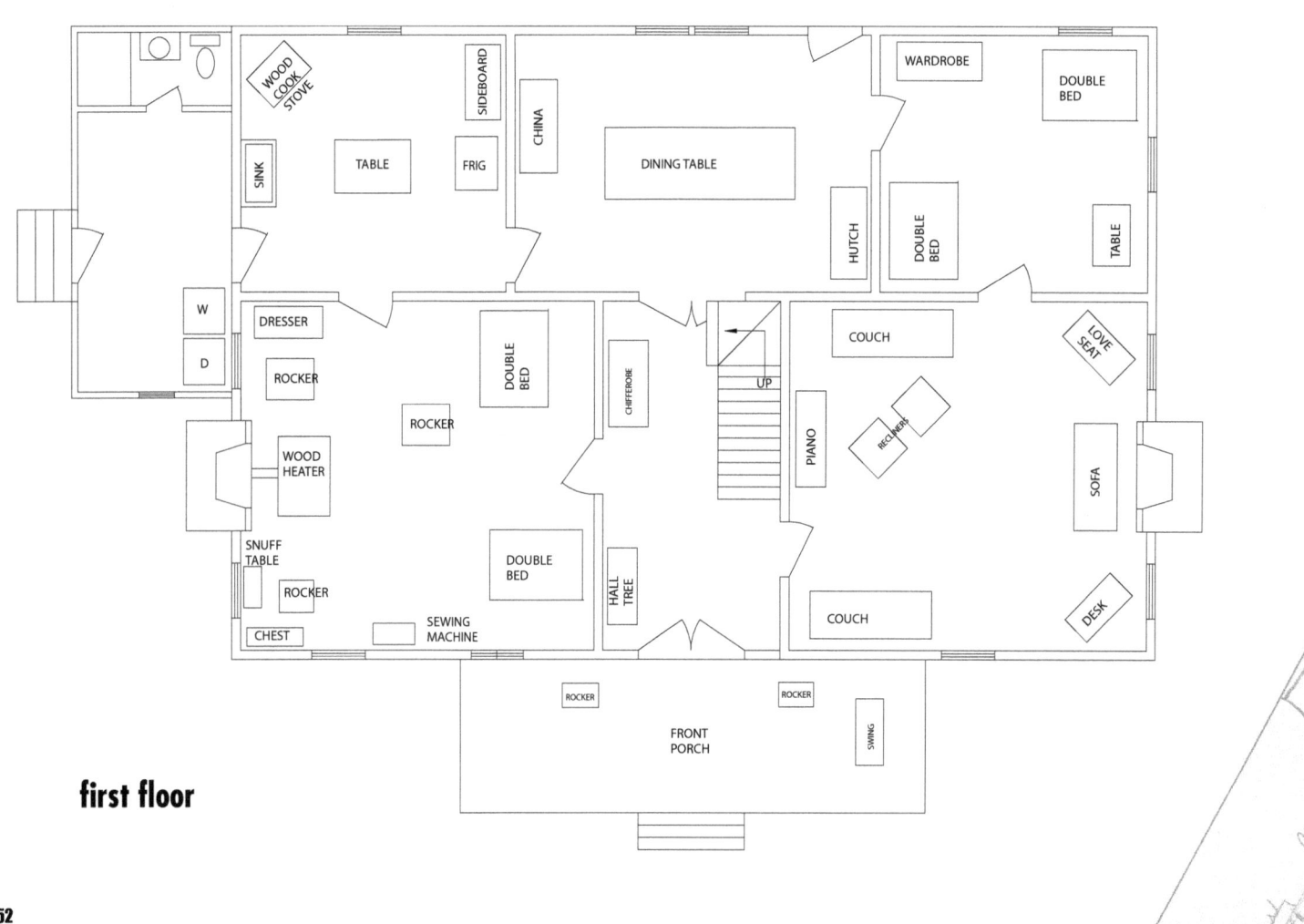

first floor

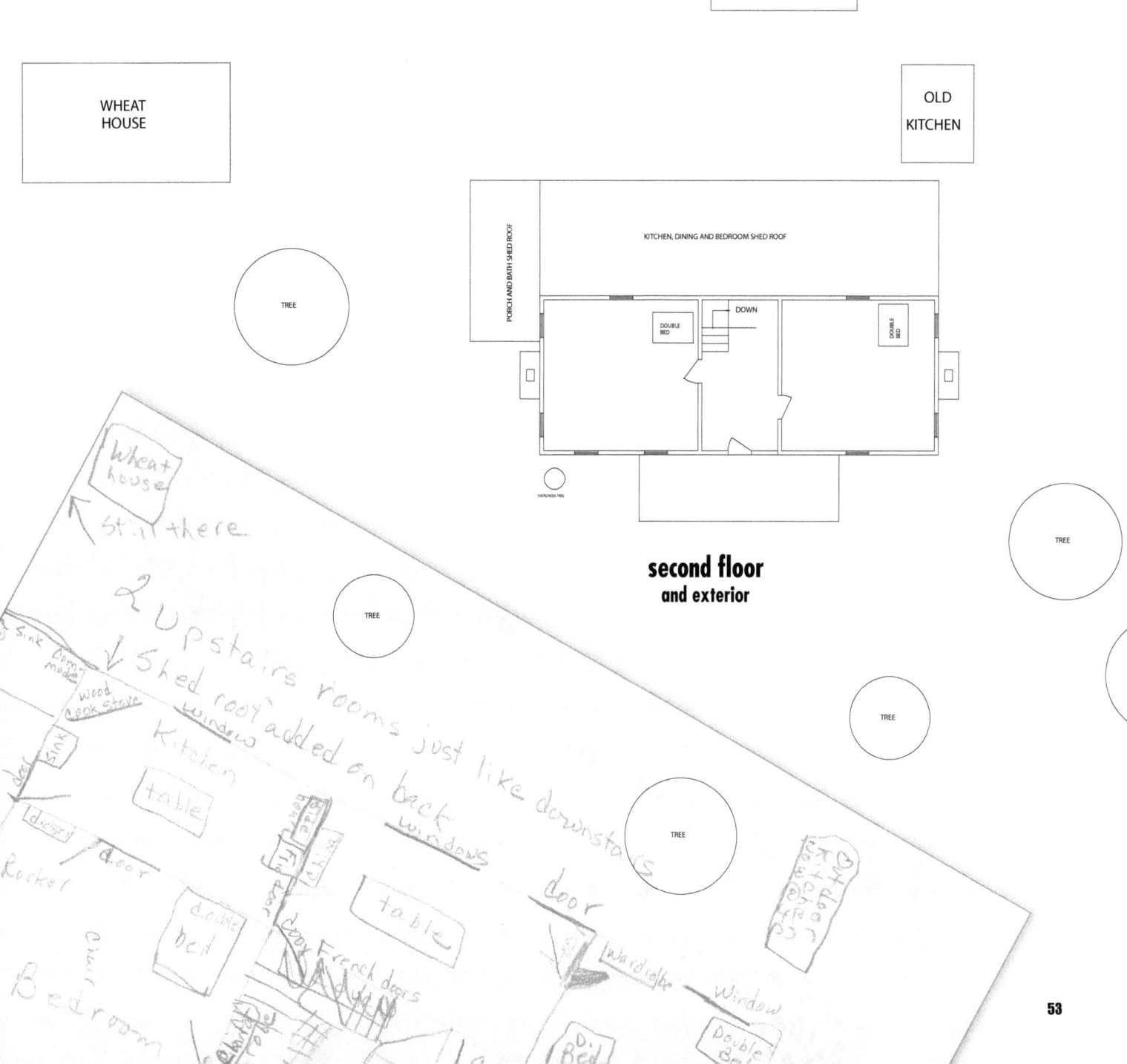

second floor and exterior

In 1957 Ben and Lizzie celebrated their 50th golden wedding anniversary. Several photos exist from this celebration. The main anniversary present was a pair of golden colored chairs (pictured on the opposite page). One of these chairs has survived and has been handed down as an heirloom. Juanita Pope, Ben and Lizzie's youngest grandchild who lives with her family on the same Pope farm today, displays the chair with pride in her home.

At the beginning of 1966 Lizzie struggled with pneumonia but a week or so into the year she appeared to be recovering. Ben himself was not well by this point, struggling with dementia. On the morning of 11 Jan, their daughter Mary was on her way to work and stopped by to check on things with her parents. Lizzie was not well and Mary knew the end was near. She stayed home from work to care for her mother. Guy was there as well. Both Mary and Guy held their mother as she slipped peacefully into the great beyond.

My mother Rhonda was at school in Home Ec class with Margie Pope, Guy's wife, that day. A school official came to the classroom and called Margie outside. My mother overheard the conversation, "Mrs. Pope, we just received news that your mother-in-law has died." This was how my mother received the news about her Grannie's death.

Ben's mind was so bad that he never really realized Lizzie was dead. Needing constant care, he lived in a nursing home in Calhoun for a while and later in Dalton. Mary would take her break from working at the spread factory to go see her father and feed him lunch. He departed this world only a few months after Lizzie on 3 May. The cause of death was atherosclerosis.

Grannie and Gramp, as they are known by their grandchildren, are laid to rest at East Armuchee Baptist Church.

Top: Lizzie feeds Ben anniversary cake at their 50th wedding anniversary celebration.

Bottom: Rhonda watches Ben & Lizzie try out their new chairs.

Opposite: The Pope family gathers around the table for a delicious country dinner. L to R: Bobbie Pope (face not seen, arms folded), Hill Pope Jr, Helen Pope, behind Helen you see the side of Mary Earl Jordan's face, Rhonda Jordan, June Pope, Joan Pope, then Mary Pope Jordan. Behind Joan is Orville Pope, to the left of him is Linda Pope, and Battie Lee Pope. To the right of Mary Pope Jordan: Jim Pope, Marie Larman Jordan, Robert Jordan, and the shoulder of J.C. Pope.

(Collection of Mary Pope Jordan)

Pope - Clement Reunion

Saturday, July 6th, 1996

 Home of Carl and Charlotte Griggs
1810 Wood Valley Drive
Dalton, GA 30720
(706) 278-7711

Old-fashioned Picnic at 5:00

Bring a picnic dinner for your family.

Drinks and utensils will be provided.

Activities beginning at 3:00 P.M.

(Swimming, Tennis, Softball, etc.)

Bring your own swimsuits, towels, racquets, gloves, etc.

And in thy seed shall all the kindreds of the earth be blessed. Acts 3:25

The Pope clan has always come together for family reunions. There have been numerous gatherings over the years.

Above left: Invitation to the 1996 reunion, designed by Jordan M. Scoggins (Collection of Rhonda Jordan Scoggins)

Above right: Siblings Martha, Guy, and Mary at the 1994 reunion. (Collection of Rhonda Jordan Scoggins)

Right: Family gathered at Ben & Lizzie's for the 1960 reunion. (Collection of Mary Pope Jordan)

Opposite: Reunion at Ben & Lizzie's about 1945. L to R: Lizzie (cut off), Guy with Ben behind, Bennie, Burke, Georgia Mae Richardson, George Hames, Charlotte with suspender straps, J.C. and Helen with Karen and Jim (and dog) in front of them, Mary Earl, Mary, Earl, Orville holding Linda's shoulders, and Battie Lee. (Collection of Mary Pope Jordan)

CLEMENT, LOVE and ROBBS families
(and SHAHAN too)

Through Ben Hill's wife Nannie Elizabeth Clement, the Pope family connects to the Clement, Love, and Robbs families. Nannie Elizabeth was the daughter of James Constantine Clement and Emily Love.

CLEMENT

J.C. Clement was born 4 Jan 1852 in South Carolina. His parents were Madison Green Clement and Emily Robbs. Madison and his family appear on the 1850 census in Spartanburg, SC. By the 1860 census they had relocated to East Armuchee. Emily died two years later in 1862. Madison remarried in 1864 to Mary Ann Amanda Keown. Shortly thereafter on 18 Mar 1864, Madison enlisted as a Private in Co K of Georgia's 39th Infantry Regiment in the Confederate army. The regiment surrendered at Greensboro, NC on 26 Apr 1865. During the time of his service, he was promoted to a Full Sergeant (Historical, Soldiers & U.S.; National Park Service). Madison died 5 Mar 1901.

After moving from South Carolina to Georgia as a child, J.C. Clement lived his entire life in the East Armuchee valley. When he married Emily Love in 1871 he built a home in the community known as Trans. While it is no longer in the family the house does still stand. I don't remember who organized the outing or if there was a special occasion, but many of us went to the old Clement place once when I was little. My Grannie Mary, my sister Julie, my aunt Charlotte, my mother, and I posed for a photo at the house.

I remember exploring the house and recall feeling an eerie sense of the past. I imagined my ancestors living there, carrying out the mundane chores of their everyday life. I pictured what the home might have been like when my family lived there, wondered what the furniture was like and how the rooms were decorated. It must have seemed perfectly ordinary to them but to me it seemed like a beautiful place. Yes, it was practically a ruin at the time. But my imagination could see beyond that.

At one point we explored the second story and were in what must have been the bedrooms. A summer rain broke through the sky, seemingly out of nowhere as the day had previously been full of sun. The sound of the water beating upon the tin roof was loud and startling. My sister and I jumped, frightened by the sound, at first not knowing what it was. When we finally realized what was happening we laughed at our skittishness.

The family photo above was taken in the late 1890's. This print was scanned and restored from a badly faded 8x10" print made by my father, Michael Scoggins, in the early 1970's at the request of Mary Pope Jordan. Mary had an original, smaller version of the photo. My dad used the original to create an enlargement which for many years was displayed in Mary's home. I do not know what happened to the original print.

Emily Love died in this home at 12:30 in the morning on Thursday, 27 Sep 1917. Just a few weeks before she had been bitten on the cheek by a spider. This led to complications and blood poisoning was the cause of death. Funeral services were held at East Armuchee Baptist Church where her body is interred (Austin 48). J.C. lived for some time longer until 14 Dec 1935. He is also buried at East Armuchee.

Above: The Clement family. L to R: George Lester Keith, Carrie Green, George Luther, Callie, Emily Love, Mary Ethel, William Madison, Nannie Elizabeth, J.C. Clement. (Collection of Rhonda Jordan Scoggins)

Opposite page: We posed in front of the same house, c.late 1980's. Also see pg 71. L to R: Mary Pope Jordan, Julie Marie Scoggins, Charlotte Jordan Griggs, Jordan Michael Scoggins, Rhonda Jordan Scoggins. Photo by Glynn Griggs. (Collection of Charlotte Jordan Griggs)

Emily Love & J.C. Clement.
(Collection of Rhonda Jordan Scoggins)

Top row L to R: Billy Clement, Clement Price, Watson Clement, Nilla Keith, Hill Pope.
Bottom row L to R: Burke Pope, J.C. Clement holding J.C. Pope, Mary Pope. (Collection of Rhonda Jordan Scoggins)

19		Benjamin F.	1	M				S.C.
20	574	538	M. G. Clement	35	M	Farmer	1500	819	S.C.
21			Emily	32	F				"
22			William G.	15	M				"
23			Frederick W.	11	M				"
24			Martha J.	13	F				"
25			James C.	8	M				"
26			Perry J.	4	M				Geo
27			Permelia E.	6/12	F				"
28			J. J. P.	48	M	Farmer	1800	10285	S.C.

Section of the page in the 1860 U.S. federal census where Madison Green Clement's family appears. The census shows he was a farmer with $1,500 worth of real estate and $819 value of personal estate. His place of birth is South Carolina. (Ancestry.com 1860)

J.C. Clement family, taken about 1894.
Top row, L to R: Carrie Green Clement, Nannie Elizabeth Clement, Callie Clement, George Luther Clement
Bottom row, L to R: J.C. Clement, William Madison Clement, Emily Love holding Mary Ethel Clement
(Collection of Mary Pope Jordan)

LOVE

Emily Love is the daughter of William Jasper Love. William was born in Haywood County, NC and came to Georgia some time before 1842 when he married Elizabeth Caldwell Sims in Gilmer County, GA. Census records show that in 1850 he resided in Murray County and in 1860 he resided in Dalton. In 1862 he moved to Walker County where he lived the rest of his life. While William's occupation was a farmer he also served as a Justice of the Peace for the 953rd district of Walker County from 1881 until his death. He died of cancer on his face (Lowe 1; Walker Heritage 260).

William's father was John Love, who was born in Ireland about 1788. His mother, Elizabeth McCarter, was born about 1795, also in Ireland.

Above: Tintypes of John Love and wife Elizabeth McCarter. (Shared by Nita Henry [bnh711] on Ancestry.com)

Right: Wm. Jasper Love's house in Villanow. The house was torn down in the late 1990s/early 2000s. (Shared by LundieDyer27 on Ancestry.com)

The large portrait above is of Wm. Jasper Love as an older man (collection of Charles Clements) while the smaller image is a tintype from his younger years (shared by Nita Henry [bnh711] on *Ancestry.com*). To the right is his Justice of the Peace certificate. (Shared by LundieDyer27 on *Ancestry.com*)

James CLEMENT
b. abt 1795
d. ?

William ROBBS
b. 19 Jul 1787 in North Carolina
d. 15 Feb 1876 in Georgia

John LOVE
b. abt 1788 in Ireland
d. abt 1880 in Georgia

↓

Madison Green[1] —— Emily
b. 11 Feb 1823 in South Carolina | b. 12 Oct 1825 in South Carolina
d. 5 Mar 1901 in Georgia | d. 15 May 1862 in Georgia

↓

Wm Jasper [I]
b. 20 Mar 1816 in North Carolina
d. 8 Jun 1891 in Georgia

↓

James Constantine ———————————— Emily
b. 4 Jan 1852 in South Carolina | b. 24 Aug 1852 in Georgia
d. 14 Dec 1935 in Georgia | d. 27 Sep 1917 in Georgia

↓

my great-grandmother Nannie Elizabeth,
my grandmother Mary Evelyn,
my mother Rhonda and then me

---

[1] Madison's first wife was Emily. His second wife was Mary Ann Amanda Keown, who connects to my father's family! See pg 222.

In her work on the descendants of John and Elizabeth, Mary Ann Lowe writes:

> "There was a boat *The Brothers* that sailed from Londonderry to Philadelphia in December of 1806. In steerage was a James Love ... and a Thomas McCarter. I have not been able to prove it, but I believe these were the fathers of John and Elizabeth" (Lowe 1).

Mary Ann recalls how her grandfather George Washington Love (son of McCarter, John and Elizabeth's youngest son), "remembered going to visit John and Elizabeth and hearing them speak in Gaelic when they didn't want the children to understand them" (Lowe 1).

The Love family is unique in my ancestral history, having arrived in this country much later than any other family line.

Top: me at the grave of William Robbs in Talley Cemetery in Trans. The tombstone of his wife, Malinda Green, is flat on the ground to my left, Nov 2010. (Photo by Michael D. Scoggins)
Bottom: a page from the original will of William Robbs. (Collection of Rhonda Jordan Scoggins)

ROBBS

Emily Robbs, my 3rd great grandmother and wife of Madison Green Clement, was the daughter of William Robbs. A receipt from the CSA dated 5 Sep 1863 shows that William sold 150 bushels of corn to the army at Green Bush (Receipt Robbs). He outlived his daughter by five years. I do not know the cause of her early death. Both are buried in Talley Cemetery in Trans.

Mary Pope Jordan had the original copy of William Robbs's will which was passed down to her daughter (my mother) Rhonda Jordan. The 1872 will is handwritten, yellowed from age, and difficult to read. Of note in my direct family line, he left $50 to his grandson J.C. Clement, my 2rd great grandfather.

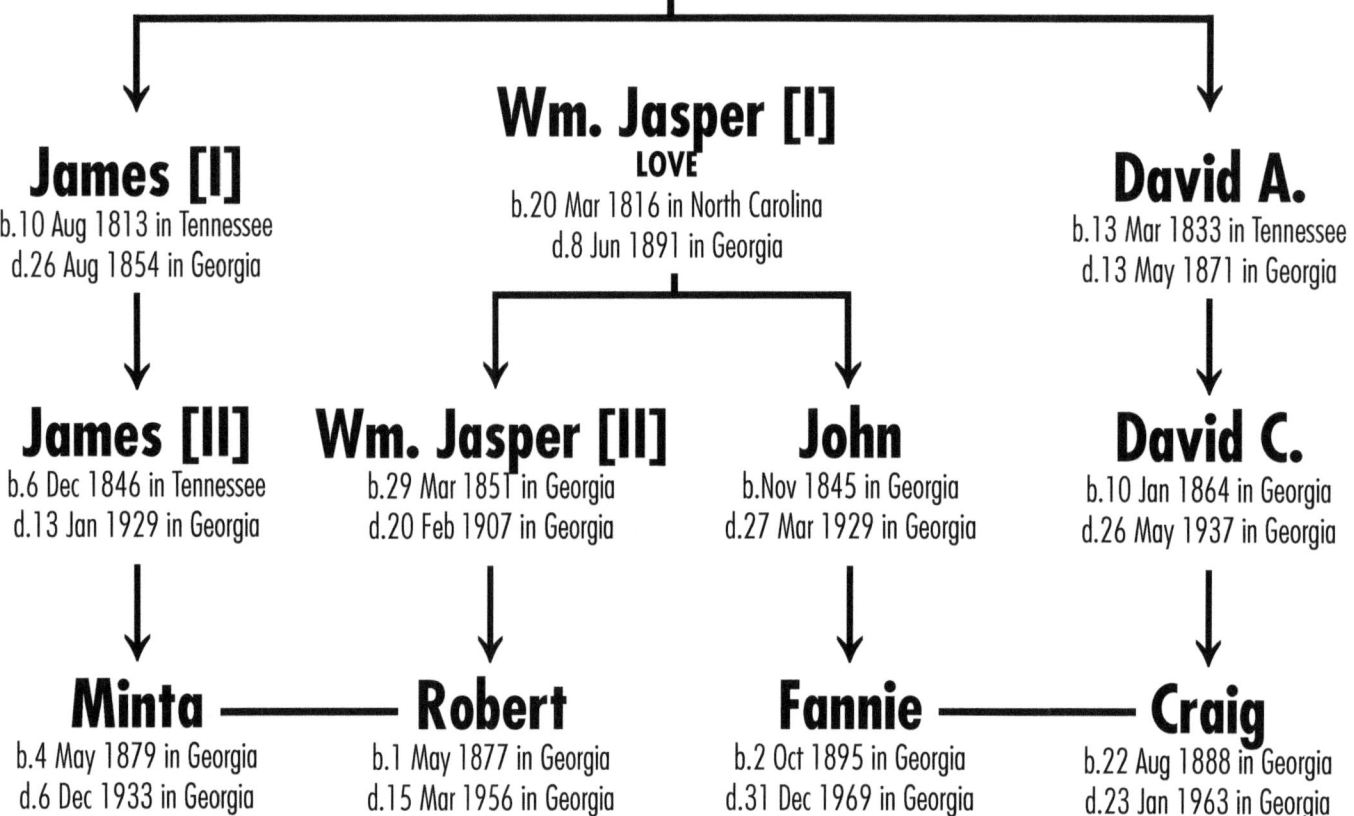

SHAHAN

Through the Love family there are a couple of connections to the Shahan family. I do not descend from the Shahan family but write about them here because of their intermingling with my family.

William Jasper Love's son John Robert (my 2nd great grand uncle) married Georgia Gober. Their daughter Fannie Jewell Love married Craig Shahan

The other Shahan connection comes through John Robert's brother William Jasper Love [II]. William's first wife was Rebecca Dobson. His second wife is Earlie Keown. William and Rebecca's son Robert Dobson Love married Minta Shahan. Minta is the daughter of James Alexander Shahan [II] and Martha Jane Keown. Earlie (Robert's step-mother) is the niece of Martha Jane (Robert's mother-in-law)! (See page 218 for more information about the Keown family).

Minta Shahan (b.1879) and Craig Shahan (b.1888) are second cousins, both descending from John Shahan. John was born in Delaware in about 1783.

This iconic barn is very old and sits on the original Shahan home place just across the road from the Shahan house in Villanow. Howard is a son of Fannie and Craig above. Ironically, after 9/11 the "H," "O," and "D" in Howard had fallen and said "WAR" for some time. May 2010. (Photo by Jordan M. Scoggins)

TRANS
by Emily Clement Payne

Ah! Trans! The Shangri-La of my childhood. For me, it was a place surrounded with love and beauty. Nestled at the foot of Dick's Ridge and on the banks of Dick's Creek for awhile it was a little hamlet with no name. There was a store, a sawmill, a cotton gin and a school. The school was on the hill across the road. I don't know if Prof. Sarten was the first teacher but I believe he was. Prof. Moore came next and named the hamlet. He came over the mountain from Everett Springs in Floyd County. He named the hamlet "Trans" which means over because he had to come "over" the mountain.

I wish I knew all the names of the people who originally lived in the 6 or 7 houses there but I don't. The Keowns first lived in the house on the hill above the spring. W. M. Clement had the original deed with the beeswax seal attached for a long time. J.C. Clement bought it from Keown. J.C. Clement sold it to Matthew Grigsby, only the chimney remains [pictured here]. On that place just south and on the left toward Richardson's store on East Armuchee Road was an empty house. I never knew who lived there. In the other direction on past the business area at the road intersection was the original Price house. Beyond them on the hill lived the Cleghorns and in the forks of the road past them the Hames resided.

Back at the road intersection going down the road through the gap to Manning's Mill where the Babbs live now, just across the creek Uncle Frank Price and Aunt Callie Clement Price had built a wonderful two-story house on the right. On the hill beyond was an empty 2 stored house with columns on the front. Empty, it was beginning to fall down and was said to be haunted. Mr. Gordon Keown (he worked at Berry College) sold some of the timbers to be used recreating the buildings at New Echota State Park in Calhoun. They did not use them there but in restoring Traveler's Rest near Toccoa.

Still further down the road, still standing in 2010 is the house J.C. Clement built for his bride, Emily Love in 1871. All their children, 2 infants who died at birth and were buried at Macedonia, Luther, Carrie, Callie, Lizzie, Billy and Ethel were born there. When some work was being done on the house in later years a little hand made, high top, leather shoe was found. It belonged to Uncle Luther and I have it at the farm. J.C. later bought the Keown place and his son William M. (Billy) Clement bought the original house when he married Leona Davis. I, Emily Clement Payne, was born there in 1920. Mother taught school in the school house on the hill.

I remember "The Spring" so well. By then Grandpa had moved into the Keown house and the spring was part of his place. There was a

Above: The chimney ruins of the Keown/Clement/Grigsby house in Trans.

Left: Talley Cemetery is in the cluster of trees in the middle of the field.

Opposite page: A close up view in the field surrounding Talley Cemetery.

(Nov 2010, Photos by Jordan M. Scoggins)

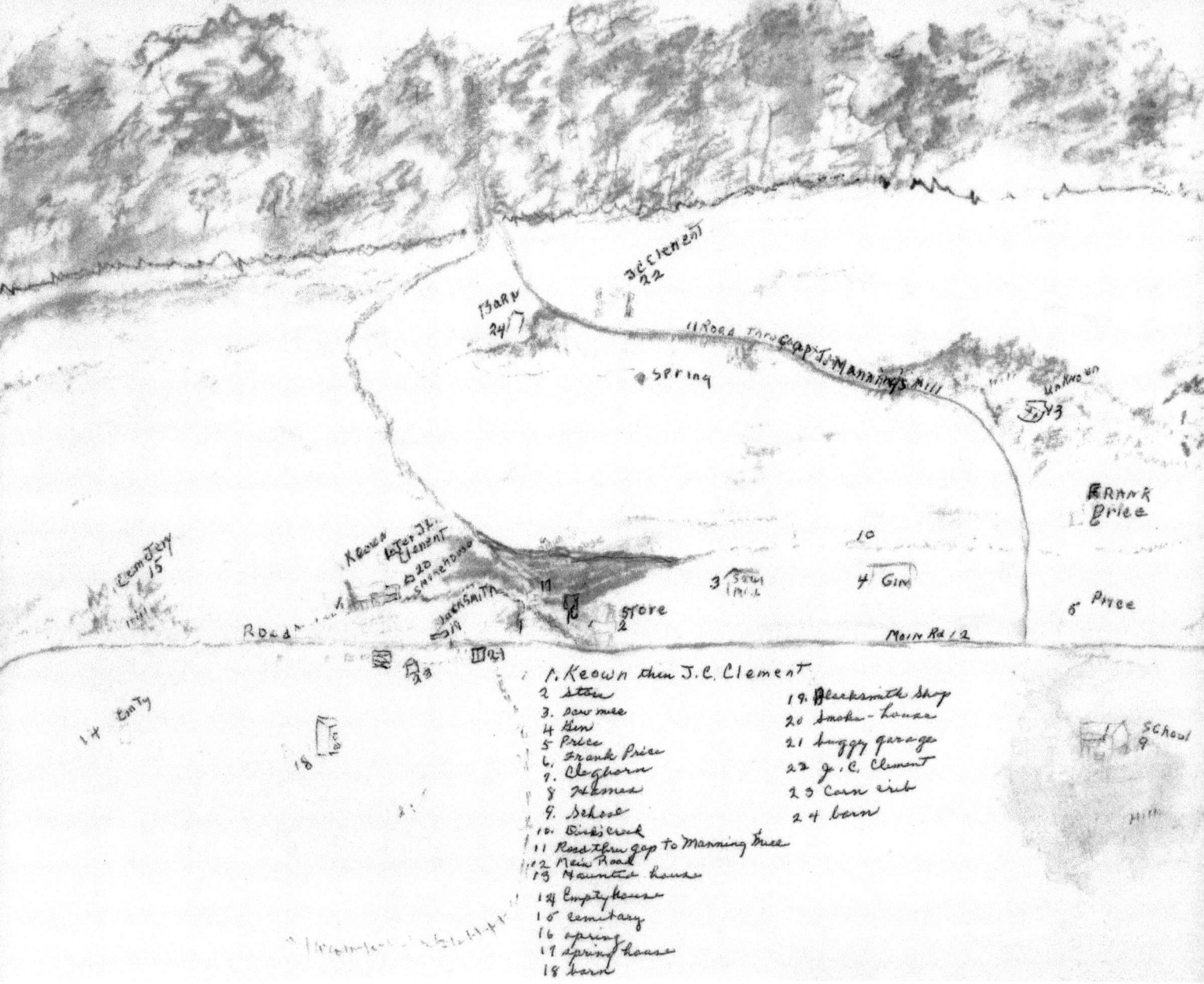

Above: Map of 1920's Trans (Drawn by Emily Clement Payne, 2010).

Opposite page: The back side of the J.C. Clement home as it appeared in the late 1980's. See photos of the front on pg 58-59. (Photo by Glynn Griggs. Collection of Charlotte Jordan Griggs)

wide beaten trail from the hamlet common to the spring. It was a gathering place for people far and near. Many a watermelon cutting, ice cream supper, picnic and family reunion was held there. Just below the spring was a community spring house. Inside there was a moat all the way around. Milk and butter were kept in the moat and anything that was to be kept just cool was placed on the island in the middle. Grandpa had installed a Ram in the stream just outside. It pumped water up the hill and into the kitchen of his house.

In my day Aunt Ethel (Clement) Clements ran the store. I was told many tales about things that happened when Frank Price ran it. Today I have the case of the wall clock and a thread cabinet from the store. The store had at least 3 rooms and a porch across the front.

In addition to the Spring the one teacher school was a place people gathered. They came to see and hear what their children were taught. The children came from far and near, walking, by horse back or mule or in a buggy. There was no such thing as a bus. The automobile had hardly been invented. All ages were taught in the same room. So much was taught by repetition aloud such as the alphabet and sound. B,a - bay, b,e - be, b,i - by, b,u - boo, bic a by bow boo was one exercise. Elocution was a part of the curriculum. My father could repeat some of the one that Felton Pope gave "I never learned to plow by watching my dear old father plow. God bless him, he was too fat to plow. I learned to plow by plowing."

In the early 20's a bond issue was held to build a school to consolidate West Armuchee, Villanow and Trans. The bond issue failed. After that one by one the people at Trans moved away until all were gone. Trans as a hamlet was no more.

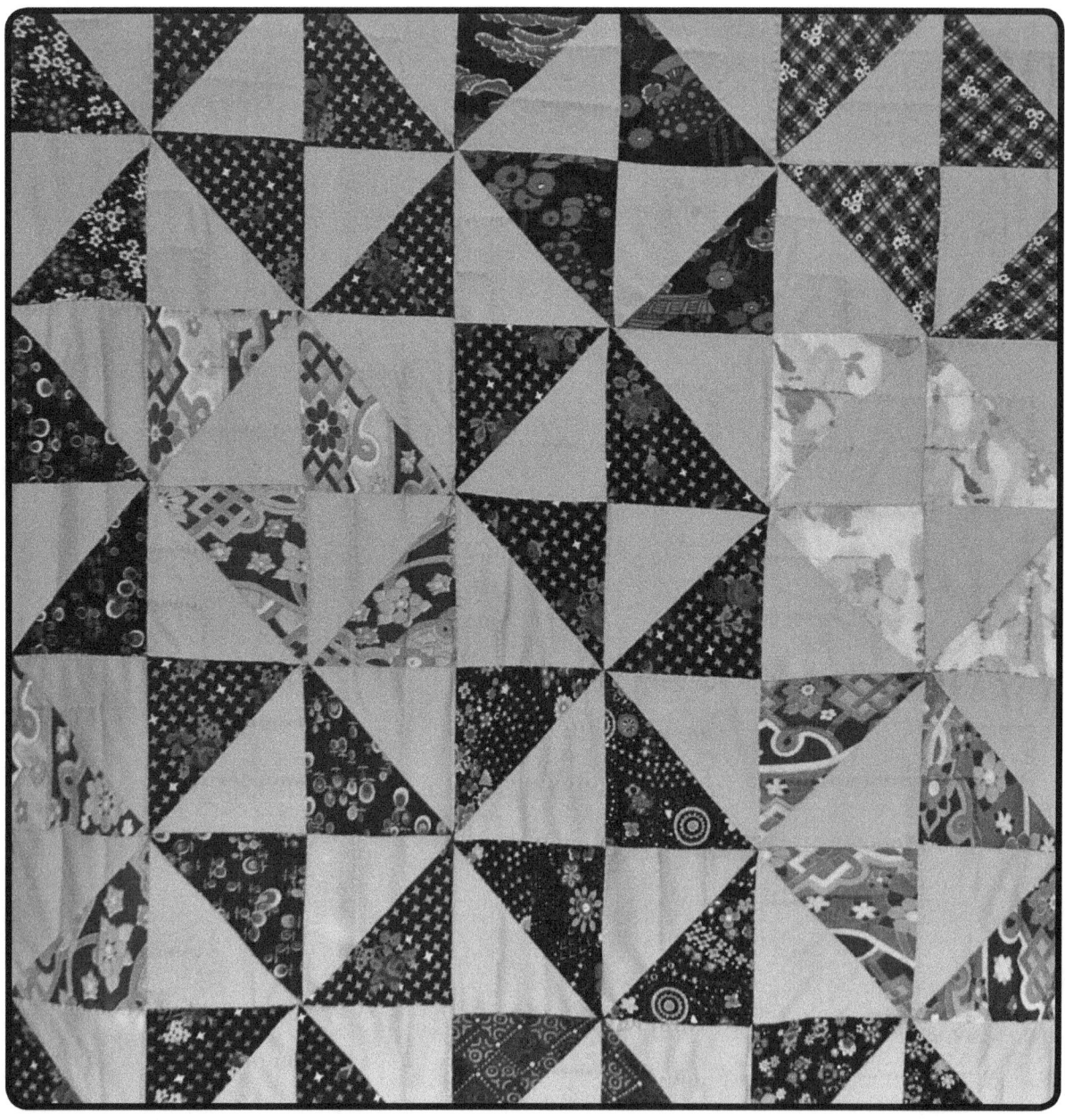

Mary Evelyn Pope
b. 13 May 1913 d. 6 Sep 2004
married
Earl Felix Jordan
b. 5 Mar 1911 d. 28 Nov 1994

Mary Evelyn Pope was born at home in East Armuchee near Villanow on 13 May 1913. Because of this she always claimed 13 was her lucky number! She was the third child of her parents, Ben and Lizzie, and the oldest daughter. From the time she was born up until about 1925—when her grandfather Micajah Felton Pope died—Mary lived in the home on East Armuchee Road where (during my lifetime) Joan Pope lived for many years. After Felton's death Ben and his family moved into the house where his father had lived and remained there for the rest of his life.

Mary married Earl Felix Jordan 4 May 1930. I will tell more of this story and their life together in the chapter on Earl (beginning on pg 104). But here I want to focus on my memories specifically about—as I called her (and as she spelled it)—Grannie.

This page: Mary always disliked this portrait of herself. It is, however, my favorite image of her. c.late 1930's early 40's.
(Collection of Mary Pope Jordan)

Opposite: Detail from a quilt made by Mary. She gave this quilt to my mom during the blizzard of '93 as we didn't have many quilts in the house to keep warm!
(Collection of Rhonda Jordan Scoggins)

I am Mary's youngest grandchild. This comes with the unique distinction of a childhood where my grandparents had more time to devote to me, being retired from regular work in those twilight years (although neither of them ever really stopped working in one way or another). I am also the only grandchild who spent almost 15 years living on the same farm, just one door away. My life circumstances provided me with a unique experience that I most certainly was not aware of there in the midst of it. At 32 years old—not even half the age my grandparents came to be—I now well know their lives were far different from my own.

I have many memories of my Grannie. Fragments, scraps, and images form a patchwork quilt as rich as those Grannie sewed herself.

Grannie would set up her quilting table in her living room. I don't know how long it actually took her to complete a quilt, but to me it seemed like an eternity. I remember laying on the floor under the quilting table so I could watch her work her magic. I never quite understood how it worked but I found it endlessly fascinating. Her thimble stands out to me. Such a simple, little tool. It was an important tool to get the job done and perhaps a reminder that—in spite of life's beauty—if you are not careful it can hurt you like the prick of a needle. I don't know how many quilts Grannie made in her lifetime but I am lucky enough that she made two quilts for me. The first was made in the early 1980's. It featured farm boys in overalls on the front. The back side was made from a patriotic pattern with eagles and stars. It is a true country treasure. The second quilt

Left,: Detail from a quilt made in the early 1970's by Mary for her daughter Rhonda. (Collection of Rhonda Jordan Scoggins)

Below: The yellow pitcher Grannie always used to make Kool-Aid for me when I was a kid. She used the same pitcher to make lemonade for my mom when she was little (Collection of Julie Scoggins Cook)

Right: Grannie's iron skillet, used to cook up her famous french fries and numerous other delicious dishes.
(Collection of Julie Scoggins Cook)

was made around 1996. My mother and I found some fabric with dogs. We thought it would be nice to decorate my room using this as a motif. Mom made some curtains from the fabric and Grannie made the quilt. At this age I had already become aware of the artistry required and the soul imbued into such a creation that I requested of Grannie to stitch a signature into the finished quilt. This is probably the only quilt she ever actually "signed". The quilt still lives in my old room at my parent's house along with the curtains. The farm boy quilt lives with me in New York as a reminder of the simpler, quieter place from where I come.

One of the traits that identified Grannie is her down home, southern cooking. Any meal that Grannie prepared was always a treat. She was famous for her apple pies. These pies were more like turnovers than a normal pie. She picked the apples from trees in her yard. In stark contrast she made the crust from Pillsbury Grands canned biscuits. I can't help but wonder if it was an old recipe that she adapted to modern convenience or if that's how she always made them. Whatever the origin, this study in contrasts represents a bit of southern harmony: appreciate the simple world around you but adapt when and where you can without sacrificing your down home roots. This sort of distinctiveness is at the heart of southern identity.

You'd never enter Grannie's home and not hear that voice croon, "Don' cha want sumthin' ta drink?" She might serve you a classic southern iced tea, a Diet Rite, or—if you were lucky—a refreshing Tang. I can even remember Grannie making Kool-Aid for me. She kept pouches of the stuff in her pantry and used a large, yellow ceramic pitcher to mix and store the drink. This was always a special treat. My mother must have made Kool-Aid for me too but I don't remember that anywhere near as vividly as when Grannie made it for me.

Not far behind Grannie's thirst quenching question, she would chime, "Fig Newton? Little Debbie?" A sweet of one kind or another was always nearby, but these two were her favorites. Oatmeal Creme Pies were the classic standard but Star Crunch, Swiss Cake Rolls, Fudge Rounds, or Nutty Bars were not uncommon. At Christmas she would always have the tasty Christmas Tree Cakes. Sometimes Papa would take more than he was supposed to have, sneaking them away when no one was looking, and you might find an empty box. But even then my overall memory is a never-ending flow of goodies.

But my favorite food memory comes from a quieter place. Picture this:

It's late evening, the sun is down and I sit at the kitchen table with Grannie and Papa. It's mostly quiet except for me (I was a talkative boy). We have finished our meal except for some cornbread. We rip the bread into pieces and stuff it into a glass and pour on some buttermilk. Spoon in hand and taste buds anxious we dig in for a delicious treat. There is a feeling of rest, a calm sentiment about, as we wind down from the day.

I can see this scene as if from afar. And somehow this vague impression fills my mind with a dim evening light: comforting, relaxing, and bittersweet. Outside the air is still as night covers the country side. All is at rest.

I am struck by the way time marches on. As a child another day could never come too soon. As an adult I cannot seem to even catch up on life in the space of a week much less a day. I know there is a lesson in what I just said. What exactly am I trying to "catch up" to? What is this ever moving target that I'm always aiming towards but never reaching? All the while so many years have passed. If only I could tuck in at the kitchen table with Grannie for some cornbread and buttermilk one last time.

TEENAGE THESPIAN

My mother tells a story, passed down to her by Mary, about how Lizzie organized the local youth to put on plays. Mary remembered playing the title role in Dot, the Miner's Daughter. Written by Lizzie May Elwyn, Dot, the Miner's Daughter is not a well known play today. From the early Vaudeville stage it was written some time in the 1880's. Subtitled One Glass of Wine, the play dealt with the subject of temperance. Although I have not located the script to read myself it seems to eerily foreshadow the role of temperance Mary would attempt to play (successfully or not) for her husband later in life. Earl Jordan, that future husband, even played a part with Mary in the play! My own mother mused, "I just can't imagine my father being in a play. He must have done it to be with mama."

I can picture it so clearly, a country play in the roaring twenties. I wonder if Lizzie and Mary ever read about the Great White Way and dreamed of seeing a show on Broadway?

If old photographs serve as evidence Mary embodied the desires of young women in the twenties. She must have been a feisty teenager, a rural country girl who admired her urban counterpart flappers. I don't know if Mary ever wanted to leave the country but the Great Depression would all but make it impossible to do so as she came of age. So Mary led a life far more reserved than I imagine she might have experienced otherwise. That is not to say, however, that it was any less fulfilled.

Above, left: I love to photograph wildflowers that grow back home on the farm. Jun 2009. (Photo by Jordan M. Scoggins)

Above, right: A fashionable Mary sporting a sophisticated look, circa 1930. (Collection of Mary Pope Jordan)

When I was in middle school I interviewed Mary about the Great Depression. She looked back on the time with fond memories, emphasizing love of family and hard work ethics.

J About how old were you when the depression began?

M Well I guess I was 17, 18 and along there. I don't think it really started until after I married and I married at 17 and that was in May of 1930. So I don't remember exactly which year it started but it was in the early 30's.

J: Do you know about when it ended and about how old you were maybe?

M: Well I think when Roosevelt came in as president he did help everything a lot because he, you know, set up all these things for what they had, what they called CC camp for the boys. And there were jobs you know. He helped the world a lot it seems like when he came in as president. I don't remember exactly what year that was but it was in the early, well he died in the 40's I believe. He died in 1941. Was that it? I believe it was. But most all in the 30's the

A view of the house built by Mary and Earl in 1935. Jun 2009. (Photo by Jordan M. Scoggins)

depression was pretty much the same.

J: Who were you living with during the depression?

M: Well I was already married when it started.

J: So you had your own home with your husband?

M: Yes, uh huh. We lived with his mother and daddy for a year [in Whitfield county] and then we moved back home and then we bought some land from my daddy. And my daddy gave Earl the timber. He cut it and had it sawed. His brothers were saw milling at that time. They sawed the lumber for him. And he stacked it and dried it. And when it got dried well we got one of my brothers and some of his kin and they helped to build the house so we just built our own home. That was 1935. We didn't have it all sealed at first but then he cut more timber and had more lumber sawed and then we eventually sealed a five or six room house and built us, you know, a pretty good country home in 1935

Mary's three oldest children in the field picking cotton: Charlotte, Mary and Robert. They are displaying the "v" for "victory" during WWII in the early 1940's. My mother was not yet born. (Collection of Jordan Michael Scoggins)

J: Did you have a job during the depression?

M: Well we worked in the fields mostly then because growing cotton was the main cash crop. Of course the whole family went to the field. We picked about enough to make two 500 lb bales of cotton in a week at least, our family would. The families would join together and help pick. Well not at first we didn't pick that much until we had children to get up of age before they were big enough to help pick. But you could very easily hire somebody to come in and pick cotton and get it picked because everybody was looking for work back then and they were willing to do seems like anything they could get to do. So that was our main cash crop was growing cotton and so we had everything else we grew to eat. We'd eat. We didn't suffer too much during the depression because we already had these things and lived on the farm and could work and make a little money that way. We had our cow for milk. We had chickens for eggs and then we could sell those chickens. Catch them when they were big enough for fryers to fry and you could sell them and we would have what you'd call a peddling wagon. He'd go around. At first they came out from LaFayette. But then when Mr. Porch got started at Villanow he had what he called a peddling wa—it wasn't a wagon. It used to be on a wagon way back yonder when I was just a kid. But then he had a truck that was closed in of course and carried groceries around and he'd come around to your house each week. You could sell him a few eggs, a few pounds of butter, and a few chickens and a get a little extra money there. And it just didn't take too much money to buy enough groceries to finish out what we would need other than what we had, you know.

J: About how much money would you make from selling stuff?

M: Oh, I don't know, let me see. It just depended on what you were selling. I mean you could go out there and pick cotton for somebody and they'd give you something like a dollar for a hundred pounds and if you could pick two hundred pounds a day you could make two dollars a day. And back then why that 2 dollars would go, you know, a long ways. So really and truly, I mean, it just didn't hurt us too much since my daddy owned quite a bit of land and we were on his farm and would help each other.

J: Money you did get, did y'all spend it on things you needed or did you spend it on pleasures?

M: Well we just usually bought what we needed. We didn't go out for much pleasure.

J: Do you have memories from the depression?

M: Well I remember all right but I don't have any bad memories. We had been taught to do all these things we had to do during the depression and it just kind of come natural and we made a few pennies. I mean, a little change was appreciated because you know it would go a long way. You could take 10 cents and go to the store and buy a big little bag of chocolate drops, it'd be just a nice little bag. And well you couldn't buy a bar now, I mean one little piece I don't guess for 10 cents. Nothing didn't cost as much. You could take 5 dollars and buy a week's supply of groceries it seems like. I guess I already told you how we'd sell to the peddling wagon.

J: Were the times really hard?

M: Well not really for us. Since my daddy had a big farm and we all worked in the field and mama had taught me sewing and I knew how to sew. She taught me to quilt and I knew how to quilt. And we would all get together, you know, and do those things and really we kind of enjoyed it.

J: Was the money ever hard to come by or did you have any problem with getting money?

M: No, not really, because everybody farmed and somebody, if you didn't have stuff together at home, you could go out and pick cotton for somebody else and make a little money if you were willing to work. And we had all been taught to work and, you know, it wasn't a problem. We never did go hungry or anything. Of course we didn't buy nice expensive clothes. We made most of them. I made most of my children's clothes.

J: Did your friends have more money than you, or less than you, or about the same?

M: Well, some had more, yes. And some had less.

J: Were you jealous of those who had more? Or if you had more than others did you show it off?

M: No, no. Families all helped each other seems like back then. Everybody would just kind of work together.

J: How has the depression affected your present life?

M: Well, it's taught me that you can get by on less if you have to if it comes down to it. Like the storm of 1993 when we didn't have electricity. We had to burn wood for heat. And really, I mean, we would have been better off if we had a cook stove then like we did back in those days because we could have cooked our food. But we managed I mean by cooking on the fireplace some, by having wood to burn you know. My grandson [Jordan Scoggins] lived close to me and pulled down the wood that was up on the side of the hill on a big plastic sheet. And really we all had fun during that depression! [she laughed]

J: Can you remember how much flour and sugar and gas might have cost during the depression?

M: Well gas, I remember when it was 17 and 18 cents a gallon. You could take a dollar and go put enough gas in your car to do a long time. And now, I mean, you know it's way over 1.00 a gall in't it? It's more than 5 times more now than it was then.

J: Did the flour and sugar come in little bags like they do now or did you get them in big bags?

M: Oh we got them in big bags. I believe it might have been, I don't remember if they were 25 or 50 pound those flour sacks. Dad would used to buy, he'd buy 4 at a time. They call that a barrel of flour. I reckon 4 sacks would make a barrel. And that would get through winter. Then we'd save those flour sacks and bleach them white and have dish towels and things out of them you know.

J: Did your family have an automobile in the depression?

M: Yes, yes.

J: For people that lived around you, did any of them suffer from the depression?

M: Well not too many I don't believe that were close around. Because families helped out families and, you know, they could always get out there and do a little work and get a little money if they had been taught to work as most families had back then.

J: So no one around you really suffered?

M: Not that I remember of. I remember one lady that didn't really have a family that when she got older had to go to the poor farm. You know, what they might call rest homes now.

J: Is there anything else you'd like to share about the depression?

M: Well just that it taught me that you can get through if you don't have all these conveniences, like the power going out you know.

Although Grannie recalled that her family didn't really suffer from the depression, general historical accounts of the Great Depression indicate the state of Georgia "was hit doubly hard" (Georgia Stories). I don't think Mary was glossing over the truth here though. The depression was particularly hard for Georgia because the 1920's had already been a time of economic crisis. This was largely due to the drop of price in cotton (in part due to the boll weevil, which arrived in 1915). Mary was born in 1913 so by the time she was old enough to be aware, the only world she ever knew was one wrapped up in widespread poverty and economic turmoil. While her hard work ethics are certainly commendable it's easy to see how it was a result of economic circumstances of the times. However, the Pope family was also somewhat sheltered as "large landowners were usually able to ride the depression out." Jamil S. Zainaldin of the Georgia Humanities Council notes:

"A small number of farmers who made the transition from cotton production to soybeans, peanuts, corn, livestock, and hogs had resources to fall back on. For the rest of Georgia's farmers (69 percent of the population was rural in 1930), the depression was a catastrophe."

Zainaldin goes on to describe the typical Georgia farm:

"[Most Georgia farms had] no electricity, no running water, and no indoor privies. Diets were inadequate, consisting mainly of molasses, fatback, and corn bread."

Mary's memories of raising chickens and milking the cow indicate her family had the extra resources needed to sustain themselves—something that was obviously not so common throughout the state at the time.

Both Georgia and the rest of the country weathered the Great Depression into the early 1940's when the United States entered World War II and finally turned the economy around. The first three decades of Mary's life—her pivotal years as a young woman—were not the best of times but certainly not the worst of times either. And to her it was all she had ever known. This ultimately made it easier to work through, but also it ensured Mary would be forever thankful for everything she had during the rest of her life. She was never a rich woman, but she lived her entire life on the farm that had been tended to by the generations before her.

Left: Mary with her little brother J.C., circa 1917. (Collection of Mary Pope Jordan)

Above: Julie's high school essay "The Person I Admire Most." (Collection of Julie Scoggins Cook)

Opposite: My portrait of Grannie during my last visit with her. 29 Aug 2004. (Photo by Jordan M. Scoggins)

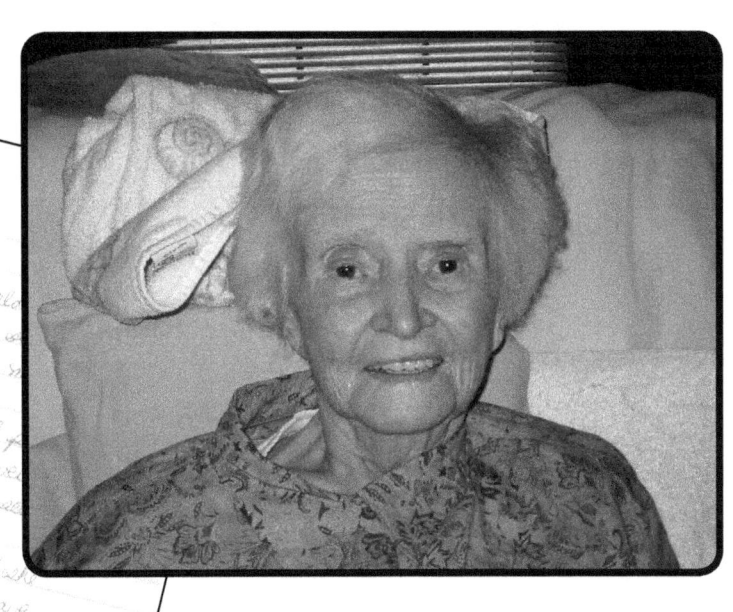

[I'll write more about Mary and her life on the Jordan farm in the chapter on Earl Jordan, beginning on pg 104]

As a woman all her own, Mary was deeply loved by the many people that made up her family and community. My sister, Julie, always had a close connection with Mary. In a high school English class Julie wrote an essay about the person she admired most. She chose Grannie. In the essay she recalls the home cooking, of course, but she honed in on Mary's sense of selflessness, writing:

"Grannie always puts others before herself. She does what ever Papa wants her to do. She cooks for us when we get sick and don't feel like cooking. Sometimes, she even cooks for us just to be cooking."

Today Julie has a spare bedroom in her home that she calls "Grannie's Room." She has decorated the room using furniture and other items that belonged to Grannie. It's a loving tribute and her way of keeping that connection alive.

When Grannie was dying in 2004 it was hard for all of us. Death is never easy. But death is particularly hard when it knocks on the door of someone you love so dearly. Living in New York and still in the trial period of my first professional job out of college, I got the call from my sister letting me know the situation. I didn't know how best to handle it. Fortunately I had an understanding boss who allowed me to take the time to go see Grannie.

She was staying in a hospital bed in her den, unable to walk or move around on her own. Weak and worn, she had lost a lot of weight. Mary had lived through nine decades, witnessing the world transform before her eyes. Yet she remained a constant force of love in that tiny valley I call home.

During that last visit I don't remember much about what we talked about. Mostly I remember just being with Grannie and holding her hand. I took some photos—probably the last photos ever taken of her. And, most importantly, I read a poem to her. Composed just days before, it was my way of saying goodbye. I knew it would be the last time I saw her. I wanted to bid her farewell, give her hope, and do my part to shine a light down that dark path looming before her. I wanted to show her that even though I now lived far away she was as close in my heart as all those years ago when I brought her firewood in the snow that now reminds us maybe we can live with a little less, for that is how Mary lived.

Grannie died on 6 Sep 2004, the week after my visit.

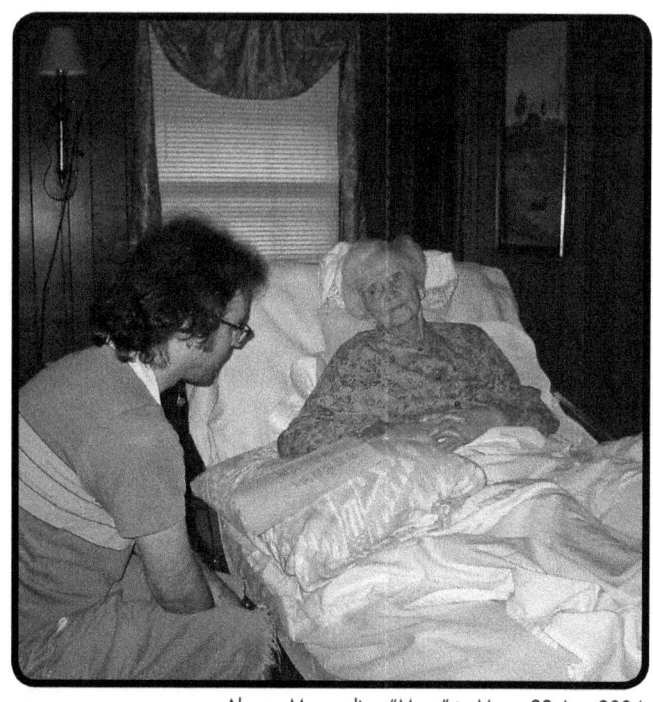

Above: Me reading "Mary" to Mary, 29 Aug 2004.
(Collection of Jordan M. Scoggins)

mary

mary, go to your garden:
there are flowers there
from seeds you planted
seasons ago, with care

and the food you grew,
tended daily with honest work,
your bonnet tipped towards the sun
to keep out the burning light

while through the night
i rested soundly in the next room
sometimes sitting up late to read,
sure to be quiet so not to wake you

mary, go to your garden:
there are flowers there
from seeds you planted
seasons ago, with care

i can only imagine
what your life was like
through the troubled decades,
two world wars and endless battles

and never mind the hassle
of raising four children,
tending to a husband who
would scarce hear a word you said

and now here you are
fragile as spinning glass,
unable to walk about;
immobile yet still noble

mary, go to your garden:
there are flowers there
from seeds you planted
seasons ago, with care

and now the cross you bear
is heavy like a load of bricks
weighing down upon your soul
waiting for the tock to tick

for the alarm to chime
for the sound of "welcome home"
as your body is released
and your soul is free

mary, go to your garden:
there are flowers there
and you can leave
your cross among them.

23 august '04 10:31pm

JORDAN

ANDERSON

William
b. 2 Jan 1762 in Virginia
d. 18 Sep 1848 in Alabama

↓

Burrell
b. abt. 1794 in South Carolina
d. 1880 in Georgia

↓

James Wm.
b. 30 Nov 1832 in Georgia
d. 24 Apr 1910 in Georgia

↓

Wm. Brownlow
b. 3 Jul 1863 in Georgia
d. 5 Jul 1956 in Georgia

↓

Earl Felix
b. 5 Mar 1911 in Georgia
d. 28 Nov 1994 in Georgia

↓

my mother Rhonda and then me

The Jordan family has roots in Colonial America like the Popes in the section before. Through the generations they migrated through the Carolinas and eventually to Georgia where I—many generations later—grew up.

Jordan Generations
The Jordan Family Origins

Like the origins of the Pope family at the beginning of this book, there is confusion about the colonial origins of my line of the Jordan family. I have been able to find fewer published accounts of this line and have had to depend on less reliable and under-documented online lineages, making this discernment all the more difficult.

Some of these online accounts identify a lineage starting with Thomas Jordan [I] (b.1600 in England, came to Virginia on the *Diana*). This lineage is documented in Meyer/Dorman's *Adventurerers of Purse and Person*, Bodie's *Seventeenth Century Isle of Wight County Virginia*, and *The Edward Pleasants Valentine Papers* (Vol. IV). Valentine goes as far as identifying Thomas [I] as the son of Samuel Jordan of Jordan's Journey, the inspiration for this book's title (2268). In contrast, Meyer/Dorman acknowledges this as only a possibility, not documented fact (379).

Descending from Thomas Jordan [I] is Thomas Jordan [II] (b.1634), then Thomas's [II] son Richard (b.1670). Richard married Rebecca Ratcliffe. They had a son named Joseph (b.1716). This constitutes the Thomas Jordan lineage (Bodie 116-23; Valentine 2268-74; Meyer 379-82)

However, there is a different Richard Jordan (b. abt 1672) of Surrey County, VA who also had a son named Joseph. This Richard Jordan [III] was the 3rd in a line of Richard Jordans. His father was Richard Jordan [II] (b.1655 in Isle of Wight County, VA), and his father was also Richard Jordan [I] (b. abt 1620). All the same names certainly make an already confused genealogy that much more confusing!

This Thomas Jordan lineage was the line I originally worked back to. But as I delved deeper I found errors in the lineage I had defined. My tree had Joseph Jordan with wife Hannah as the son of Richard Jordan (b.1670) and wife Rebecca Ratcliffe. In the Thomas Jordan lineage this Richard and Rebecca do indeed have a son named Joseph (Valentine 2269). The Joseph I originally had in my tree was born in 1716 while the actual Joseph in my line (what turns out to be the Richard Jordan [I] line) was born between 1694 and 1719. Based on birth date alone it could be the same person. But the Joseph (from the Thomas line) born in 1716 died in 1789. The Joseph (from the Richard I line) born between 1694 and 1719 died in 1770. This means I had Richard and his son Joseph from the Thomas Jordan lineage in my tree, with Joseph married to Hannah—Joseph's wife in the Richard Jordan [I] lineage. It was in combing this detail that I finally realized there are two distinct Jordan lineages with a Richard Jordan and son Joseph. But these lineages have become confused and mixed up, propagated by shared online trees. I

describe this mix-up here in order to point out the two separate lineages and hopefully help prevent future confusion!

It appears that this is the accurate lineage for my line:

> Richard I > Richard II > Richard III > Joseph (b. btwn 1694-1719 in Surry County, VA, d. btwn 11 Oct -20 Nov 1770 in Surry County, VA. He married Hannah in VA) > William > Burrell

And that the following, while an accurate lineage in and of itself, is not my line (nor have I found documentation that shows these two Jordan family lines are related even though they lived in the same area of the country):

> Thomas > Thomas > Richard > Joseph (b.18 Jan 1716 in VA, d.21 Feb 1789 in NC)

It's easy to see how the two Josephs, both with fathers named Richard, have been confused. Brazier's *Descendants of Richard Jordan I Family Website* and Baird's *Bob's Genealogy Filing Cabinet* have been my primary sources for understanding this lineage. Both of these sites contain numerous references to sources that illustrate the necessary evidence. While I have not yet been able to directly verify the sources myself, the work is logically sound and therefore it is what I have subscribed to here. I am not recounting the numerous land records and other items but rather providing a brief overview of the lineage for the purpose of gaining a general impression of my ancestors:

Richard Jordan [I] was born around 1620. It is not clear whether he was born in England or Virginia. He married Elizabeth Reynolds in Isle of Wight County, VA. Elizabeth died some time between 1668-78 in Isle of Wight. After Elizabeth's death he married Alice. She died around Mar of 1685/6. Richard outlived both wives and died in Surrey County around the beginning of May 1687.

I descend through Richard [I]'s son Richard [II]. Richard [II] was born abt 1655 in Isle of Wight and married around 1672 a woman named Elizabeth (b. abt 1655).

Richard [II] died before 3 Oct 1699 in Surrey County. He lived little more than a decade longer than his father. Elizabeth died after 1699.

Following my line of descent, Richard [II] and Elizabeth's oldest child, Richard [III], was born around 1672 in Surrey County. The name of Richard [III]'s wife is not known, but they married around 1694. He may have had other wives as well. Richard [III] died before Nov 1751 in Surrey County at about 78 years old.

Finally my line deviates from the name Richard and things get a little easier to follow! Joseph is Richard [III]'s youngest (known) child. Joseph was born between 1694 and 1719 in Surry County, Virginia. He married a woman named Hannah (her last name is unknown). Still in Surry County by the end of his life, Joseph died between 11 Oct and 20 Nov in 1770.

Opposite: Cotton growing on an Isle of Wight Farm.

Spanning the pages: Driving around the Isle of Wight countryside helped me get an impression of the general area where my Jordan ancestors lived.

Oct 2011 (Photos by Jordan M. Scoggins)

William Jordan
b.2 Jan 1762 d.18 Sep 1848
and his wife

Delilah
b.1760 d.12 Oct 1854

William Jordan is my 4th great grandfather and the youngest son of Joseph Jordan. He was born in Surry County, VA.

In late 1779 or early 1780, William was drafted into the army during the Revolutionary War. He was in a skirmish at Ashley Ferry and served as a cook for Col. Lowry. Honorably discharged in Apr 1780 after three months of service, William returned to his home in Edgecombe County (Pension).

Again in Feb or Mar of 1781 William was drafted into the service. He was at the battle of Guilford Courthouse. After that battle he was taken prisoner by Tories, "by whom he was deprived of all his clothes except his shirt & pantaloons." After he was turned loose he was sent home by an army captain to retrieve clothes for himself. He did as such, making his way back to Edgecombe, and then returned to the service. After three months of service since this drafted term, William employed a man named George Harris to serve out the remainder of his term. William's brother (name unknown) paid George, "a Horse worth about $100.00 dollars, a Beaver hat worth about $20.00, a coat, shirt & pair pantaloons worth about $6.50." George served for William for 12 months. Col. Hart provided a written discharge for William at the end of the term (Pension).

In his 1844 deposition, William claimed his total military service was 9 months in person and 12 months by substitute, for a total of 17 months. Unfortunately he had no proof for this as his home in Edgecombe burned about 1785. All documentation of his military service was destroyed, as well as any proof of his birth date (Pension).

After his service in the war, William married a woman named Delilah (last name unknown). They had four known children:

1. Elizabeth Betsy (b. abt 1780, m.Stephen Center Key, d.18 May 1883)
2. Burrell (b.abt 1794, m.Keziah, d. abt 1880)
3. William [II] (b.8 Aug 1798, m. 1st Elizabeth Davis, 2nd Nancy C. Murphy, d.4 Dec 1884)
4. Sarah (b. abt 1805, m.Samuel Nunis, d. aft. 1860)
5. Christopher Edward (b.21 Jun 1809, m.Mary Ann Knowles, d.7 Nov 1895)

According to Brazier's *Descendants of Richard Jordan I* web site there are several other children which have yet to be identified.

William and his family dispersed quite far from his original Virginia roots (the last four generations of his line having lived

Below: Two pages from William's pension claim file. (Obtained from Fold3.com)

> Bowdon, Geo.,
> Apr. 21st 1860.
>
> Dear Sir,
>
> My father was a Revolutionary Soldier from North Carolina served under Col. John Lowry — his name was Mr. Jordan & he was entitled to a Pension. I engaged some time since S R Boller of Ala. to attend to this for me, but I cannot learn anything about it. Please let me know immediately whether Mr. Boller or anyone else has ever drawn a Pension or not &c. I am a poor widow lady & I hope you will not fail to give me the information I desire,
>
> Respectfully,
> Elizabeth Key
>
> Direct your letter to me at Bowdon Carroll County, Georgia.
>
> Elizabeth Key

out their lives in Virginia's neighboring Surry & Isle of Wight counties). Around 1786, William and his family moved to Edgefield District, SC. He resided in Edgefield for 35 years. Around 1820 he moved to Elbert County, GA where he is counted on the 1820 and 1830 censuses. Some time in the early 1830's he moved to Newton County, GA. The deposition for his first pension application (#R5770) took place there on 22 Jun 1835. In 1840 William was counted in Newton County, and the pension file indicates he was living there in 1841. Some time after that he moved to Randolph County, AL, where he was living at the time of the deposition for his second pension claim (#R5773) (Pension).

The pension was ultimately rejected on the grounds that William's time as a cook "was not construed to be 'military service'" and therefore he did not meet the 6 month minimum requirement to receive a pension. William was unable to receive compensation for time spent serving his country (Pension).

In 1856, several years after his death, William's children Elizabeth, Burrell, Sarah (represented by her husband Samuel Nunis), and Christopher attempted to obtain the pension as William's heirs. They were also unsuccessful.

Both he and Delilah died in Randolph County, AL, as did their daughter Elizabeth. William [II] died in Wesobulga, Clay County, AL. Christopher traveled even further west, ending up in Arkansas. Burrell, my 3rd great grandfather, seems to have taken the safer route, remaining closest to the homeland and living the majority of his life in Georgia.

Burrell Jordan
b.abt. 1794 d.1880
and his wife

Keziah
b. abt 1805 d.1880

The Brick Store in Newton County stood at the crossroads of two major stagecoach routes, marked by the stone monument standing to the rear left of the building. The monument was erected 14 Jun 1933. Sep 2011 (Photo by Jordan M. Scoggins)

Burrell Jordan is one of those allusive ancestors who slips just far enough out of your grasp to *really* pique your curiosity. Born about 1794 in Edgefield County, SC, he later lived in Newton, Murray, and Whitfield Counties in Georgia. He married Keziah, born about 1805, in 1825 (probably while in Edgefield).

Keziah is even more of a mystery. Her maiden name and parents are completely unknown.

Burrell and Keziah had the following children:

1. Unknown daughter (b.abt 1823)
2. Faitha Caroline (b.14 Jul 1825, m.John Harrison Hackney, d.22 Nov 1904)
3. Anna Delano (b.abt 1827, m.Spencer B. Davis, d.21 Sep 1884)
4. Susan P. (b.Dec 1828, m.Joseph B. Hackney, d.?)
5. James William (b.30 Nov 1832, m.Mary Jane Evans (or possibly McRachen), d.24 Apr 1910)
6. Keziah Delilah (b.24 Jul 1836, m.Jesse Hawkins Tatum, d.23 Nov 1919)
7. Mary T. (b.Sep 1840, m.George Creekman, d.?)
8. Arminda J. (b.abt 1842, d.?)
9. Sarah J. (b.abt 1845, m.Lee Higdon, d.abt1904)

In 1830 Burrell was counted living in Newton County, GA. This census doesn't indicate where in the county he lived. However at that time there was an area called Winton, where today stands the oldest brick building in the county. Built in 1821, the Brick Store was a general store serving the needs of the community. What makes the Brick Store even more interesting is that it stood at the crossroads of two major stagecoach routes—from Charleston to New Orleans and from Ruckersville to Milledgeville. The route from Charleston is probably how the Jordan family migrated from South Carolina. Indeed, even with today's roads, if you use Google to plot the route from Edgefield, SC (where Burrell was born) to New Orleans, LA it takes you right through this area of Newton County. I don't mean to indicate any specific link between Burrell and the Brick Store. I present it as an example of a place that, as "the center of the area's activity," he would have known—and maybe even a place he shopped (Morris; Talley-McRae; Newton Historical).

It is interesting to note that the Brick Store was deeded to Newton County Historical Society by Charles Malvin Jordan (b. abt 1893) in 1971 (Newton Historical). The Newton County Tax Assessor shows this listed as parcel 1240-00000-

006-000. The adjoining property's (parcel 01240-00000-001-000) owner is listed as the Jordan Family Trust (Newton Tax). Charles Malvin is the son of Charles Jordan (b. abt 1858). I do not know if this Jordan family is related to my Jordan family.

I have been unsuccessful in locating Burrell and Keziah in 1840 but in 1850 they appear on the census in Murray County. By 1860 they had moved yet again to the neighboring Whitfield County, appearing on the census there in 1860 and again in 1870. By the 1880 census Burrell had died and Keziah was a widow living with her daughter Keziah Delilah. Her death followed later that year.

My grandfather Earl Jordan often spoke of an Indian ancestor

The Jordan, Anderson, and Boling lines are documented well enough that I can confidently say there is no trace of Native American ancestry here. Evans, Hackney, and Mattox are less well documented. And of course there are the two with unknown maiden names—Keziah and Mary. At this point in time there is just not enough information to determine the true story. This is one of those family mysteries that could be rooted in an all-too-common genealogical fairy tale, or it could be completely true. Without the documentation to support or deny the story I will never know for sure. Maybe this will come to light eventually!

Burrell and Keziah's final resting places are unknown. I have searched cemeteries in and records for Whitfield County—

and claimed he was one-eighth Cherokee. If this is true that means his full-blooded Cherokee ancestor would have to be one of his great grandparents:

- Burrell Jordan and his wife Keziah
- Lee L. Evans and his wife Charity Hackney
- Abraham Anderson and his wife Elizabeth Mattox
- William Boling and Mary unknown

where they would have been living—and have yet to uncover a clue. After Burrell's death Keziah lived with her daughter Keziah Delilah's family. Keziah Delilah and her husband (as well as her sister Faitha) are buried in Mt. Olivett Cemetery. Perhaps Burrell and Keziah are laid to rest there in an unmarked grave.

James William Jordan
b. 30 Nov 1832 d. 24 Apr 1910
married

Mary Jane Evans*
b. 22 Nov 1838 d. 27 Mar 1917

James W. Jordan was the oldest son of Burrell and Keziah. James was born in Newton County, GA on 30 Nov 1832. At age 25 he married Mary Jane Evans* on 31 Dec 1857 in Whitfield County. Census records show they lived in Whitfield County for the rest of their lives.

James and Mary had the following children:

1. Louisa Frances (b.23 Oct 1858, m. 1st John Cole, m. 2nd William Bruce, d.29 Jun 1908)
2. Faith C. (b.8 Feb 1860, m. John William McAlister, d.7 Nov 1950)
3. William Brownlow (b.3 Jul 1863, m.Isabell Anderson, d.5 Jul 1956)
4. Henry Alonzo (b.17 Mar 1865, m. 1st unknown, 2nd Martha Creasman, d.8 Dec 1944)
5. Sara A. (b.1869, d.?)
6. Charity (b.14 Jul 1870, m. Jesse T. Ledford, d.30 Mar 1950)
7. John B. (b.abt 1873, m. unknown, d.26 Nov 1946)
8. George Washington (b.23 Aug 1874, m.Emma Octavia Anderson, d. 21 May 1951)
9. Adeline Keziah (b.6 Apr 1876, m. Thomas Milburn Whitson, d.3 Mar 1956)
10. James W. (b.1 Jul 1878, m.Etta Louisa Cole, d.12 Jun 1952)
11. Lucy (b.Nov 1880, m. unknown Bruce, d.?)

* Some suggest Mary Jane is a McRachen. I have found no proof of this but document it here as another theory to be aware of.

Prater's Mill has no specific connection to the Jordan family. However, being established in 1855, it was founded during the same period that Jordans lived in the general area. Sep 2011.
(Photo by Jordan M. Scoggins)

James is of the correct age to have served in the Civil War. While there are military records for a James W. Jordan from Whitfield County, I have been unable to verify for sure that this is my James. The James who fought in the war first enlisted on 16 Dec 1861 in Co G of the 10th regiment, GA State Troops. On 15 May 1862 he transferred to the 34th Georgia Infantry, Company A (Historical, Soldiers). His service records reveal his enlistment in the 34th happened in Dalton for a term of three years (Service records James).

While at first this matches up with my James, the birth of his children makes it a little more difficult to say for certain. Two of James's children were born during this time frame: William Brownlow (3 Jul 1863) and Henry Alonzo (17 Mar 1865). William would have been conceived in roughly Oct 1862. The 34th was fighting in Kentucky during that time. Unless James was on furlough this does not seem to match up—and unfortunately his service records are minimal and shed no light on his whereabouts during this time period. The next child, Henry, would have been conceived in roughly Jun of 1864. During this time the regiment was fighting in Northwest Georgia so it is conceivable James was able to visit his wife while in the area. Unfortunately I have uncovered no records that provide any additional clues here. I cannot say for certain whether or not my James, my 2nd great grandfather, fought for the CSA or not (Historical, Regiments).

Through James I have discovered some interesting connections to the Hackney family:

James William Jordan's sister Susan P. Jordan married Joseph B. Hackney. Joseph's sister was Charity Hackney. Charity was married to Lee L. Evans (m.6 Jan 1850). Their daughter Mary Jane Evans married Burrell Jordan's son James William Jordan.

This makes Charity Hackney my 3rd great grandmother. But she is also the sister-in-law of my 2nd great grand aunt Susan P. Jordan in a different line of the family.

The Jordan/Hackney connection doesn't stop there and goes back even further. The oldest daughter of Burrell Jordan (and Susan and James William's sister) is Faitha Caroline Jordan. Faitha married Joseph B. Hackney's brother, John Harrison Hackney.

What a web we weave! All this means that Mary Jane's aunts Susan and Faitha are also her sisters-in-law. So, then, Susan and Faith's children are Mary Jane's first cousins while she is simultaneously their aunt!

At 78 years old, James died on 24 Apr 1910. Mary lived for another 5 years until 27 Mar 1915. They are buried in Varnell Cemetery.

William Brownlow Jordan
b. 3 Jul 1863 d. 5 Jul 1956
married

Isabell Anderson
b. 18 Oct 1871 d. 20 Mar 1946

The oldest son of James W. Jordan, William Brownlow Jordan was born on 3 Jul 1863. He married Isabell "Belle" Anderson on 16 Oct 1892 in Whitfield County. They spent their entire life together in Whitfield County and had the following children:

1. unnamed infant (b. & d. 1894)
2. Henry Lee (b.8 Aug 1895, m.Ella A. Pangle, d.2 Jan 1953)
3. James Abraham "Abe" (b.7 Feb 1898, m.Lillie Bryant, d.12 Dec 1982)
4. John William "Bill" (b.3 Jul 1899, m.Jewie Robinson, d.9 Jul 1985)
5. Cora (b.13 Oct 1901, m.John Wesley Wiggins, d.13 Jul 1983)
6. Estelle (b.30 Oct 1903, m.Harvey Turner, d.3 Jan 1999)
7. Carl Earnest (b.29 Apr 1906, d.8 Nov 1923)
8. Mary Jane (b.18 Sep 1908, m.John Wiggins, d.28 Mar 2006)
9. Earl Felix (b.5 Mar 1911, m.Mary Evelyn Pope, d.28 Nov 1994)

When the children were growing up they lived in the Dawnville area of Whitfield County. They first lived in the Anderson home on top of the hill. Their water source was a spring at the bottom of the hill. William fixed a way to draw water from that spring up to the house. Later William and Isabell built their own house at the foot of the hill near the spring. That house still stands on parcel no. 09-001-01-000 (Whitfield).

A couple of years before Earl—William and Isabell's youngest son and my grandfather—died, my aunt Charlotte took Earl back to his childhood home to see it one last time. Earl showed Charlotte the old spring which still ran with fresh water!

Charlotte has vivid memories of her Papaw and Mamaw Jordan:

"The thing I remember most about Papaw was how lovingly he attended to Mamaw as she was an invalid for many years before she died. She had rheumatoid arthritis and was confined to a wheelchair [for about the last 15 years of her life, as she had once stepped in a hole and badly hurt her back or hip]. They would come to spend about a month with us each summer. Mamaw would not

William and Isabell's family, c.1915. L to R men on back: Henry Lee, Abe, John William. Seated on the edge of the porch L to R is Cora, Carl, William Brownlow, Isabell Anderson, Estelle (bow in hair). Earl is the boy in front and to the right is Mary Jordan.

Opposite page: William and Isabell, circa late 1930's or early 1940's

(Collection of Rhonda Jordan Scoggins)

Left and below: My mom and I visited the Jordan/Anderson home place in Sep 2011. The photos show the Jordan house as it appears today. The large tree was probably already growing when William and Isabelle lived there.
(Photo by Jordan M. Scoggins)

Opposite: William and Isabell, circa late 1920's or early 1930's.
(Collection of Mary Pope Jordan)

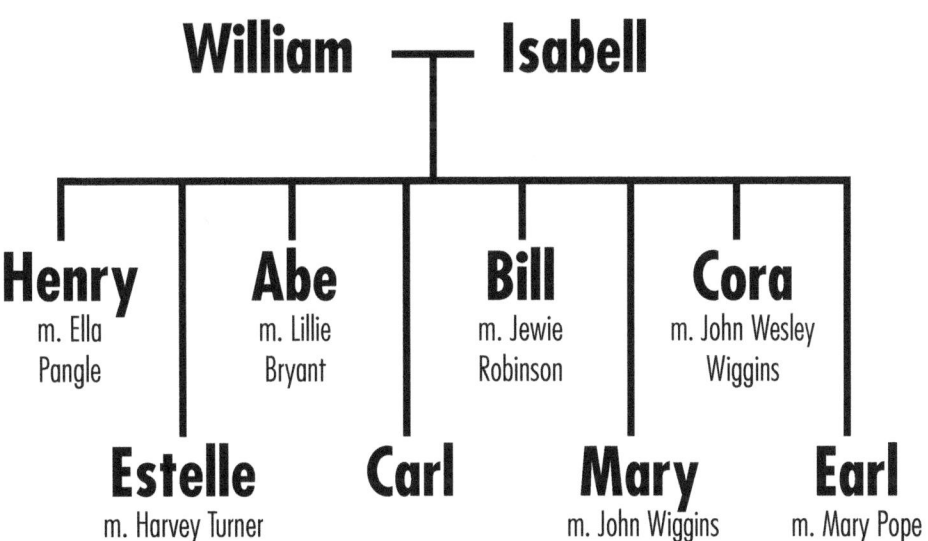

Right: The Jordan family gathered for a reunion and also celebrated William's birthday. This was taken in Bill's living room at Villanow (which was the old Love home, pictured on pg 62), Jul c.1955. L to R: Cora, Bill, Abe, Earl, Mary, Estelle. William Brownlow is seated. (Collection of Mary Pope Jordan)

let many people push her wheelchair, but she let me and I felt honored! Papaw had to lift her out of her chair at bedtime and put her to bed. I can still see in my mind how gentle and kind he was to her. He had so much patience. Mamaw could be irritable at times (I guess due to her condition), but Papaw never failed to treat her kindly! I think he was an inspiration to me and maybe I remember that now as I look after Carl!

"When I was a young girl, Daddy had let me claim a calf and take care of it. One evening I took Papaw to see my calf and as we were standing by the fence watching it, Papaw remarked that it sure was frisky! I thought he was saying something bad and I told him it was no more friskier that he was! He was probably in his eighties then! I remember he just died laughing at what I had said and that probably made me mad also" (Griggs)!

My aunt Mary Earl also remembers Papaw and Mamaw coming to visit each summer:

"I just remember that they came over and would stay with mom and dad for a week or two some times. Papaw was so good to her and he loved the country I could tell. He would just walk out through those fields just north of the house, that little terrace part that looked down on the bottom land and the creek. I remember seeing him just walking out looking around the farm" (Manis).

Mary also told me that she remembers when Mamaw was upset about something she would exclaim, "Sha-sha!" Mary laughed when I asked if she knew what it meant. She said she never did know, and she never thought to ask either of her parents what it meant. She just remembered the sound and spelled it out for me.

In the 1940's William and Isabell moved to a home on North Glenwood Avenue in Dalton. Their daughter

Cora lived with them and was their caretaker. Charlotte remembers Cora fondly:

> "Aunt Cora was a dear saint! She also took care of Aunt Mary until she could no longer do it. Aunt Cora used to baby sit for me sometimes and she made Anne's cheerleading outfits for her" (Griggs).

Mary Earl remembers that house which was near the railroad tracks. She recalls:

> "We'd go visit them and go out and sit on the bank. We'd sit and watch for trains, you know, the big steam trains" (Manis).

The Jordan family was a close knit bunch, always looking after each other.

Isabell died 20 Mar 1946. William lived for another decade until 5 Jul 1956 when he died. They are both buried in Dawnville Cemetery in Whitfield County.

Charlotte remembers when Papaw died:

> "I had gone on a date with [my husband-to-be] Carl and when I got home Mother told me Papaw had died. I was sad because I loved him very much" (Griggs).

Charlotte's memory illustrates how life dangles by a thread, lingering and teetering, ready to break at any moment. Our bodies are frail but the soul prevails. On this earth the memory of the departed will live as long as we will honor it.

Below: The Jordan family at a reunion. Back row: Bill holding grandson Steve, Abe, Gene, Earl, Jack. Middle row: Mary Jane, Vivian holding one of her babies, Charlotte holding another of Vivian's babies, Mary Earl, Carolyn, Sarah, Delene touching Wm Brownlow, Cora, Estelle, Patsy holding baby. Front row: Jennifer West, unidentified, Rhonda, Miriam, Miriam's brother, Wm Brownlow, girl, Ernestine holding baby with boy in front, Elizabeth Wiggins [West], Jerry holding baby, Gene's son. Taken at Bill Jordan's house in Villanow, Jul c.1955. (Collection of Mary Pope Jordan)

ANDERSON family

The Jordan family connects with the Anderson family through my great grandmother Isabell Anderson. I have traced the Anderson line back to 17th century Great Britain. Richard Anderson [I] was born abt 1585 in England. According to information printed in the *William and Mary Quarterly*, Richard [I] migrated to Virginia about 1635 (Adams 62-3). This matches with a record in the *Passenger and Immigration Lists Index* by Gale Research. In contrast, a study of the Andersons by Marion Pettigrew and Newton Brightwell does not claim Richard [I] came to Virginia, but only his son. While this detail is not clear, it does seem apparent that Richard [II], at the age of 17, sailed to Virginia in 1635 on *The Merchants Hope* (Adams 62; Gale; Pettigrew 214). Richard [II] remained a Virginian for the rest of his life. His son Robert and Robert's son Thomas established a solid foundation in the Virginia colony of the New World. Thomas's son Gideon left behind the Virginia roots, dying in Georgia about 1802.

Gideon's arrival in Georgia marks the beginning of a long line of Georgian Anderson descendants. Gideon's son William [I], born 8 Jan 1763 in Buckingham, VA, also came to Georgia. At the age of 14 he enlisted under Captain Burwell Smith and served in the Revolutionary War. At the time of his enlistment he lived in Wilkes County, GA. He served with Captain Smith for two and a half years. He also served additional time after that, including "in the expedition against the Cherokees" (Widow's Pension W.512). Given the time frame, this expedition seems to have been part of the Chickamauga Wars (1776-1794). Later William lived in Baldwin County where he is counted on the 1820, 1830, and 1840 censuses. He died on 6 May 1844.

While my line undoubtedly descends through this William Anderson [I], there is some confusion surrounding which of his sons is in my direct line. There seem to be two theories.

William's [I] oldest son Abraham Marshall Anderson was born about 1791 in Georgia. In 1850 he lived in Gilmer County. He died 24 Dec 1854. Abraham Marshall's children are documented in T.J. and Frances Anderson's book *Anderson Records*. Among his children they identify Abraham M. Anderson, Jr. with details that align with my 2nd great grandfather. This is the Gilmer County theory.

Anderson Records also records William's [I] youngest son with his first wife, William [II]. (7) No further information about William [II] is explored in that particular work. However, the information about his descendants recorded in *Heritage of Lumpkin County, Georgia 1832-1996* is in direct conflict with the *Anderson Records* lineage (56). I do know that William [II] and his family are living in Lumpkin County on the 1850 census. This, in contrast with the above Gilmer theory, is the Lumpkin County theory.

These two individuals, Abraham Marshall Anderson (the Gilmer theory) and William Anderson [II] (the Lumpkin theory), are brothers, both with sons named Abraham. The correct identity of those sons is the point of dispute. One of those Abrahams is my 2nd great grandfather, born 12 May 1837 in Lumpkin County and died 1 Feb 1905 in Whitfield County.

Normally we genealogists would look to census data to shed light on these relationships and make a positive identity. Unfortunately each of these Abraham sons not only have the same name but were born about the same time—so census data alone does not fit the bill here. The fact that my Abraham was born in Lumpkin county in 1837 (something documented clearly in his Civil War service records) seems—at first glance—to support the Lumpkin County theory (Service records, Abraham). However, a deeper examination provides more clues. Abraham Marshall Anderson (father of son Abraham in the Gilmer theory) lived in Coweta County in 1840. His pension file shows that he lived there up until about 1850 at which point he moved to Gilmer County, where he is counted on the 1850 census of the Gilmer theory. The pension papers also show that Abraham Marshall died in Pickens County (which was formerly part of Gilmer County) on 24 Dec 1854.

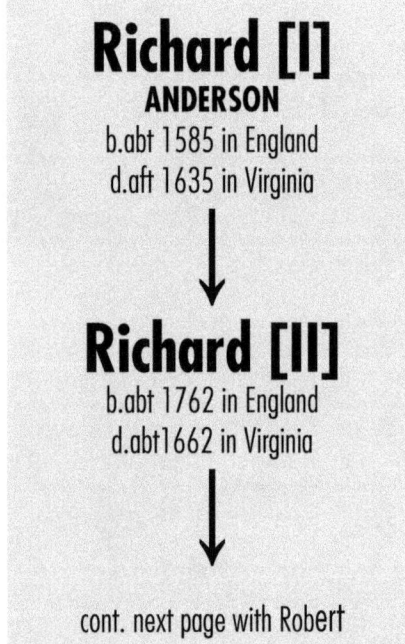

Richard [I]
ANDERSON
b.abt 1585 in England
d.aft 1635 in Virginia

↓

Richard [II]
b.abt 1762 in England
d.abt 1662 in Virginia

↓

cont. next page with Robert

Earl and Mary visited the old Anderson/Jordan home place in Whitfield County in 1994. (Collection of Charlotte Jordan Griggs)

But perhaps the most interesting item—and an easy to overlook detail—is the signature of Solomon Anderson on Elizabeth Mattox's widow claim in Abraham Marshall's pension file. Elizabeth lived with her son Solomon in the latter years of her life, enumerated in his household on the 1880 census. Solomon's daughter Emma Octavia Anderson married George Washington Jordan. George is the brother of William Brownlow Jordan, who married Isabell Anderson… daughter of Abraham Anderson (see these relationships illustrated on the next page). According to census data these allied Anderson/Jordan families were all based in Whitfield County, where we know my Abraham lived and is buried, therefore tying this all together and strongly supporting the Gilmer theory lineage.

While the details from Abraham Marshall's pension files do not prove conclusively the Gilmer theory on their own, when paired with the census data, as well as son Abraham's (my 2nd great grandfather) pension files and service records, the correct lineage does come together. Therefore, I am in support of the Gilmer theory and will state here that Abraham Marshall Anderson (b. abt 1791) is my 3rd great grandfather. However, genealogy is always a work in progress and it is possible I will eventually find documentation that sways the balance. We must always keep an open mind!

It's easy to see how this lineage became confused given the both Abraham Andersons are associated with Lumpkin County. Likely somewhere along the way someone knew of the son Abraham in my line, knew that he was born in Lumpkin County, and found the 1850 censuses in Lumpkin with Abraham son of William. Based on dates, locations, and names alone it matches up. This is a prime example of the constant need for detailed documentation in genealogical research—even when you think you already have everything correct.

So, then, my 3rd great grandfather Abraham Marshall followed in his father's military footsteps and served in the War of 1812 and the Creek War. For the War of 1812 he entered Captain Howard's Co, GA Militia, on 24 Jun 1812 and served until 15 Oct of the same year. In the Creek War he served

Robert
b. 1640 in Virginia
d. 1712 in Virginia

↓

Thomas
b. abt 1672 in Virginia
d. 25 Oct 1757 in Virginia

↓

Gideon
b. abt 1737 in Virginia
d. abt 1802 in Georgia

↓

cont. next page with William

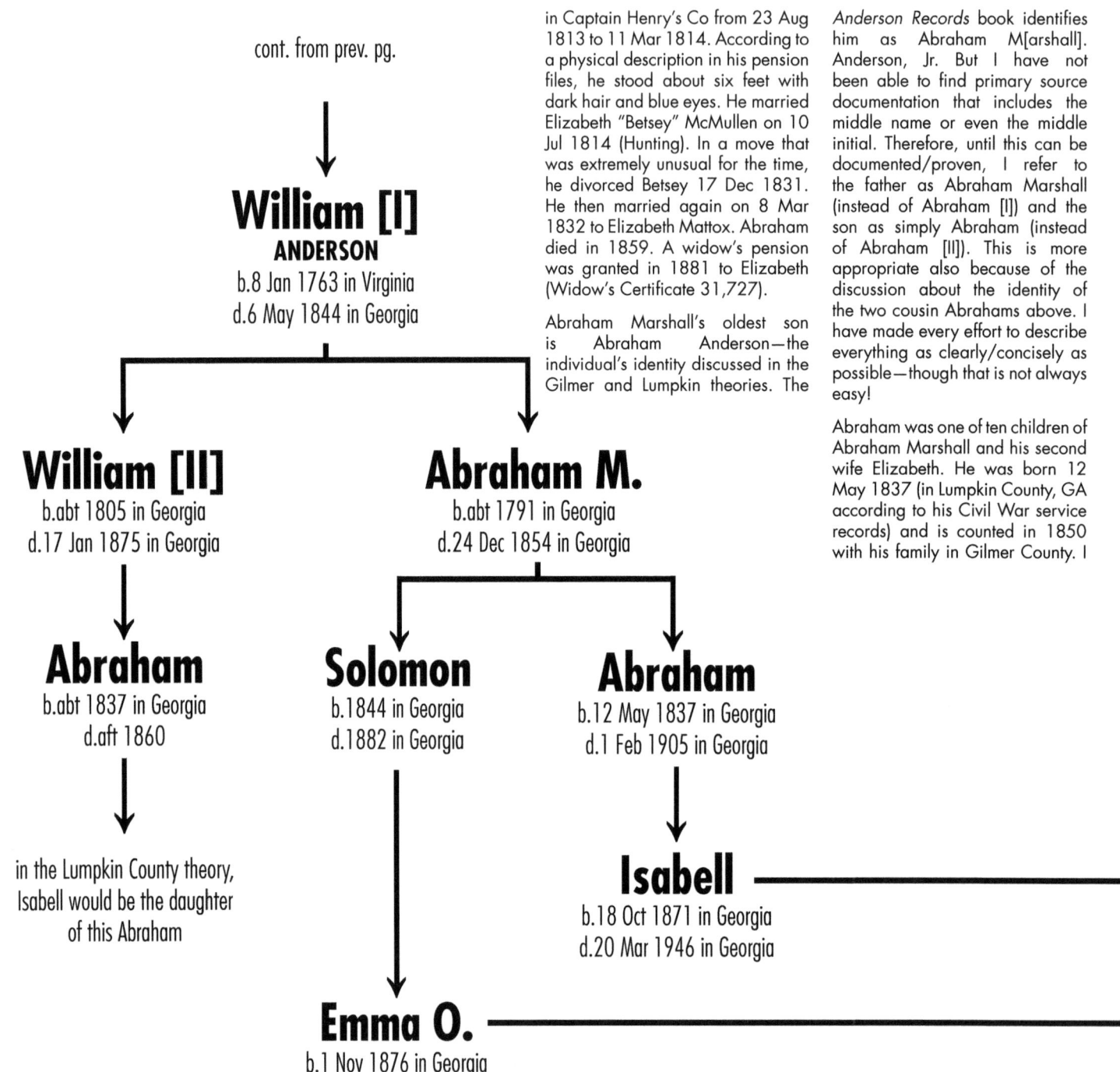

cont. from prev. pg.

William [I]
ANDERSON
b. 8 Jan 1763 in Virginia
d. 6 May 1844 in Georgia

William [II]
b. abt 1805 in Georgia
d. 17 Jan 1875 in Georgia

Abraham M.
b. abt 1791 in Georgia
d. 24 Dec 1854 in Georgia

Abraham
b. abt 1837 in Georgia
d. aft 1860

Solomon
b. 1844 in Georgia
d. 1882 in Georgia

Abraham
b. 12 May 1837 in Georgia
d. 1 Feb 1905 in Georgia

Isabell
b. 18 Oct 1871 in Georgia
d. 20 Mar 1946 in Georgia

Emma O.
b. 1 Nov 1876 in Georgia
d. 14 Mar 1952 in Georgia

in the Lumpkin County theory, Isabell would be the daughter of this Abraham

in Captain Henry's Co from 23 Aug 1813 to 11 Mar 1814. According to a physical description in his pension files, he stood about six feet with dark hair and blue eyes. He married Elizabeth "Betsey" McMullen on 10 Jul 1814 (Hunting). In a move that was extremely unusual for the time, he divorced Betsey 17 Dec 1831. He then married again on 8 Mar 1832 to Elizabeth Mattox. Abraham died in 1859. A widow's pension was granted in 1881 to Elizabeth (Widow's Certificate 31,727).

Abraham Marshall's oldest son is Abraham Anderson—the individual's identity discussed in the Gilmer and Lumpkin theories. The *Anderson Records* book identifies him as Abraham M[arshall]. Anderson, Jr. But I have not been able to find primary source documentation that includes the middle name or even the middle initial. Therefore, until this can be documented/proven, I refer to the father as Abraham Marshall (instead of Abraham [I]) and the son as simply Abraham (instead of Abraham [II]). This is more appropriate also because of the discussion about the identity of the two cousin Abrahams above. I have made every effort to describe everything as clearly/concisely as possible—though that is not always easy!

Abraham was one of ten children of Abraham Marshall and his second wife Elizabeth. He was born 12 May 1837 (in Lumpkin County, GA according to his Civil War service records) and is counted in 1850 with his family in Gilmer County. I have not been able to locate him in 1860 but he married Mary Frances Boling in Cherokee County on 26 Dec 1861.

After the marriage but before they started having children, Abraham went to Cleveland, TN where he joined up with the army to fight in the Civil War. He did not support the Confederacy and enlisted in the 5th regiment of the Union's 5th Tennessee Mounted Infantry on 22 Nov 1864. It was a new regiment having only just been organized (Goodspeed 511). Abraham served in both Companies H and F. He mustered out on 17 Jul 1865 in Nashville (Service Records A. Anderson). Abraham's half-brother Francis Marion Anderson (son of Abraham Marshall Anderson and his first wife, Elizabeth McMullen) also served the Union in the 1st Tennessee Mounted Infantry as Captain (Service Records F.M. Anderson).

Reunited with his wife and having finally started a family, Abraham and Mary are counted on their farm in Whitfield County in 1870. Francis and his family are also living nearby. Although Abraham suffered from piles ever since his service in the war, he made a go of life as best as he could. He worked as a farmer for about 25 years until the physical burden became too much. He described his situation on an affidavit dated 12 Mar 1892 in his pension file:

> "I contracted piles while I was in service from cold and other exposure which has grew [sic] worse on me and for the past 12 months I have been nearly entirely disabled and for past 5 months have not been able to do any work and it seems that I git [sic] worse daily my legs and feet cold with rheumatism and weakness of the back. While I was able to work I asked for no help. I do this because I can't do better" (Soldier's Certificate Anderson).

I get the sense that Abraham was a proud man. Probably to him seeking help was admitting defeat. A 15 Jun 1892 medical report from his pension files—showing he stood 5'10.5" and weighed 137 lbs—describes his condition:

> "I have suffered with piles for eighteen years. I have rheumatism in both legs and feet. My piles pain me, bleed, and protrude. I am disabled from doing manual labor two thirds" (Soldier's Certificate Anderson).

In a follow-up report two years later from 20 Jun 1894, he is half an inch shorter and seven pounds lighter and shows his turn for the worse:

> "I have had piles since the war. I am troubled with rheumatism in my back and limbs which gives me much pain. I am totally unable to do manual labor" (Soldier's Certificate Anderson).

Abraham was ultimately granted a pension of $12 a month. Unable to work this must have been the primary means of support for the family which in 1900 consisted of four of his five daughters as well as his 15 year old son, Samuel. His son Henry's family is counted next door on the census so they probably lived on the same farm. Abraham's daughter Isabell had married William Jordan in 1893 and they made their home on the Anderson farm (see page 96 for a photo of the Jordan home). They probably all worked the same farm and were bonded together as a family like so many in those days.

Abraham's house is no longer there but my grandfather Earl remembered it from his childhood having grown up in the Jordan home. In 1994, only months before his own death, Earl went back to the Anderson/Jordan home place one last time. Several family members went that day, including my sister Julie. Where the Anderson home stood on top of the hill still blooms every spring beautiful jonquils leftover from Abraham and Mary's time, a sure sign of days gone by.

In 1904 death must have been at Abraham's doorstep as he transferred his property to Mary in Jun 1904. The farm consisted of about 160 acres (land lot No. 36, 9th District, 3rd Section of Whitfield County, GA) (Deed Anderson). Abraham died 8 months later on 1 Feb 1905. His pension having been the only source of income, Mary was left behind with no means of support. She applied for a widow's pension which she was also granted (Soldier's Certificate Anderson).

On 11 Apr 1912 Mary's doctor, A.M. Jones, made a house call. She was in bad health and required constant attention over the next few days until she died of gastritis on 16 Apr (Soldier's Certificate Anderson).

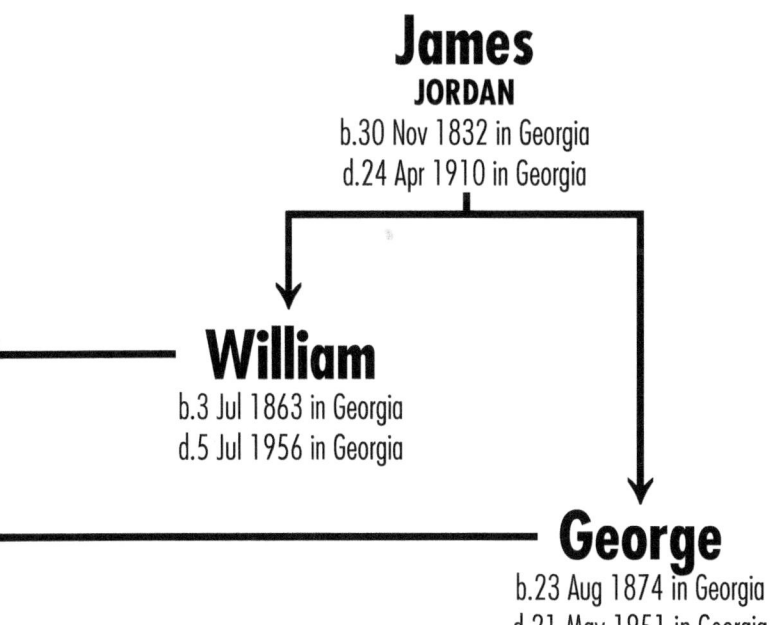

James
JORDAN
b.30 Nov 1832 in Georgia
d.24 Apr 1910 in Georgia

William
b.3 Jul 1863 in Georgia
d.5 Jul 1956 in Georgia

George
b.23 Aug 1874 in Georgia
d.21 May 1951 in Georgia

Earl Felix Jordan
b. 5 Mar 1911 d. 28 Nov 1994
married
Mary Evelyn Pope
b. 13 May 1913 d. 6 Sep 2004

Earl and Mary had been teenage sweethearts from an early age. I don't know how or when they met but they must have known early on that they wanted to be together. They didn't meet at school. Earl always said he went to high school at Ringgold... "in the front door and out the back!" While Mary did stay with one of her relatives in LaFayette in order to go to high school, she never graduated. Her parents found out that she had gone to the Chattanooga fair with Earl and another boy and girl. Furious about this they made Mary drop out of school and move back to the farm. I don't know if Ben and Lizzie had a specific objection to Earl or were just being overprotective of their daughter in general.

The rebellion continued and Earl and Mary eloped on 4 May 1930, bucking tradition of a formal wedding. After they married they lived with Earl's parents in Dawnville about one mile south of where Abraham Anderson is buried. Mary and Earl stayed in the front bedroom of the house.

After Mary became pregnant they returned to the Pope farm in East Armuchee and lived in a small house on Concord Road. Presumably any objections Ben and Lizzie had over Earl had eased by now. The house was still standing when my mother was a little girl and she describes it as "a shack". The shack stood where Anita Pope and her husband Mark Dunn live today. (After Earl & Mary, Homer Watkins & Fannie Pope and J.C. Pope & Helen Grigsby lived in the shack too).

Earl and Mary had four children:

1. Robert Alton (b.31 Dec 1930, m. Marie Larmon 24 Jul 1954, d.21 Sep 2001)
2. Mary Earl (b.9 Apr 1934, m. Thomas Watson Manis 25 Sep 1954)
3. Charlotte Alexa (b.28 Jun 1936, m. Carl Lloyd Griggs 2 Sep 1956)
4. Rhonda Verlyn (b.12 Jul 1949, m. Michael David Scoggins 15 Jul 1967)

Earl and Mary looking stylish, circa late 1920's. Mary always told a story about Earl's fast driving. Whenever her knee was acting up she would say to her daughter Rhonda, "Yeah, I hurt that knee. One time your daddy was driving around that corner [near the bridge on E Armuchee Rd] and he slung me out of the car and hurt my knee."
(Collection of Mary Pope Jordan)

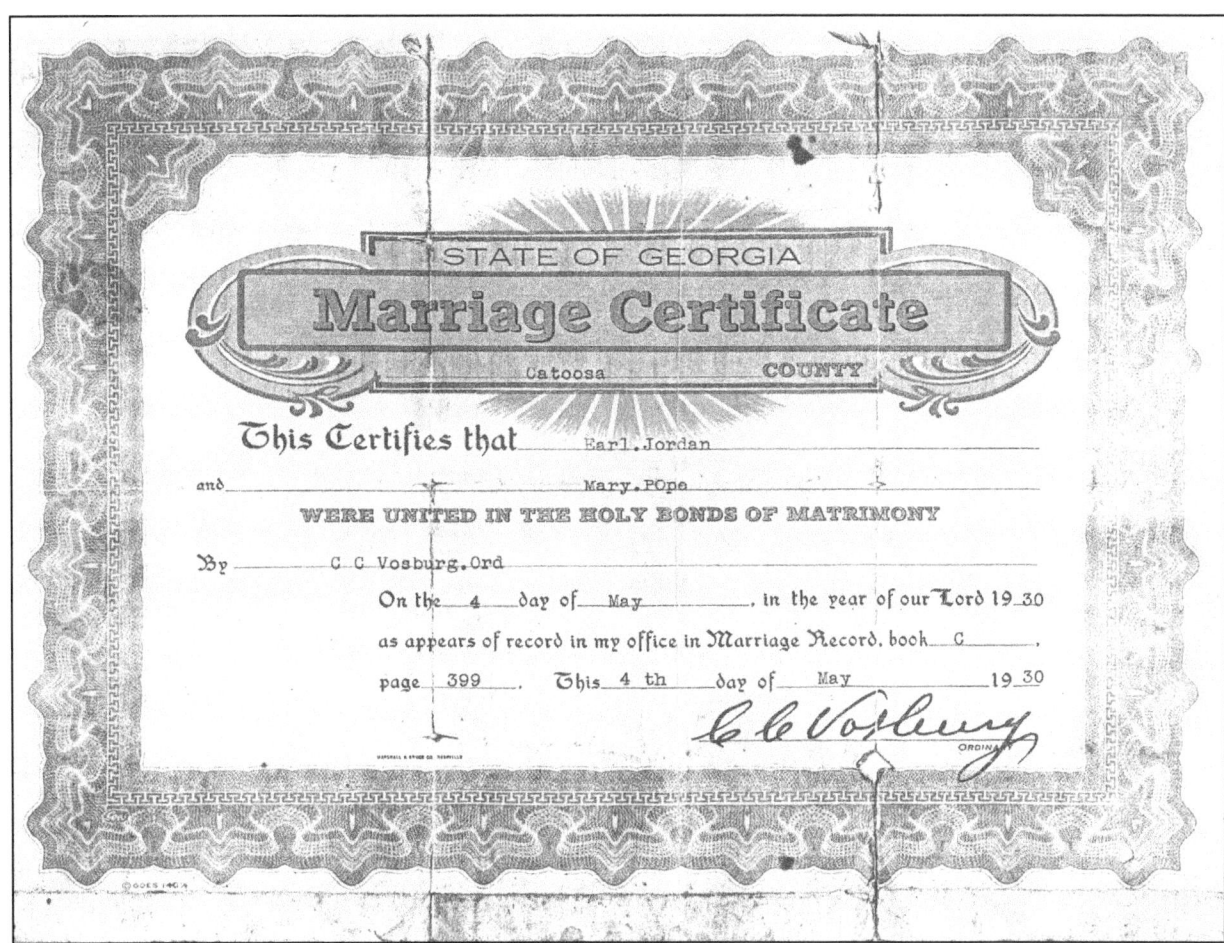

Earl and Mary were married on 4 May 1930, as seen in their marriage certificate above. (Collection of Mary Pope Jordan)

The first child, Robert Alton, was born at home on the Pope farm. He was named after Alton McDaniels, the owner of a clothing store in LaFayette where Mary had a job. Robert's birth date is less than 9 months after Earl and Mary were married. I once pointed out this fact to Grannie who was quick to explain that Robert was born premature! While this easily could have been the case Mary's teenage rebellion suggests that, just like teenagers today, she and Earl might have resisted convention in more ways than one! I love this kind of story because it shows that no matter how much change we go through generation to generation certain things remain the same. Teenagers are teenagers. My dear Grannie, always revered as a grand woman with a spotless name was a rebellious teenager along with the rest of us. And that is a beautiful story to know, a story that paints a more human portrait than any tale of contrived perfection ever could. My ancestors were human. They all loved and laughed and suffered and sinned in the same ways I have. And that core thread of humanity is what connects us more than any direct blood line.

A second child, Mary Earl, followed in 1934 (also born at home on the Pope farm). Her name is a combination of both of her parents' names.

With a growing family on their hands Earl and Mary bought a portion of the Pope family farm from her father. They built a new home down the road in 1935. This is the house that over the years the family came to call "the white house" due to its white siding. The lumber for the home was given

Earl — **Mary**

Robert
m. Marie Larman

Mary E.
m. Tommy Manis

Charlotte
m. Carl Griggs

Rhonda
m. Mike Scoggins

Opposite: Robert and Mary Earl, taken about 1940. The portrait of Earl and Mary was taken about 1966.
(Collection of Mary Pope Jordan)

Left: Charlotte and Rhonda pose in their front yard on Easter 1954. The spot on the hill across the road directly behind Charlotte and Rhonda is where Earl and Mary built their brick house in the 1970's.
(Collection of Mary Pope Jordan)

Below: The Earl Jordan family poses for a photo at an Aug 1987 family reunion at the William Madison "Billy" Clement/Emily Clement Payne home in Shannon, GA. L to R: Rhonda, Charlotte, Mary, Earl, Mary Earl, and Robert.
(Collection of Rhonda Jordan Scoggins)

to Earl by Mary's father Ben and saw-milled by Earl and his brothers. When the family first moved in the house had only two bedrooms, a living room, a dining room, a small kitchen, and a back porch. For the bathroom they had an outhouse. There was also a car shed which had a smoke house on the back corner. In the winter this is where they hung salted meat to keep it cool.

After settling in at their new home, Charlotte Alexa (after Mary's cousin Alexa Price) was born (all 10.5 pounds of her!) in the front bedroom of the white house in 1936. My mother, Rhonda, wasn't born for another 13 years in 1949. Born at Kitchen's Clinic in LaFayette, she was the only child Mary did not have at home. Rhonda's name comes from Rhonda Flemming—a 1940's movie star admired by Robert.

The Jordan children first went to school at Villanow and later Subligna. Robert went to Dalton High School for his senior year and graduated from there in 1948. Mary graduated from Subligna in 1950. Charlotte graduated from LaFayette High School in 1953. My mother went to school through the 8th grade at Armuchee Valley (where she met my father) and then LaFayette High School, graduating in 1967.

Earl's main occupation was farming. Cotton was an important crop in the earlier years and the Jordan children all took part in the harvest (see pg 78 for more about this). Although my mother was too young to help out in the fields at that time, she does remember her father growing the cotton. "About the time that I got ten-ish or something like that they quit growing cotton," says Rhonda. She continues:

> "It wasn't profitable. The boll weevils were a pest that would get into the cotton bulb and damage it and so it didn't do as well. I can remember riding on the back of the wagon full of cotton, or the big truck that he would put it in after everybody weighed in, and riding on the back of it when he would take cotton pickers home wherever he hired somebody that was helping him pick cotton" (R. Scoggins, interview)

Wheat was another important crop. "I can remember when he would combine the wheat in the summer he would catch baby rabbits because there would be rabbit beds out in the wheat fields," Rhonda recalls. "He would bring me a rabbit and I would try to keep it alive but it didn't usually live very long" (R. Scoggins, interview).

The biggest crop I remember Earl growing was corn. As a child the corn fields seemed like a sea of green. I would often play out in the fields, making my way through the corn as if it were a thick jungle forest. It itched the skin but a country boy like me didn't care. Come harvest time after the corn had been picked it was time to shuck it. I remember being in the shed with piles of corn as tall as I was. We'd all gather around and make an afternoon of it. Sometimes you might find worms in the corn

silk which I always enjoyed and sometimes went fishing with.

"Daddy grew the vegetables, but Grannie did a lot of hoeing and picking of the garden as well," says Rhonda (R. Scoggins, interview). Even I remember quieter, more intimate moments of breaking green beans or shelling peas with Grannie. It was a slow meditation, a way to connect with the food that would nourish our bodies. Most people today put fork to mouth and never even consider where that food came from much less how it grew. I miss those moments of simple quietude and contemplative reflection out in the country.

Earl and Mary grew many other foods: watermelons, cantaloupes, squash, peppers, peas, okra, tomatoes, potatoes,

Above: Corn grown by my parents just like in the olden days, Jun 2009.

Opposite: The Earl Jordan barn is not as old as some in the area. The original barn was destroyed in the 1960's due to a fire caused by an electrical problem with Earl's Chevy truck. This barn was built shortly thereafter. Sep 2011.

(Photos by Jordan M. Scoggins)

and more. A feast for the eyes and the mouth, whenever I see fresh vegetables I think of the farm back home.

Beyond the fields, Earl sometimes did other work to help support his family. Guy Pope recalls:

> "I remember Earl, he helped put these lines [the electric lines when the valley first got electricity, about 1939] in. They used his truck and had all the gear on it. I can remember Earl'd come up here and eat dinner at our house [Ben and Lizzie's house, as Guy was still a teenager living at home], I guess Mary was working, and me and Robert would be here and he had a big water jug on the back of it. He had these little old v funnel cups. Me and Robert would go out there and just drink water all the time he was in there eating dinner" (G. Pope).

Sometimes people who needed to move house would hire Earl and his farm truck to move their things. Guy also remembers that Earl would sometimes travel to Florida and come back with his truck loaded full of oranges. This was during the winter when he could sell the oranges while there were no other crops (G. Pope).

But Earl wasn't the only helping hand around the Jordan home. Mary worked just as hard. She had a job in Dalton working in a spread factory. Since gas was expensive Mary and her brother J.C.—who also had a job in Dalton—would take turns driving. They carpooled, picking up a few others along the way who would contribute money for gas. By the time my mother came along and was too young to stay home alone during the summer—and her siblings were no longer living at home—she rode in the carpool to the factory with Mary. From the factory Mary would send my mom in a taxi to Charlotte's house. My mom would spend the day with her sister, helping look after Charlotte's young children. When the day was over Mary would pick up Rhonda before heading back to the country. In the evenings Mary would tend to the household chores. It was a constant cycle of hard work and elbow grease (R. Scoggins, interview).

Indeed, there were many things to tend to. They had cows for milk and chickens for eggs. Mary churned butter and canned beans, cucumbers, tomatoes and other vegetables. She used buttermilk to make cornbread. She picked fruit from the yard to make blackberry preserves, pear preserves, and apple jelly. She made much of the family's clothing—sometimes from flour sacks! She even made their soap using a black wash pot. But not everything was quite so Martha Stewart. Some practices of the Jordan farm seem far removed from life as we know it. My mother remembers:

Robert Alton Jordan
1951

Mary Earl Jordan
1950

Charlotte Alexa Jordan
early 1950's

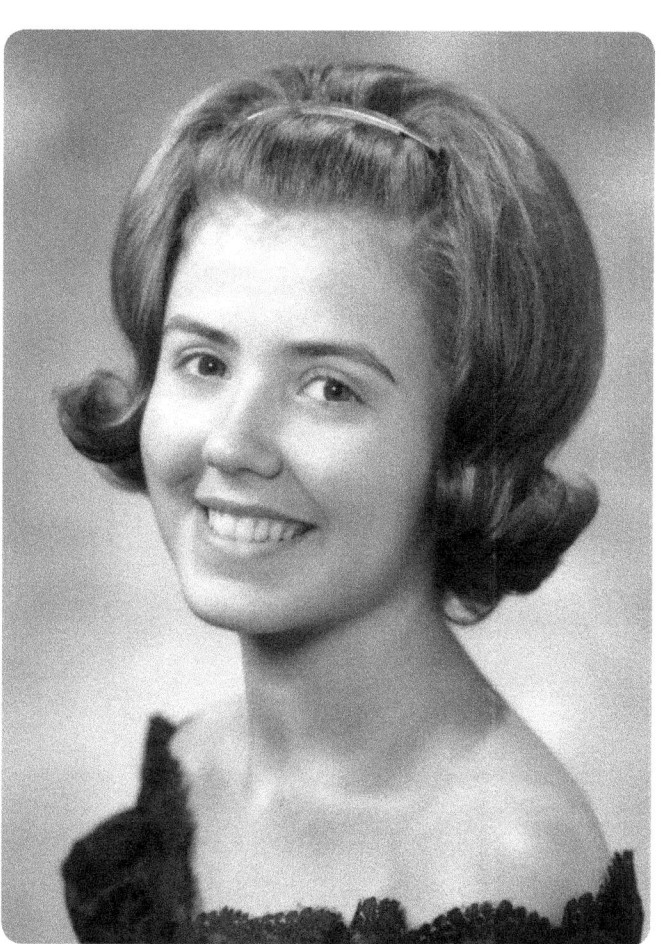

Rhonda Verlyn Jordan
1966

"Every winter when it got cold, they had hog killings. Mother ground part of the meat into sausage. The hams were salted for a while in a salt box in the smoke house part of the shed. Then they were hung to cure and sliced up to fry and eat later. The fat of the pig was cooked in a big black wash pot outside and made in to what is called cracklins. She would then put them in her buttermilk corn bread. The skins were fed to the dogs and the lard was used to fry food in" (R. & M. Scoggins, correspondence).

By today's standards we refer to using the "whole animal" as an alternative, more sustainable practice to the mainstream habit of buying only the "best"/"desirable" parts. But living on a farm—especially for farmers with a lifestyle rooted in the Great Depression—meant making use of everything that you had. (For more about Mary's experience coming of age during the Great Depression, see my interview with her starting on page 76).

Charlotte shares similar memories:

"I can remember Mother working so hard all day in the fields and come home and cook supper and then can beans, etc. I remember one night going to bed and I could see her in the kitchen breaking up green beans. I got up and helped her. Mother really sacrificed a lot for us and would go to work at the bedspread plant to make money to buy things for us for school. I don't remember her getting herself anything.

"I guess a lot of my memories involve picking cotton, killing hogs, cooking on a wood stove, heating water in a black pot outside to wash clothes in a wringer machine, rinsing them in two big tubs of water, each time running each piece through a wringer. We

Rhonda remembers her mother canned vegetables and "put the jars on concrete ledges in the basement to keep them cool" (R. & M. Scoggins, correspondence). I took this photo in 2009—the same ledge in the basement of the white house. These jars had probably been sitting there since before Mary moved out of that house in the 1970's. (Photo by Jordan M. Scoggins)

hung them outside on a clothes line. I still remember how good the sheets smelled" (Griggs)!

The chores of farm life were endless but modern inventions eventually helped ease the burden. My mother Rhonda recalls:

> "In the old days there were no electric irons and everything was all cotton and had to be ironed. She had to heat an old heavy iron on the wood stove. After we would gather the clean clothes off the clothes line, we would dampen what needed ironing and roll it in a ball and put it in the freezer. Then it would be damp when we ironed it and that helped the wrinkles come out better. By my era, there were electric irons though.

> "The first washing machine that mother had she bought with her mother Lizzie," Rhonda continues. "They hauled it back and forth every month. It was an old wringer type washer. They hung the clothes on the line to dry" (R. & M. Scoggins, correspondence).

Even when I was a boy I can remember Grannie hanging her wash out. She had a laundry line strung up between two trees with an old piece of wood that helped support it in the middle. I can see the texture of that wood with such clarity and it instantly takes me back. It's funny the mundane objects that make up the textures of memories old and lives past.

These country memories live on throughout the family. Charlotte has landscaped her yard using Mary's black wash pot as a decorative planter. Mary Earl keeps the large pan that her mother used to cook big roasts for Sunday lunches. My mother, Rhonda, has the meat grinder Mary used to make sausage. My sister, Julie, cooks with the iron skillet Mary used throughout her life and she has an old bottle used by Mary to roll dough for biscuits. She even repaired and refinished Mary's old sewing machine and uses it as a night stand in a guest room in her house. Called "Grannie's Room," Julie dedicates that space to the memory of our Grannie. These items are artifacts of an ancestral past. When paired with the stories and memories they begin to build a history all their own, enriching our view of the past.

As the country emerged out of the Great Depression so, too, did the Jordan family. Recreational travel became more common and "between 1945 and 1960 the number of cars in the country increased by 133 percent" (Chafe 118). In 1949 Earl took his family to Florida. At the time Mary was pregnant with Rhonda. Again in 1959 Earl and Mary visited the Sunshine State with Rhonda. Robert and his wife Marie went on the trip as well. My mother has fond memories from this trip and it is probably a large part of why—even to this day—escaping to the beach in Florida is her favorite way to "get away." The 1950s were a decade of immense cultural change even beyond the highways: electricity use tripled, advertising increased 400 percent, and consumerism was on the rise (Chafe 119). Even the idyllic East Armuchee valley and the Jordan family farm would not go untouched by these changes.

As the decades moved on—and the Jordan children had all grown up and moved away—Earl and Mary remained on the farm.

Two photos of Earl and Mary from their 1959 trip to Florida. In the top photo, Robert's wife, Marie, peeks out from behind the palm tree. (Collection of Robert Jordan/Collection of Mary Pope Jordan)

On 4 May 1980 Earl and Mary celebrated their 50th wedding anniversary. The entire family gathered at their daughter Charlotte's home in Dalton to honor the couple that had been a part of so many lives. Mary's sister Martha came from Louisville. All of Mary's children and grandchildren were there.

Opposite: Anniversary celebration invitation framed with dried flowers. Mary's friend Irene Bowen made the arrangement with dried flowers she collected on a trip with Mary and others to Europe and the Middle East.

The black and white photo is of Earl and Mary cutting their anniversary cake, 4 May 1980.

Mary's sister Martha holds me, looking through the decorated window, 4 May 1980.

(Collection of Mary Pope Jordan)

Above: All eight of Earl and Mary's grand children, 4 May 1980. L to R: Back row: Carl "Bubba" Griggs, Jr.; Donna Manis; Mark Griggs; Glynn Griggs; Thomas "Little Tommy" Manis, Julie Scoggins, Anne Griggs holding Jordan Scoggins.

(Collection of Michael & Rhonda Scoggins)

Just a few short years after that golden celebration my parents moved our family back to the farm to live next to mom's parents. Both Earl and Mary were still active, always working on the farm. Papa plowed the fields with his tractor and I followed behind combing through the newly turned up soil searching for any trace of arrowheads. Grannie hoed in the garden, covered from the sun—she had photodermatitis—in long sleeves and a bonnet. One time I was inside the house, probably watching TV, and didn't know where Grannie had gone. I went outside and yelled, "Grannie where are you?"

"I'm up here in the okrie patch," she hollered back.

I made my way to the garden and promptly corrected her, "It's okra, Grannie, not okrie."

I remember helping Grannie gather eggs from her chickens. I was very little the last time she had chickens, but I can remember the chicken pen and the old metal screen door she used as a gate. I would go in with her and reach into the coop to get the eggs. I remember being slightly afraid of the chickens but loved going to see them nonetheless.

I can see Papa's cows even clearer, as he still kept cows when I was a little older. In 1987 when he was ill, my father took care of the cows for him. I would go with Dad to help make sure they were fed and tended to. The thing that sticks out in my mind the most is that I had worn a red or orange cap. Several of the cows gathered all around me and huddled up very close. I was just a small thing and it was terrifying. My father came to my rescue and told me not to wear that cap—that the cows were attracted to that color! I also remember the cows grazing up on top of the hill one day. We called out for them so they would come eat... and soon there was a stampede coming down the hill with us in the path between the cows and the barn. I remember being scared, afraid that they would trample us. One of the cows even gave birth while Papa was sick. My father and I took our video camera and recorded the calf so that Earl could see.

It wasn't long after that Earl finally retired from cattle farming, gradually working less and less. But he never stopped working completely. Just a couple of weeks before he died he was plowing the fields, working hard until the end. He didn't have to work like that in his twilight years. He didn't have to toil and labor. But he did it because it's what he knew and it's what he loved.

But I can't tell the story of Earl without acknowledging his darker side. Let me be very clear that while I may relate some things here that are connected to difficult memories for some, my intent is to portray the humanity of my grandfather. We all have much more to learn from such difficult experiences than any story we could tell to gloss over the less attractive parts.

Earl was an alcoholic. From the stories I always heard it was not that he drank all the time. He couldn't afford to drink all the time. But when he could he didn't hold back. In typical Southern fashion, the family didn't talk out in the open about Earl's struggle with alcohol abuse. But my mother has become more open about it over the years. She once told me that when she came home from school if Earl was drinking she would hide in her room until her mother would come home. She was afraid of her father when he was drunk.

One time my mom, ever wanting her father to give up the bottle, took the Mason jars of moonshine and poured them out. She refilled them with water. To the eye it looked the same. She was just a child and didn't want her father to drink anymore. She must have seen this as the only thing she

Above: Grannie's chickens, about 1976 (Collection of Michael & Rhonda Scoggins)

To the right: I met these bovines in Nov 2010 when I visited Talley Cemetery in Trans. They remind me of Earl's cows from so many years ago. (Photo by Jordan M. Scoggins)

could do to keep him from drinking. When he found out, of course, it did nothing but provoke anger.

His abuse was verbal and psychological. Mother says he never physically harmed her. This shows that at his core Earl was not a bad man. I knew him well enough to know he had a sweet and loving soul even if he had a thick-skinned exterior. But something in his life must have weighed heavy on him and alcohol was his coping mechanism. We all have our vices. Unfortunately, Earl's vice had all too strong an impact—probably much more than he ever realized—on his family.

There was one way that Earl's alcoholism was a blessing in disguise. When he was drunk, Mary and Rhonda would often go stay with Mary's mother Lizzie. For my mother this helped build a special bond between her and her grandmother. Mom and Grannie even stayed with Lizzie the last three weeks before her unexpected death—time they would not have shared together if it were not for Earl's drinking.

I feel lucky that I got to see a part of Earl that not many others witnessed. I often stayed with Grannie and Papa after school before my parents came home. And I would spend the night with them sometimes as well. I spent hours upon end with Earl in the late afternoons and evenings. Often he would sit and read the paper while I watched the TV. I didn't have the kind of relationship with him where you would sit and talk or do things together. But we did spend a lot of time together. It was the kind of relationship where it was ok to just be present. There were no expectations of what the other was supposed to do… except be.

In his later years Earl became increasingly hard of hearing. It was not unusual to hear Mary yelling at Earl… not out of anger but rather in an effort to be heard! It could be quite comical at times to hear them banter back and forth, the stereotype of an old married couple. When Earl came to church, always decked out in a stylish fedora, sometimes his hearing aid would start humming during the middle of the service. I could hear the screeching and looked across the way, knowing it was my grandfather. It might take him a few moments to realize what was happening. He would fumble with the controls and try to adjust it. Mary sat by his side, dignified as ever, and tried not to be embarrassed. I chuckled under my breath.

Some of the funniest memories are the things he would do and say. At the dinner table when he was finished he would put down his plate for my dog, Rounder, to lick clean. He would look at me across the table and proclaim with a laugh, "Well she [Mary] don't need to wash that plate now." He might reach for a "Debbie Little" (as he called them) for dessert. When it was time to go to bed he would announce, "Well I believe I'll turn in now!" As he made his way to the back of the house to his bedroom he would exclaim, step by step, "Ohhhh me. Ohhhh me." Later when I would go to bed in the guest room you could always count on hearing him in the middle of the night, moaning and exclaiming. I always joked that he sounded like an elephant. My favorite saying is when he would tell Grannie, "I don't know what you'd do without me." He liked to say the opposite of what he really meant.

Earl was always expressing himself, always displaying his eccentricities—even in his sleep!—without a care for what anyone else might think. And that is the quality I admire most in him. He was a bit of a rebel, defying convention in his own way. It may not have always served him well—his struggles with alcohol definitely left a mark on the family—but he seemed certain of who he was and wasn't going to let anyone else's expectations take that from him.

Earl farmed with his 1952 Ford 8N tractor. He also had a 1970's Massie Ferguson 165 and always drove Chevrolet trucks throughout his life.

In 1994 my cousin and friend Glynn Griggs wanted to photograph our grandparents in their natural setting on the farm. He spent the day with us and shot some of the most striking images that exist of Mary and Earl. Glynn's photos capture the down home essence of simple farmer folk. When I look at these images, I see the Mary and Earl that I knew best.

This spread: Earl and Mary working on the farm, photos by Glynn Griggs, 1994 (Collection of Michael & Rhonda Scoggins)

Earl died later that year, only months after Glynn's photos. He had been in the hospital for a number of days struggling with pneumonia that November. But the worst news came on Thanksgiving day: lung cancer. He died around 1am the following Monday.

My memory of his death is best described in an excerpt from "The Impermanent Flesh"—an unpublished story/prose-poem I wrote in 2003:

The rain poured with careless precision; a fierce storm raged. My grandfather was dying. I was sleeping. Mother stirred. Father followed mother.

I was wakened by swift hands—whose hands I don't remember. I sat in the back seat of the car, father driving as always, mother agitated and restless, the side of my face pressed against the glass of the window, cold from the rain. The din of the storm floated through the air sharp as a carving blade. My cheek bled—unnoticed—soft as the belly of a fish, fresh and full.

Dark skies, black tires, asphalt road: drenched, shadowed with tears from heaven; we hid in my parent's Chrysler, but eyes were not dry.

Being thirsty with so much water, but none I could partake. Tears in excess, fear, and hope. But the greatest of these...

"I love him, mother."

"We all do... we all do."

"I'm tired of watching him suffer."

At once, Papa was in the car with us, the night still, family packed like sardines.

"Whya et luk like em lights on th' line!"

I giggled enormously. "Yeah! How's it do that?"

Father was still driving, my small body squeezed between him and Papa, women somewhere in the back.

"They're reflectors, placed on the center line so you can see it in the dark."

"It looks like lights!"

"Et do!"

Here in the rain, on this night, there were no lights, no happily cramped family, no Papa, all innocence lost, the car an empty tomb.

When we arrived, the car slowed and we emerged dry under the large hospital awning. The rain slickened, full of regret. Through the stoic sterile halls we rushed to Papa's side. I slowed around the corner, through the door, into the room. Grannie stood quiet and forlorn, hand rested upon his, my aunt by her side, Papa stretched out, as if he were flat, across the bed. His jaw hung low, false teeth removed to prevent swallowing, lips enormously caved, wide and gaping, a large sunken mixing bowl dirty from cooking.

I saw Grannie standing in her kitchen, preparing a Sunday feast, mixing her famous apple pies in large bowls, adding the eggs, beating them with a whisk. Papa slouched in his worn armchair, half sleeping, until called to dinner. Afterwards he would take his plate and set it on the floor for the dog to clean.

But now the dogs would starve. And Grannie, using two eggs instead of three, would use her new, modern bowls. She sat the old bowls outside to catch rain for the dogs to drink.

Above: Earl and Jordan
(Collection of Michael & Rhonda Scoggins)

SCOGGINS

CHAPMAN • LAWRENCE
RAMBO • PECK

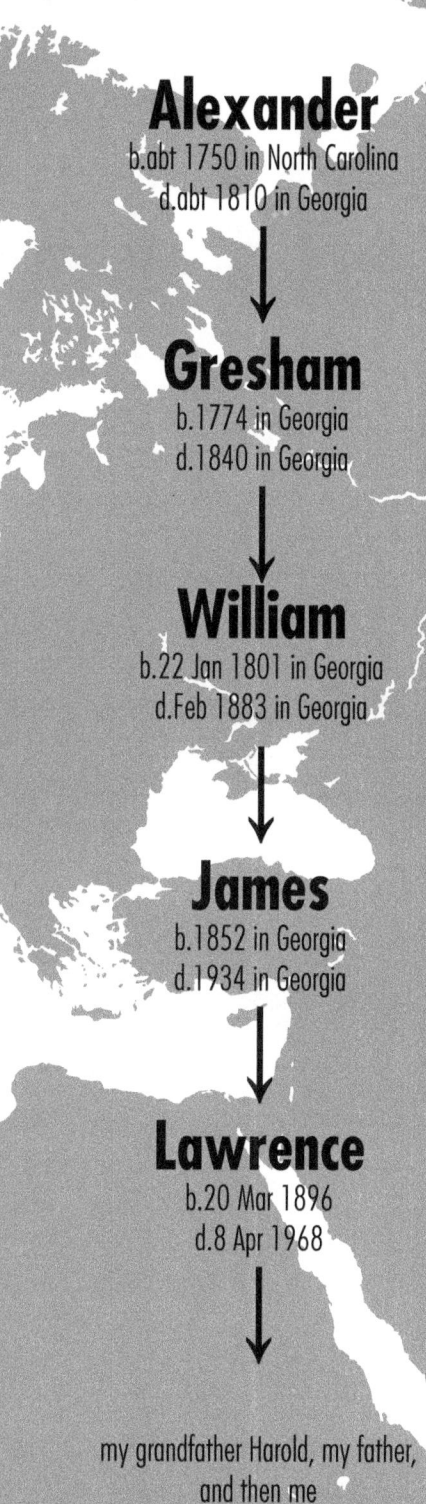

Alexander
b.abt 1750 in North Carolina
d.abt 1810 in Georgia

Gresham
b.1774 in Georgia
d.1840 in Georgia

William
b.22 Jan 1801 in Georgia
d.Feb 1883 in Georgia

James
b.1852 in Georgia
d.1934 in Georgia

Lawrence
b.20 Mar 1896
d.8 Apr 1968

my grandfather Harold, my father, and then me

My oldest documented Scoggins ancestor is Alexander Scoggins, born about 1750 in North Carolina. He migrated to Georgia in the 1780's or 90's where I was born a 7th generation native Georgian Scoggins.

Scoggins Saga
The Scoggins Family Origins

The first few generations of my Scoggins family in this country are a bit difficult to track. While it has proven thus far impossible to verify a specific immigrant, the Scoggins family likely originates in England and there are at least two possible immigrant ancestors to consider. The name has been spelled numerous ways even within the same family lines. Some spellings include Scogin, Scoggin, and Scoggins. My family, as far back as memory serves us, spells the name Scoggins.

The most commonly identified individual is George Scoggin, born about 1830 in England. This lineage appears in multiple places online, most prominently in Kevin Skoglund's *My Family History* as well as the *Scoggin and Kin Home Page* (the author is not identified). The lineage is as follows:

- George Scoggin (b. abt 1630)
- Richard George Scoggin (b. abt 1665)
- Richard Scoggin (b. abt 1695)
- Nathan Jonathan Scoggin (b. abt 1721)
- Alexander Scoggin (b.1750)

Although the above sites do not document any sources (unfortunately), the theory on George Scoggins may be rooted in information from the book *Cavaliers & Pioneers* by Nell Marion Nugent. Nugent describes the arrival of a George Scoggin in Virginia in 1653. A man named William Tidner paid for George's passage. The reason for this is not mentioned but George could have been an indentured servant (230).

George, however, is not the only possible original immigrant for my Scoggins line. Information from the research files of Merle, Lou, and Charlotte Scoggin from Jul 1979 (shared with me in 2011 by Nelda Scoggin Reynolds) identify a man named Thomas Scoggin. This Thomas was "granted land by the King of England in 1641 on Lawns Creek located on the south side of the James River in Surry County, Virginia" (M. Scoggin). Dates and locations alone identify Thomas as a potential ancestor. The line provided in these notes descends as follows:

- Thomas Scoggin
- Richard Scoggin I
- Richard Scoggin II
- John Scoggin (b.1721)
- Alexander Scoggin (b. abt 1750)

If Thomas was granted land by the king, it seems pretty clear he couldn't be the same person as the George whose passage was paid by William Tidner. It is interesting, though, that with the exception of George and Thomas, the rest of the generations (with Nathan Jonathan and John being the same person) down to Alexander are the same in these lineages.

Unfortunately at this point my sources do not go beyond what is described here. Further research is needed. Therefore I have chosen to present these theories as a suggestion, a jumping off point if you will. Whether or not the necessary records to prove a specific lineage even exist remains to be seen.

Left: me looking through the Civil War section in the Milstein Division at the NYPL, Dec 2011.
(Photo by Andrew P. Jones)

Alexander Scoggins
b.abt 1750 d.abt 1810
father of

Gresham Scoggins
b.8 Oct 1778 d.1840

The lineage becomes much clearer as we move forward from Alexander. Alexander "Elick" Scoggins, my 5th great grandfather, was born about 1750 in either North Carolina or Virginia. He married Mary Gresham about 1775 (Lovvorn 1; West, Individual). While there is no firm consensus on the number of Alexander's children, researchers "agree that it was between six and ten" (N. Reynolds, "Alexander"). Here I follow James Lecil Lovvorn's work and list eight children:

1. Millington (b.abt 1771, d.May 1841)
2. Gresham (b.8 Oct 1778, d.1840)
3. Rhoda (b.abt 1779, d?)
4. Gilliam (b.18 Dec 1780, d.12 Mar 1862)
5. Sarah "Sallie" (b.abt.1783, d. 11 Mar 1856)
6. Cynthia "Sinia" (b.abt 1790, d.9 Jul 1845)
7. Wiley (b.23 Jun 1794, d.19 Jan 1873)
8. J. Davis (b.abt 1794, d.bef 1860)

Alexander is counted in Orange County on the North Carolina census of 1779 (Jackson, NC) and just a few years later he "sold land in Orange Co, NC 24 Mar 1783 to John Edwards". After that, Alexander's whereabouts for the next seventeen years are unclear. By 1800 he was living in Oglethorpe County, GA, counted there on the state census in that year (Jackson, GA) and appears on Oglethorpe County tax lists from 1795 to 1800. His will was written 5 Jun 1809 and recorded 9 Jan 1811, placing his death (most likely) in 1810 in Cloud Creek, Oglethorpe County (Lovvorn 1; West, Individual).

Apart from these few details, I know very little about Alexander's life. One story has been passed down by Susie Scoggin Mahaffey (2nd great granddaughter of Alexander) and recounted by Nelda Scoggin Reynolds in an essay on Alexander:

> "When Alexander was a young man he and his friends went hunting. They came upon a group of wild boars who chased the boys into the woods. The boys threw down their rifles and climbed into the trees to escape the hogs. They were forced to stay treed for hours as the hogs kept guard until a rescue party came looking for them" (Mahaffey qtd. in N. Reynolds, "Alexander").

While the geographical setting is quite different, images from *Lord of the Flies* fill my head!

I descend through Alexander's son Gresham. Gresham was born 8 Oct 1778 (Lovvorn 3; West, Individual; West, Births; Yates). He married Winney Rene Watson Jun 1800 in Oglethorpe County. The date is recorded as 10 Jun in most sources (West, Individual; Dodd; Hunting), just the year in Yates, and 1 Jun in Lovvorn (3); I think Lovvorn's is a simple typo/error.

We can follow Gresham's migration path clear

Above: A page from the 1830 US census that counts Gresham in Capt Britain C Tyars District in Troup County, Georgia. (From Ancestry.com)

The photo overlapping the census is Yellow Jacket Creek just outside of Hogansville in Troup County. This represents the general area where Gresham lived. Summer 2011. (Photo by Gene Morgan, Collection of Nelda Scoggin Reynolds)

According to Nelda Scoggin Reynolds, this photo of Winney Watson "came from the collection of ... Della and Stella Scoggin, descendants of Elisha Harrison Scoggin ... [The photo] is authentic because we can trace it straight back to a member of the family in Chattooga County where Winney was living in 1880." This copy of the photo was shared by babydowhat on Ancestry.com. Unfortunately no known photo exists of Gresham.

across the state of Georgia. In 1820 he was living in Putnam County. In 1830 he had relocated to Troup County. He is listed as a soldier in his entry the 1832 Georgia Cherokee Land Lottery (Ancestry.com Cherokee). The *History of Troup County* also lists him as a soldier on a roster of men in Captain Stewart's regiment, LaGrange District, from the period near 1836 (Ancestry.com Troup 83). By 1840 he was living in Heard County.

Gresham and Winney had eleven children:

1. William Delaney (b.22 Jan 1801, m. 1st Mary Cleckler, 2nd Elizabeth Ann Sewell, d.Feb 1883)
2. Gillum (b.21 Dec 1802, m.Margaret Dowling, d.28 Mar 1856)
3. Cynthia (b.7 Jun 1805, m.Josiah R. Reeves, d.2 Oct 1902)
4. John Watson (b.6 Jun 1808, m.Eliza G. Gillespie, d.26 Mar 1854)
5. Rhoda (b.14 Oct 1810, m.Edmund Baker, d.20 Mar 1905)
6. Sinia Ann (b.6 Jul 1813, m.Thomas Anderson Lawrence, d.28 Aug 1871)
7. Levi Sanford (b.29 Sep 1817, m.Nancy Matilda Steward, d.25 Mar 1901)
8. Elizabeth Caroline (b.Aug 1819, m.George W. Moore, d.aft 1900)
9. Elisha Harrison (b.Aug 1823, m.Martha Barron, d.aft 1900)
10. Wiley Gresham (b.7 Feb 1826, m.Lovica Barron, d.9 Nov 1909)
11. Zillian A. (b.20 Dec 1828, m.James F. Barron, d.26 Oct 1893)

Every one of these children was involved either directly or indirectly in the Civil War. See the next page for an illustration.

Gresham's descendants alone do not represent the extent of the Scoggins family in the Civil War. His siblings also had sons who served in the Civil War. The Scoggins family was heavily entrenched in the conflict.

Gresham died in 1840 (Lovvorn 3; West, Deaths; West, Individual). Winney lived another 40 years at least and migrated to Chattooga County with some of her children. She is counted there in 1870 living with her son William and in 1880 living with her daughter Rhoda, widow of Edmund Baker.

Scoggins Soldiers
Gresham's Sons, Grandsons, and Sons-In-Law
who served in the Civil War

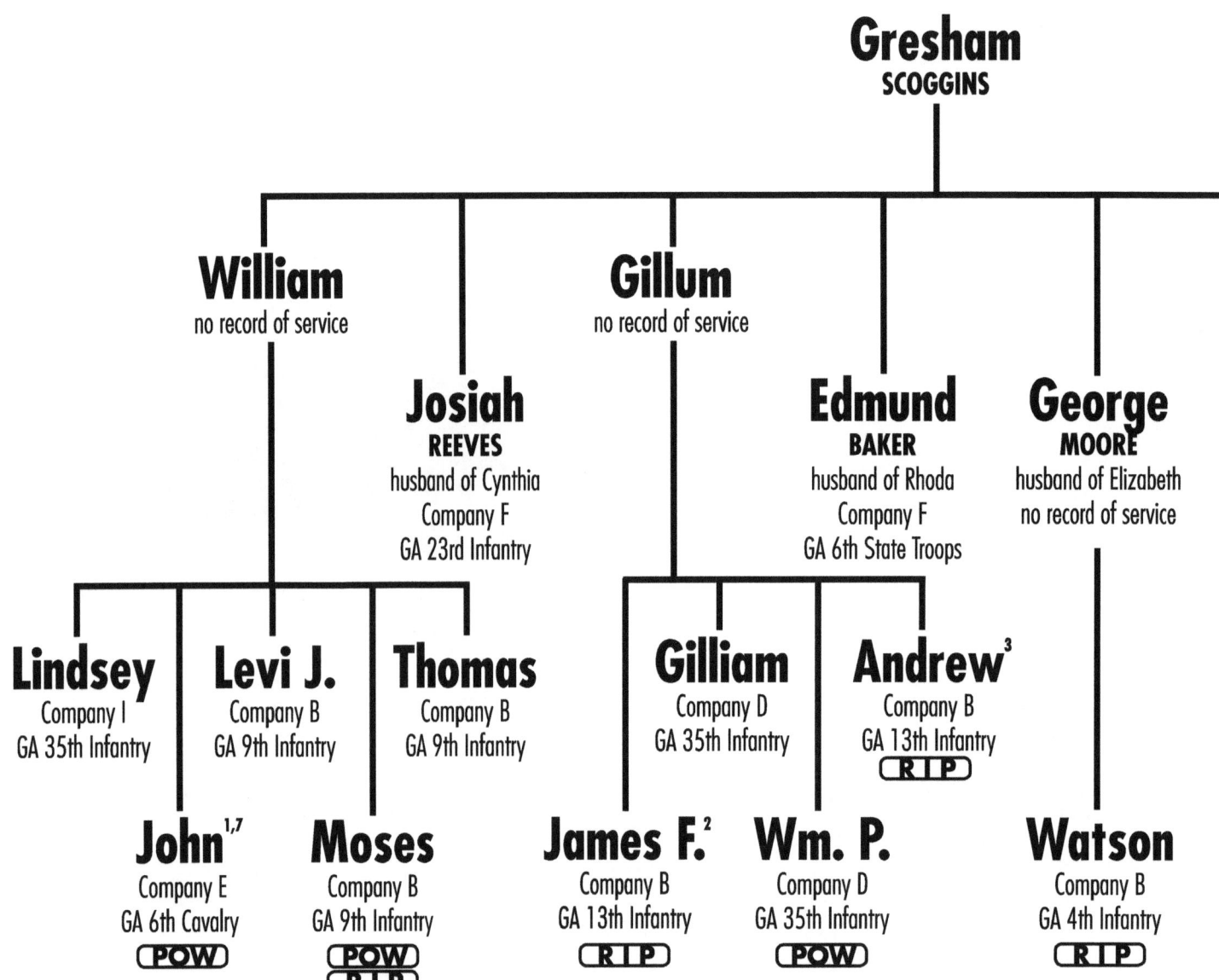

Gresham SCOGGINS

- **William** — no record of service
- **Gillum** — no record of service
- **Josiah REEVES** — husband of Cynthia, Company F, GA 23rd Infantry
- **Edmund BAKER** — husband of Rhoda, Company F, GA 6th State Troops
- **George MOORE** — husband of Elizabeth, no record of service

Grandsons:

- **Lindsey** — Company I, GA 35th Infantry
- **Levi J.** — Company B, GA 9th Infantry
- **Thomas** — Company B, GA 9th Infantry
- **Gilliam** — Company D, GA 35th Infantry
- **Andrew**[3] — Company B, GA 13th Infantry (RIP)
- **John**[1,7] — Company E, GA 6th Cavalry (POW)
- **Moses** — Company B, GA 9th Infantry (POW) (RIP)
- **James F.**[2] — Company B, GA 13th Infantry (RIP)
- **Wm. P.** — Company D, GA 35th Infantry (POW)
- **Watson** — Company B, GA 4th Infantry (RIP)

This chart is not an exhaustive tree of the Gresham Scoggins family, but rather an illustration of his sons, grandsons, and sons-in-law who served in the Civil War. A total of 22 men from the Gresham Scoggins family fought. Three men either died in battle or as a result of sickness from their service and four were prisoners of war. In a war with upwards of 618,000 American lives lost, it's astonishing so few of Gresham's family died from the conflict. The unsung heroes, though, must be the women and children who kept the farms going and tended to life without the traditional husband/father figure.

All of these soldiers are documented in *American Civil War Soldiers* and *U.S. Civil War Soldier Records and Profiles* (both by Historical Data Systems) and the National Park Service's *U.S. Civil War Soldiers, 1861-1865* except as noted. As with all people in this book, please see my tree on Ancestry.com for additional details.

POW = Prisoner of war
RIP = Died due to service

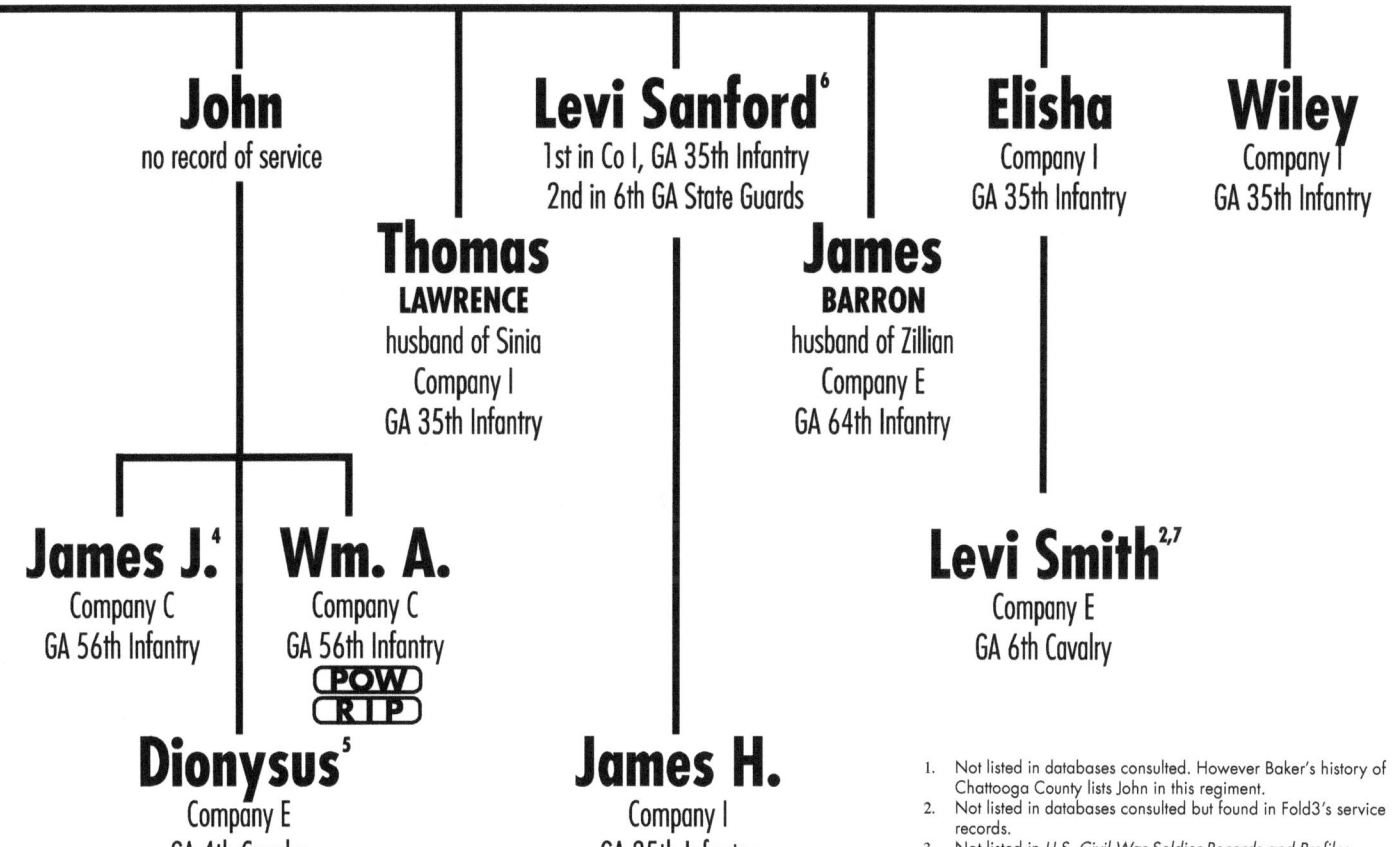

1. Not listed in databases consulted. However Baker's history of Chattooga County lists John in this regiment.
2. Not listed in databases consulted but found in Fold3's service records.
3. Not listed in *U.S. Civil War Soldier Records and Profiles*.
4. Not listed in *U.S. Civil War Soldiers, 1861-1865*.
5. Not listed in databases consulted but found in Ancestry.com's *Georgia, Confederate Pension Applications, 1879-1960*.
6. Not listed in *U.S. Civil War Soldier Records and Profiles* for his 2nd regiment only.
7. Confederate Muster Rolls available online at Georgia Archives

William Delaney Scoggins
b. 22 Jan 1801 d. Feb 1883
married 16 Sep 1839
Elizabeth Sewell
b. 1810 d. 1879

Elizabeth was the second wife of William. His first wife was Mary Clecker (b. abt 1805, d.1838). I descend through Elizabeth.

William "Billy" Delaney Scoggins was born on 22 Jan 1801 in Georgia. Some sources state he was born in Jasper County (Biographical Souvenir 753), however Jasper County was was not created until 1807 when it was split from Baldwin County. Other sources identify Oglethorpe County as the location (Lovvorn 7). It's difficult to say for sure which account is correct given that county boundaries were somewhat fluid over time. Census records, of course, only identify the state (not county) of birth.

William's first wife was Mary Cleckler with whom he had four children:

1. Lindsey Hamilton (b.9 Apr 1823, m.Julia Ann Lawrence, d.25 Jul 1907)
2. Levi Jackson (b.20 Jul 1825, m.Lucy Lawrence, d.1 Jan 1895)
3. William Delaney [II] (b.abt 1827, d.?)
4. Mary Jane (b.abt 1829, d.?)

The first two children were born in Newton County, Georgia. Two of my ancestors in the Jordan line, William and Burrell, also lived in Newton County around this time (see pgs 88-91). No further details are known about William Delaney [II] and Mary Jane. They died probably as youngsters and family stories say William [II] died of disease and Mary Jane burned to death. There is, however, no documentation to verify these stories (N. Reynolds, correspondence).

By 1830 William and his family had moved

Above: Looking towards Little Sand Mountain from Farmersville Cemetery, Sep 2011. (Photo by Jordan M. Scoggins)

Opposite: These two images are crayon portraits of William Delaney Scoggins and Elizabeth Sewell. (Collection of Frances Scoggins)

A RESEARCH NOTE

Don't be confused by the name! There is another man by the name of William D. Scoggins living in Georgia at the same time as my William. This other William is counted in Baldwin County on the 1830 and 1840 census. He is the son of Smith Scoggins and the father of John Scoggins. John is immortalized on the Georgia monument in the Chickamauga Battlefield. Some researchers suggest this family is related but as yet there is no documentation to prove any relationship between the Scoggins family in Baldwin County and my own Scoggins line (Chattooga Heritage 310; Reynolds, correspondence).

on to Troup County Georgia, an area that only a few years before had been Creek territory. After a series of corrupt treaties the Creek had been forcibly removed and were no longer in the area by 1827 (Worthy).

According to the Confederate pension application for William's son Levi, William and his family lived in Chattooga County beginning Sep 1835 (Ancestry.com, GA Pension). William's first wife, Mary, died there in 1838. He also married his second wife, Elizabeth "Betsy" Sewell, in that county on 16 Sep 1839. William and Elizabeth had the following children:

1. Thomas Newton (b.Oct 1840, m.Evaline Clarissa Lawrence, d.17 Oct 1917)
2. Moses Gresham (b.abt 1841, d.19 Oct 1863)
3. Harriett C. (b.abt 1843, d.?)
4. John Weston (b.11 Aug 1845, m.Mary F. Johnson, d.21 Mar 1933)
5. Winney Emily (b.10 Dec 1847, m.William Booker Foster, d.4 Nov 1937)
6. Gilliam Terrell (b.18 Jul 1850, m.Phebe Ellen Valentine Mathis, d.23 Jan 1923)
7. James Harvey (b.30 Jun 1852, m.Drucilla Chapman, d.14 Dec 1934)
8. Martha Ann (b.17 Oct 1862, m.Cyrus Montague Herndon, d.30 Oct 1920)

The family lived in Dirt Town Valley, where so

many of my ancestors lived (and some cousins still do). I have not been able to track down the precise location of his farm yet, but it is said to be "at the foot of Little Sand Mountain in Dirt Town Valley, not far from where Pleasant Grove Baptist Church was established" (Baker 1131). Notes from the research files of Merle, Lou, and Charlotte Scoggin show that a creek runs north to south on the west side of William's property (M. Scoggin). Little Armuchee Creek is the main creek that runs through this area.

Five of William's sons fought in the Civil War. From his first marriage, Levi and Lindsey served. Of Elizabeth's sons, Thomas, John, and Moses served. See the chart on pages 128-129 for more details. And while William did not serve in the war himself, records show he did play his part by providing supplies. He sold 10 bushels of corn to the Confederacy in Nov 1863. William's brother Levi provided a wagon and horses (Receipt, W D & L S).

Family lore, too, adds to the story of the Scoggins involvement in the war. Nelda Scoggin Reynolds recounts the following story:

"When the Yankees swept through Chattooga County, they came to the

Above: Little Armuchee Creek in Dirt Town Valley near the foot of Little Sand Mountain, Sep 2011.

Right: William Delaney's commemorative tombstone in Farmersville Cemetery. Note the alternate spellings. Sep 2011.

(Photos by Jordan M. Scoggins)

farm of Lindsey Hamilton and Julia Lawrence Scoggin. Lindsey had been sent home because of illness. At the time, Julia and Lindsey had eight children. The Yankees attempted to take their milk cow. Julia confronted them armed with a broom and declared that they were not going to take the milk cow which was the only source of food for her eight children. The Yankees left the cow" (N. Reynolds, correspondence).

The women of the Scoggins family had to be particularly strong. Not only were many of the Scoggins men away at war, but often the men from their maiden families too. Nelda continues her story about Julia:

"Frankly, I don't know how in this world Julia lived through it all. Her brother Malachi Columbus Lawrence died in July 1862 in Virginia while serving in the Confederate Army. Her father, Malachi Lawrence, died in September 1862 followed by the death of her mother, Isabelle Grimsley, in October 1862. Lindsey was sent home because he was too sick to serve any longer in October 1862. Julia must have been made of iron to withstand all of the pressures of living through that terrible time" (N. Reynolds, correspondence).

After the war had subsided and the surviving men had returned home life began to regain some normalcy. Most of William's children remained in the Chattooga County area, raising their families close to home. Lindsey was the pioneer of the bunch, migrating to Texas in the 1870's. Nelda, a descendant of Lindsey, tells a story passed down by each generation:

"It took eight wagons to move all of Lindsey's family and goods to Texas in November 1875. William Dulaney drove one of those wagons. At that time William would have been seventy four. Keep in mind that he had to go back to Georgia as well. That's quite a feat for a man of that age" (N. Reynolds, correspondence).

Lindsey ultimately settled in Grayson County, TX. His half brother John joined him there in the 1880's.

William must have been fairly well off for his day as he had several slaves. On the 1860 slave schedule there are 7 slaves to his name (Ancestry.com 1860 Slave). Stories handed down by the family tell us that one of William's slaves was named Hester. Even after emancipation, Hester remained with the Scoggins family. She helped with the children and was called Mammy Hester. She appears on the 1880 census as Hester Scoggins, the head of her own household of 13 people (including herself along with children, grandchildren, nephews, and a boarder). William had allowed her and all his slaves to take the family surname. With Hester's large number of offspring yet no record of a husband, I can't help but wonder if William fathered at least some of her children. This would not have been uncommon and it would be interesting to make contact with a descendant of Hester and perform DNA tests. This could also account for family stories of Hester's affection towards

William's family—perhaps there was a love triangle at play, all but lost to history now.

William died in February of 1883 in Walker County (Biographical Souvenir 753; Lovvorn 7). The location of his burial is not documented but family tradition says William is buried in Farmersville Cemetery. When I visited the cemetery in Sep 2011, along with my grand aunt Frances, she recalled that her mother, Ida Mae, would always point out the cemetery when they drove by, telling her, "That's where your great grandfather is buried." Ida would not have known William herself, but she was passing to Frances what she knew through her husband Lawrence and her father-in-law James. Commemorative stones for William and Elizabeth were placed in Farmersville Cemetery by Leonard Pritchett Scoggins and relatives around 1985 (N. Reynolds, correspondence).

James Harvey Scoggins
b.30 Jun 1852 d.14 Dec 1934
married 25 Nov 1880

Drucilla Chapman
b.20 May 1859 d.1 Jun 1922

Below: This photo of Harvey in his later years is one of the only surviving images of him. It was most likely taken at his home in Green Bush. (Collection of Dot Scoggins)

Opposite: Scoggins & Sons, circa 1905. See the main text for more about this photo. (Collection of Robert Paul Maloney)

James Harvey Scoggins was born 30 Jun 1852, the youngest son of William Delaney. Commonly known as Harvey, he grew up in Dirt Town Valley and married Drucilla Chapman on 25 Nov 1880.

Drucilla is the daughter of William Jack Chapman and Clarissa Lawrence. According to tradition she was born in the James Edward Lawrence house in West Armuchee. Her name is one of those you find written a number of different ways. It is spelled "Drucilla" on her tombstone. Other common spellings include Druscilla, Drew Cillar, and sometimes just Drew.

James and Drucilla had the following children:

1. Jesse (b.16 Nov 1881, m. 1st Viven Inez McWilliams, 2nd Mary Neal, d.11 Mar 1968)
2. Ellen (b.12 May 1883, d.15 Dec 1883)
3. Fred (b.24 Nov 1884, m.Corinthia Addie Bagwell, d.3 Jul 1968)
4. Annie Lee (b.5 Oct 1886, d.5 Feb 1904)
5. Joe Ben (b.9 Jul 1888, d.15 Mar 1967)
6. Unnamed Infant (b.24 Mar 1890, d.25 Mar 1890)
7. Clyde (b.4 Sep 1891, d.15 Feb 1893)
8. Lee Roy (b.12 Jan 1894, m.Jayme Coulter, d.9 Jun 1945)
9. Lawrence Chapman (b.20 Mar 1896, m.Ida Mae Rambo, d.8 Apr 1968)
10. Dennis (b.23 Jul 1898, m.Nelle Smith, d.16 Mar 1943)

The *Georgia 1890 Property Tax Digests* lists Harvey in Green Bush with an estate valued at 55 dollars—among the poorest of the community (Ancestry.com, 1890). He is counted again in West Armuchee on the 1900 census; his occupation is farmer. His house still stands on present day Scoggins Lane on parcel number 0539 005B (Chattooga Tax).

In addition to farming, Harvey worked in saw milling and cotton ginning. Family tradition says he was also a cobbler.

A news item in the 20 Mar 1902 *Walker County Messenger* shows he was in the milling business with an unknown McKnight:

> "Last Thursday while sawing at Scoggins and McKnights mill the governor belt broke and the engine came near leaving the ground. It was funny after it was over with, everything ran but Mr. Scoggins" (Grigsby, Transcriptions).

Like milling, ginning was dangerous work. Another item in the *Messenger* (30 Oct 1902) shows Harvey in the ginning business with an unknown Horne:

> "A bad accident occurred at Horne and Scoggins gin last Friday. While ginning Bob McGill who was at work went to raise the gin breast and touched the saw accidentally. All of the fingers were split and his hands cut considerably, but Dr. R.E. Talley who dressed his hand says he thinks he will be alright in a few months" (Grigsby, Transcriptions).

A 27 Apr 1905 reference in the *Summerville News* refers to Scoggins and Sons for the first time:

> "Scoggins and Sons have their new engine and other machinery in shape and are doing good work ginning, sawing, grinding, etc" (Grigsby, Transcriptions).

The Scoggins and Sons building was located in Subligna (at the northern extreme of Dirt Town Valley and just before you enter West Armuchee Valley to the north). After Harvey it was operated by his son Lawrence Chapman Scoggins for many years. At some point Will White had a share as did Leland Coulter Scoggins. Subligna Baptist Church bought Leland's share to use for the church parking lot (R. & M. Scoggins, correspondence).

The above image is the only known photograph of the gin. Taken around 1905, fifteen workers are pictured in front of the gin building. In Oct 2011, Robert Paul Maloney (grandson of the Paul Maloney pictured) and I worked off two almost-identical versions of the photo, each labeled with different clues, to analyze and determine as best we could the identity of each man. Left to right:

1. Dick Rackley
2. Harry Shropshire
3. Elias B. Rackley
4. James Harvey Scoggins
5. Bryant (one of the Bryants is Tom)
6. Lawrence Chapman Scoggins (seated on the ground)
7. Bryant (one of the Bryants is Tom)
8. D(?) Watkins
9. Robert Paul Maloney
10. Ben Scoggins
11. T? Hill
12. Fred Scoggins
13. James Keown
14. Jesse Scoggins
15. Sam Watkins

Robert Paul Maloney in this photo is a descendant of William Jack Chapman (see pg 142), which makes him related to the Scoggins men in the photo. He is also related to the Watkins men. Paul's half-brother William Harvey Maloney married Cora Alverson. Cora was the sister of Mary Victoria Alverson who is the wife of the Andrew Watkins pictured here. And to top it all off, Mary is a daughter of Frances E. Robbs—a descendant (through a different direct line) of my 4th great grandfather William Robbs (see pg 65)!

Another accident was reported in the 20 Jul 1905 *Summerville News*:

> "A bad accident happened at Scoggins and Sons mill last Saturday. While a line shaft was running 200 revolutions per minute Lawrence Scoggins, a nine year old boy who was playing in a seed house with a string to the end of the shaft, was caught by the sleeve and came very near having his arm twisted off" (Grigsby, Transcriptions).

Lawrence Chapman is my great grandfather.

See page 150.

When Lawrence's daughter Frances was a little girl, she remembers "walk[ing] to the gin and the wagons would be lined up in a row waiting their turn for their cotton to be ginned" (F. Scoggins).

The *Summerville News* noted in Jan 1906 that Drucilla and her boys Roy and Lawrence "spent Sunday with [Drucilla's] mother [Clarissa Lawrence, widow of William Jack Chapman] of West Armuchee" (Grigsby, transcriptions). It may be funny to think that

such an item was newsworthy but, if you think about it, it's a precursor to today's social media status updates… just not quite as instantaneous! Everybody is always interested in what everybody else is doing.

In 1926, along with J.C. Young and R.E. McWilliams, Harvey was elected School Trustee for West Armuchee (Grigsby, Transcriptions). The school, only a few years old at the time, was located on the main West Armuchee Road about 2.5 miles from Harvey's home.

There is confusion about James's early life. A veterans stone placed at his grave in Chapman Cemetery indicates that he served in the GA 35th Infantry of the Confederate army. Unfortunately this is an innocent error. While there is a James H. Scoggins that matches these details, a close examination reveals that the record is for James Harrison Scoggins (son of Levi Sanford Scoggins). Levi's own service record show he enlisted in Co I, 35th GA Infantry Regiment on 25 Sep 1861. He was later discharged, furnishing a substitute on 4 Sep 1862, and transferred to the 6th Battalion, Cavalry

Below: Scoggins Lane is in the southern part of the West Armuchee valley and is part of the community of Green Bush. This is the house where Harvey lived. May 2010. (Photo by Jordan M. Scoggins)

Left: A crayon portrait of Drucilla Chapman
Below: A page from the James Harvey Scoggins Bible.

(Collection of Frances Scoggins)

(GA State Guards). The record for James H. matches this and shows he enlisted as a substitute to the same company and regiment on that date (Historical, Soldiers & U.S.; National Park Service). It would be unusual for James Harvey to be the substitute for Levi Sanford and more likely that Levi would supply his own son, James Harrison, as a substitute. Additionally, James Harrison was 8 years older than James Harvey. In 1862, James Harvey was only 10 years old—not even close to the legal age to serve—while James Harrison would have been an appropriate age to join up. It's an easy mistake to make given the lack of detail in Civil War records.

Drucilla died on 1 Jun 1922. Her death certificate lists diabetes, from which she suffered for two years, as the cause of her death (Death). Family memories passed down tell of Drucilla's sons carrying her coffin to the grave. Leland Coulter Scoggins remembers Harvey's passing and recalls he died in the south west bedroom of his home on Scoggins Lane on 14 Dec 1934 (L. Scoggins). Drucilla and Harvey are buried together in Chapman Cemetery.

James and Drucilla lived through the death of four of their children. Three of the children did not survive infancy, and the only other daughter died at 18. On the opposite end of the spectrum, four of the brothers died in an eerie span of two years in 1967-68, all in their 70's/80's. By the end of 1968 James and Drucilla's family was no more.

GREEN BUSH

Green Bush (or Greenbush) was a community in the West Armuchee valley region of Walker County, GA. It was originally called Vicksburg after the first European settler in West Armuchee, Mr. Vick (Sartain 307). The community was home to a post office, blacksmith shop, grist mill, cotton gin, and at least two stores. Exact locations of all but the mill are unknown. The mill and store were located very close to each other about a mile and a half up the road from the home of James Harvey Scoggins. Like the locations, other details about Green Bush have almost completely vanished from the memory of the community as well as the history books.

There were a few different churches in the Green Bush and West Armuchee area. The earliest of these, Shiloh Baptist Church, was formed in 1839. Several of the first families to live in the area helped form the church, including McWilliams, Suttle, Wood, and Young. The first pastor was William Catlett. The original building was a log structure and stood about a mile from the present site. The first building at the present site was constructed in the 1850's and served as a Confederate Hospital during the war. That building was torn down and a new one constructed in 1949. Other pastors include Artemus Shattuck, a native of Connecticut, and his son William Shattuck. Other churches of the area are Pleasant Hill Methodist, which was established in 1847, and Prospect Baptist Church, formed by the black population of the valley (Grigsby, papers).

The Green Bush postmaster was Spencer Bomar. He ran the post office, as well as a general store, from a room in the front of his house. Spencer was also the church clerk for Shiloh Baptist Church (Walker Heritage 96). James Perry McWilliams was a local physician who practiced medicine in the area during the late 19th and early 20th century (Ancestry.com Directory).

The earliest schools were held in vacant farm houses. The churches were also used as schools in the early days. Eventually dedicated school buildings were constructed and Pleasant Hill stood at the north end of the valley with Green Bush at the south end (Grigsby, papers). In 1923 a consolidated school was built and called West Armuchee School. It was a "large building with four classrooms, two office rooms, an auditorium and a hall" (Grigsby, transcriptions). But that school too eventually closed. Today the West Armuchee Community Center stands where the West Armuchee School used to be.

Suttle's Mill was a grist mill in Green Bush that was operated by the Suttle family. The earliest documentation I have found comes from the *Walker County Messenger* in the 1880's and 1890's and show that the mill was owned by James Thomas Suttle. During this time the mill was frequently used as a point of reference to describe locations nearby. It is possible the mill pre dates back to James's father John Byars Suttle. (John Suttle was among the original settlers of the Armuchee Valleys and was also one of the largest slave owners). J.T. also operated a gin while the Suttle women ran a successful dairy business. A writer in the *Walker County Messenger* in 1888 referred to the Suttle home place as "one of the most beautiful places in North Georgia" and claimed "no better butter goes to Atlanta than furnished by this model dairy" (Grigsby, transcriptions).

A barn on Cantrell Road in the Green Bush/West Armuchee area. This is a typical barn of the Armuchee Valleys. May 2010. (Photo by Jordan M. Scoggins)

One store in Green Bush was called Jackson & Blackwell. In 1910 the store was burned by a man named Melton Robbs (of no known relation to my ancestor Robbs from pg 65). Melton was arrested in Chattanooga when trying to change the money and aroused suspicion. He confessed and explained he had broken into the store, stole $50, and "set fire to the store to conceal the robbery" (Confesses). I do not know if this store reopened, or how long it had existed before the arson.

The other store at Green Bush was Puryear & Hunt General Merchandise. Evelyn Morgan Shahan recorded some details on the back of a photograph of the store and identified the central figure in the photo, the man sitting in the doorway of the store, as Francis Marion Puryear. The remaining men—and even the identifies of the "Hunt" in the store name—are unidentified.

It is unclear if Puryear & Hunt are the original proprietors. A biographical sketch of Capt. Reece Neal describes "ledgers from an antebellum store at Green Bush show repeated visits by Capt. Neal and his mother to purchase equipment prior to his service in the Confederate Army as Lieutenant and later Captain in Co. H 23 Regt., Georgia Volunteers." (Walker Heritage 311). This may be the Puryear & Hunt store. A later ledger dated 1879-81 from Puryear & Hunt is in possession of Jodie, daughter of Louis Hunt and granddaughter of Georgia Ward. The dates are much too early for Francis Marion (b.1873) to have been working there at the time, much less to have owned it. J. Puryear is written on the front of the ledger. I can not make a certain correlation between the 1879 ledger and any of the three (at least) J. Puryear men living in the area during this time period.

However, census records assist in determining who operated the store in its later years. The 1900 census lists Francis living with the Georgia Ann Hunt (daughter of John Byars Suttle) family in West Armuchee. Francis Puryear and J[ohn] Suttle Hunt (son of Georgia) are both listed as merchants, corresponding to the Puryear & Hunt name. By 1910 Francis had moved to Indian territory and was living in Bixby Township, Tulsa County, Oklahoma as a farmer. His wife, Emma, is a Native American. Back in West Armuchee, John (still counted in his mother's household) remained a retail merchant. His brother Ben had joined him in the business by this time, listed as a salesman. By 1920 Ben had moved to Cane Creek and was farming. John remained in West Armuchee and ran the store, counted on the census as a retail merchant of dried goods. Finally, by 1930 Suttle was no longer operating the store, now listed as running a grist mill—the previously mentioned Suttle's Mill. He had probably operated the mill along with the store for many years, but by 1930 the store had closed.

The store building is long gone, remembered only by

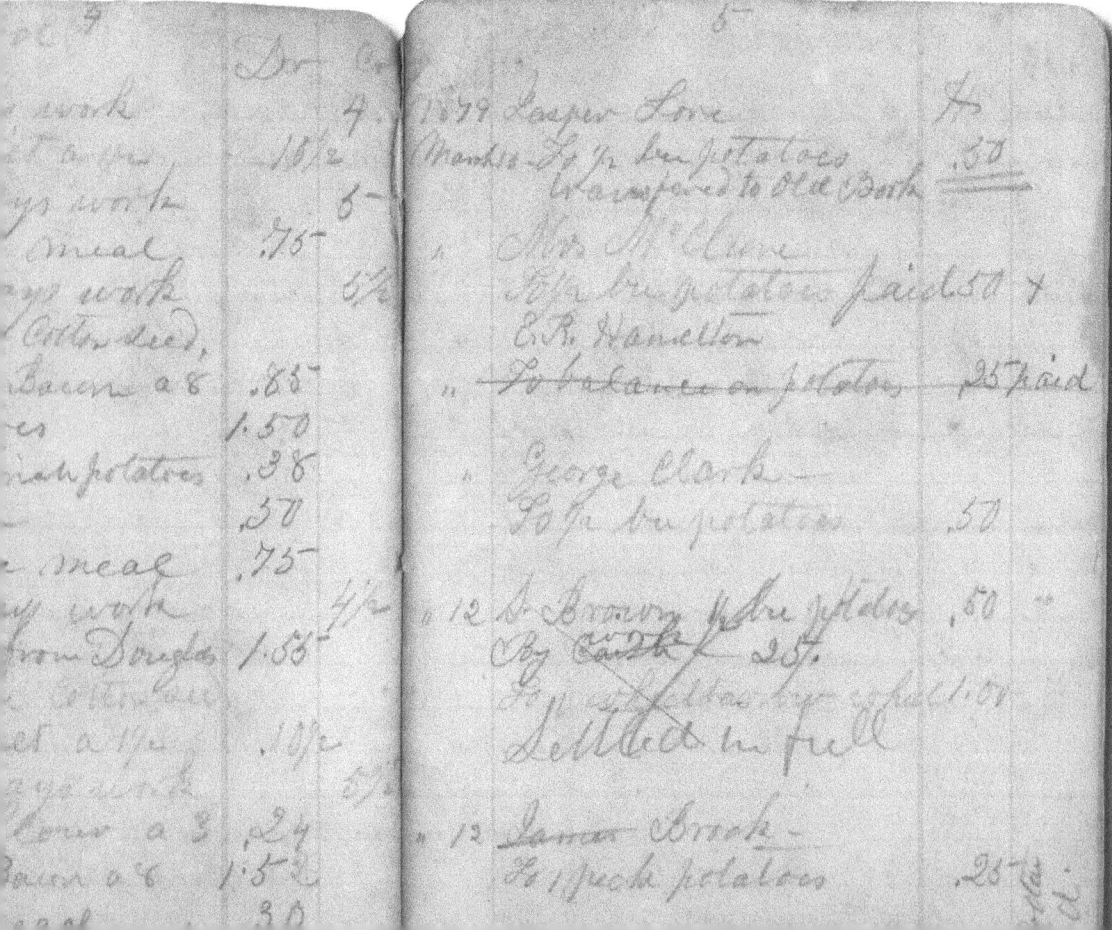

Left: A page from the 1879-81 ledger for Puryear & Hunt. Jasper Love (see pg 62) shopped there in Mar 1879. (Collection of Jodie Hunt Bell)

Above: Evelyn Morgan Shahan estimated this photo was taken about 1910, but it is probably slightly earlier since the man seated in the doorway, Francis Marion Puryear, was living in Indian Territory by 1910. The other men are unidentified though my best guess is that the young man to the right of Francis is one of the Hunt brothers. Advertisements for Friends' Oats and Monarch Tobacco hang on the store. Above the entrance a sign reads: "To Cure a Cold in One Day take Laxative Bromo Quinine Tablets." To the right rear of the store you can make out Suttle's Mill. (Collection of Evelyn Morgan Shahan)

the sole known photograph. Suttle's Mill remained many more years. By the mid 1960's it was no longer in operation but the building was still there. My parents—high school teenage sweethearts—would go to the creek there to swim. My mother remembers going for an afternoon swim one summer and sitting on top of the dam with Mike. I can picture the romantic country scene: the sound of running water and the touch of teenage hands.

"I'm afraid to get in the water, Mike. There are snakes in there."

"Oh those snakes are in the trees. They won't hurt you as long as they're in the trees and you're in the water."

I don't blame my mother for not wanting to swim that day.

Today the mill is long gone and teenagers probably don't go there to swim anymore. The dam, however, is still there and remains a fading remnant of the forgotten community of Green Bush.

CHAPMAN and LAWRENCE families
(and GRIGSBY, RICHARDSON, RAMSEY, and MALONEY too)

John [I]
CHAPMAN
b.abt 1737 in Virginia
d.10 Oct 1816 in Virginia

↓

William
b.abt 1773 in Virginia
d.16 Feb 1855 in South Carolina

↓

John Henry
b.24 Apr 1779 or 99 in Virginia
d.24 Sep 1862 in Georgia

↓

Wm. Jack
b.10 Jul 1825 in South Carolina
d.28 May 1896 in Georgia

↓

my 2nd great grandmother Drucilla, great-grandfather Lawrence, grandfather Harold, father Michael, and then me

CHAPMAN

Drucilla Chapman allies the Scoggins family with the Chapman family. Shared trees on Ancestry.com suggest the Chapman ancestors date back to 17th century Connecticut, and England before that. These connections not well documented and seem questionable to me. I have not been able to verify or disprove the lineage so therefore have not included it here. And I fully acknowledge that the lineage I do describe is not documented as fully as I would prefer. As with everything else, this is merely a starting point for future expansion.

John Chapman begins the line. I do not have clear birth or death dates. In fact, the only records I have for him are two censuses. In 1782 he was counted in the Continental Census in Amelia County, VA (Jackson, VA). On the 1810 US census he is found there again. There is one male listed as 45 and older, one male 16 to 25, and one male under 10. There are also two females 45 and over, and 12 slaves, for a total of 17 household members. Assuming John is the male over 45 he would have been born in 1765 at the latest—though possibly many years earlier as well. According to *Generations Gone By*, John was born about 1737 and died 10 Oct 1816.

John's son William was born about 1773 in Amelia County. He married Ann Jones on 23 Dec 1792. They had moved to Spartanburg County, SC, by 1810 where they appear on each census until 1840. I have not located them in 1850. William died 16 Feb 1855 (Generations).

The next in my line is John Henry Chapman. John Henry's birth is slightly confused. His tombstone in Chapman Cemetery in West Armuchee reads b.24 Apr 1779. However the 1850 census in West Armuchee (Walker County, Georgia) lists his age as 51 years old (a birth year of about 1799). The 1860 census (also in West Armuchee) indicates the same approximate age. While certainly census records can be unreliable, it seems unusual for his stone to state a birth year with 20 years difference. Yet I am certain, given the household members (including John's wife Lucy Jones and their children) and burial location, these two censuses and the stone belong to the same person. Either both censuses or the tombstone are in error. Arriving in West Armuchee before 1850, John Henry and his family were among the

Me posing with the wreath I placed at William Jack Chapman's grave at the dedication of his Civil War marker in 1991. See me almost 20 years later with the same graves on the next page. (Collection of Frances Scoggins)

(cont. from Henry Hardy to the right)

James Ed.
b. 9 Aug 1799 in North Carolina
d. 11 Dec 1860 in Georgia

↓

Clarissa
b. 12 Nov 1827 in Georgia
d. 2 Jun 1907 in Georgia

first European settlers of that valley.

The Chapmans hit upon hard times in 1862. John Grigsby, husband of Eleander Chapman and John Henry & Lucy's son-in-law, enlisted in the GA 23rd Infantry Regiment on 16 May 1862. Fifteen days later on 31 May he was killed in the Battle of Seven Pines in Virginia where he is also buried (Service Records J. Grigsby). Eleander died of yellow fever only a few months later on 6 Sep (Baker 1010). No doubt grief also took its toll. Less than three weeks later on 24 Sep 1862 John Henry also shuffled off his mortal coil. John Henry and his daughter Eleander are buried in Chapman Cemetery in West Armuchee. A commemorative stone for John Grigsby also stands there. At the age of 53 and in the space of less than four months, Lucy lost her only son-in-law, her only daughter, and her husband.

John and Eleander left behind four children—ranging in age from 7 years to about 1 year. Lucy is counted on the 1870 census in Rock Spring as the head of the household with all of these children as well as three other children bearing the name Grigsby (likely other grandchildren, though I have not yet been able to confirm their identity). By 1880 she is back in West Armuchee living with the oldest child, Robert Chapman Grigsby, as the head of the household. Lucy died 9 May 1886 and rests with her husband in Chapman Cemetery.

The next Chapman in my line of descent is William Jack Chapman. Born 10 Jul 1825, William Jack had migrated

Margaret
LAWRENCE
b. abt 1709 in England
d. bef 1739 in Virginia

↓

Thomas
b. abt 1733 in Virginia
d. abt 1797 in North Carolina

↓

Henry Hardy
b. 12 Jun 1771 in Virginia
d. 8 Apr 1855 in Georgia

↓

(cont. to the left with James Ed.)

to Walker County with his parents by 1850. There he married Clarissa Lawrence—another family among the first settlers in West Armuchee. They had four children, including my 2nd great grandmother Drucilla Chapman in 1859, before he left the family to serve the Confederate army. He joined Co A of the 1st Regiment, GA Light Duty Men (National Park Service). Two of his brothers, Abraham P. (Cos A & H) and Benjamin F. (Co H) both joined the GA 23rd Infantry and fought for the Confederacy as well (Historical, U.S.; National Park Service). Men from Clarissa's Lawrence family were also involved in the war so it was a particularly difficult for the women who had to run the farms and raise the families on their own.

After the war William Jack returned home and family life resumed for the Chapmans. However, the hardships of those years are well remembered even today. On 2 Nov 1991 the Chickamauga Chapter of the United Daughters of the Confederacy held a ceremony for the dedication of markers honoring the three Chapman brothers who served in the Confederate army as well as Moses Gresham Scoggins. It was a simple grave side service with readings and music. My cousin Leland Coulter Scoggins, Jr. gave a personal history of the soldiers we were honoring. I was given the role of placing a wreath at the graves. At the time I don't recall really understanding exactly what the purpose of it all was—I just knew it had to do with some long dead grandfather and the Civil War. But looking back it was probably the earliest connection I made to my ancestors and I'm glad I got to be a part of it.

GRIGSBY, RICHARDSON and RAMSEY

While the Chapman family is in the direct family line on my father's side of the family, it actually connects up with my mother's family through marriage!

William Jack Chapman, my 3rd great grandfather on my father's side and the father of Drucilla Chapman, had a sister named Eleander. Eleander married John Grigsby. Their oldest son is Robert Chapman Grigsby [I] (b.1855). Robert [I]'s oldest son is Robert Chapman Grigsby [II] (b.1887). Robert [II]'s oldest child is Helen Grigsby... who married J.C. Pope, my great uncle (see page 43)! This makes Helen my great aunt on my mother's side and my third cousin twice removed on my father's side of the family.

That's not all—connections abound in this line. John and Eleander's second son is William David Grigsby (b.1856). William David married Frances Richardson. Their youngest child is William Rice Grigsby. William Rice is the father of Martha Delle Grigsby. To see how Martha Delle connects with the Richardson and Keown families through her husband, see page 220.

Above left: A view of the Chapman Family Cemetery in West Armuchee, May 2010. (Photo by Jordan M. Scoggins)

Above right: My great aunt Frances Druscilla Scoggins, my father Michael David Scoggins, and I pose with the tombstones of William Jack Chapman and Clarissa Lawrence. Together we represent three generations of descendants. William Jack's original stone matches Clarissa's. It is still there but has fallen. May 2010. (Photo by Rhonda Jordan Scoggins)

Yet there's still more! The Richardson connections go back farther still—connecting to both the Lawrence and Chapman families too. Frances Richardson is the daughter of Matthew Berry Richardson and Frances Ramsey. Matthew Berry Richardson is the son of Moses Richardson and Elizabeth Chapman. Elizabeth's grandfather is John Chapman [I] (discussed at the beginning of the Chapman line on pg 142) and her father is also John Chapman [II] (brother to William Chapman in my direct line) (Landrum 413).

But surely you didn't think I'd let you off the hook that easy? Stepping back to Matthew Berry Richardson, he married Frances Ramsey. Frances is the daughter of Rice Ross Ramsey and Ann Chapman. Ann is the brother of John Henry Chapman discussed in my direct line.

The final connection involves the Lawrence family. Frances Ramsey's sister Martha Ramsey married Malachi Columbus Lawrence (son of Malachi Lawrence, brother of James Edward Lawrence in my direct line) who is the first cousin of Clarissa Lawrence, my 3rd great grandmother.

(And if all that wasn't enough to make your head spin, the Richardson family also connects to the Keown family. See page 220 for more about that!)

William
b. abt 1773 in Virginia
d. 16 Feb 1855 in South Carolina

James Ed.
LAWRENCE
b. 9 Aug 1799 in North Carolina
d. 11 Dec 1860 in Georgia

John Henry
b. 24 Apr 1799 in Virginia
d. 24 Sep 1862 in Georgia

James D.
GRIGSBY
b. 7 Jul 1804 in Tennessee
d. Oct 1888 in Georgia

Clarissa
b. 12 Nov 1827 in Georgia
d. 2 Jun 1907 in Georgia

Wm. Jack
b. 10 Jul 1825 in South Carolina
d. 28 May 1896 in Georgia

Eleander
b. 11 Dec 1833 in South Carolina
d. 6 Sep 1862 in Georgia

John
b. 21 Jul 1831 in Georgia
d. 31 May 1862 in Virginia

descends to me
as seen on on pg 142

Wm. David
b. 11 Sep 1856 in Georgia
d. 2 Jun 1929 in Georgia

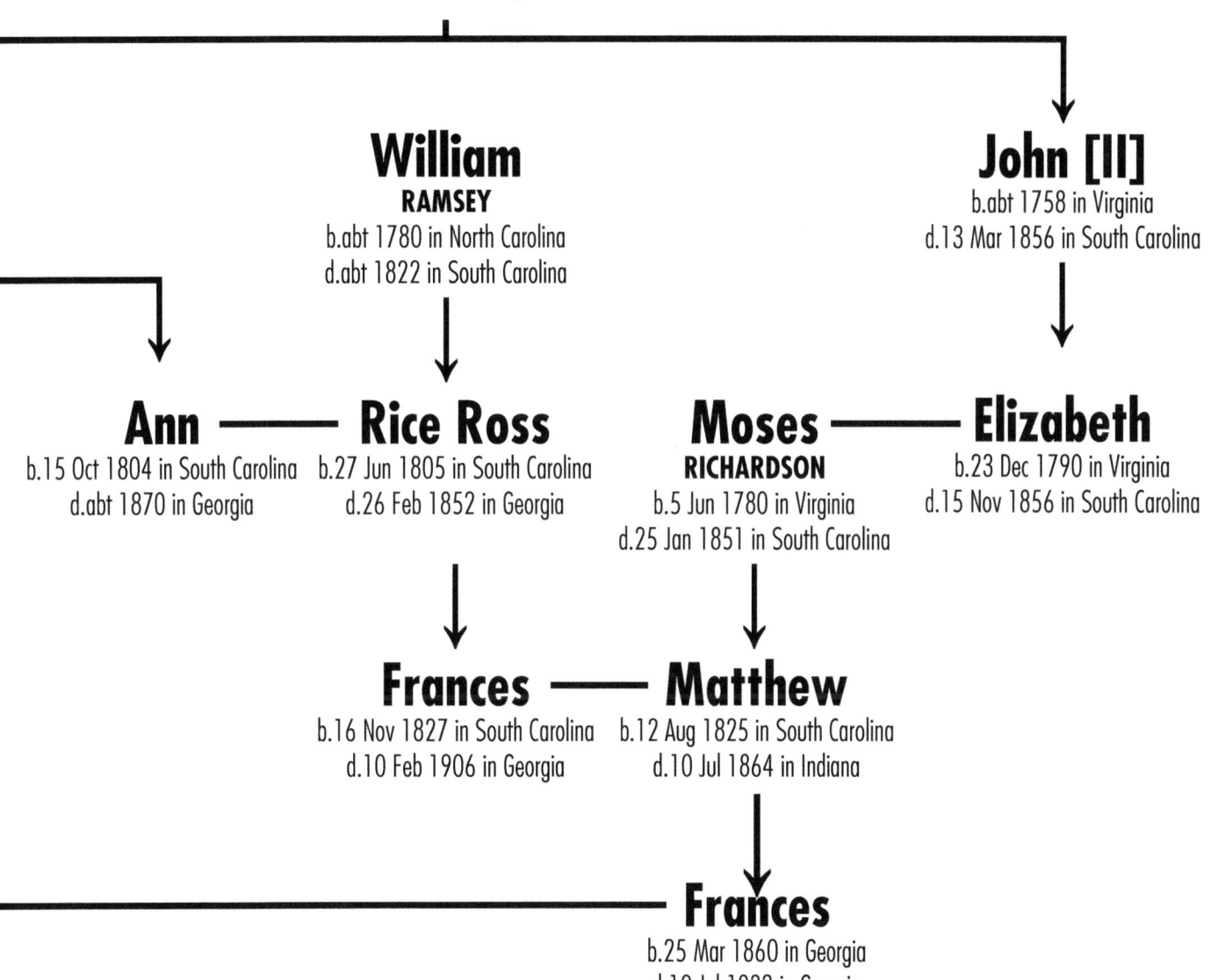

Left: The Lawrence home in West Armuchee, Jan 2011. Built in 1855, the house was once part of a 1,000-acre plantation that had been awarded to James Edward Lawrence for helping remove the Indians from North Georgia. The house has a secret tunnel which the Lawrences used to hide valuables and slaves from the Union army during the Civil War (D. Wood).

Opposite: A close-up shot of James Edward Lawrence's tombstone. Carved by hand, it can be difficult to read but has stood up amazingly well over the years.

(Photos by Robert Paul Maloney)

MALONEY

The Maloney family hooks up in a couple of different ways.

Selete E. Chapman was the sister of Drucilla Chapman, my 2nd great grandmother. Selete married Robert Weston Maloney. Their son Robert Paul Maloney [I] married Susie Ella Harlow. Robert [I] and Susie's son Robert Harlow Maloney married Margaret Eugenia Cole. Robert Paul Maloney [II] is their son.

The second connection comes through the Sewell family. My 3rd great grandmother Elizabeth Sewell (see more about her on pg 131) had a sister named Sarah E. Sewell. Sarah married Samuel B. Maloney and they are the parents of Robert Weston Maloney mentioned above.

LAWRENCE

The Lawrence family is unique among all other family lines in my tree. The original Lawrence immigrant in my family line is a woman. Therefore all my male Lawrence ancestors trace back to this matriarch, my 7th great grandmother. William Lawrence Pritchett's book *A Southern Branch of the Lawrence Family* is my primary source for recounting Margaret's story.

Margaret Lawrence was born about 1709—probably in either Shropshire County or Middlesex County, England (7). On 9 Jul 1729 she was indicted on a felony charge, apparently of thievery, in Middlesex. As she awaited trial, "she was confined to the infamous Newgate Goal in London" which was "one of the oldest and most notorious prisons in the country" (9). William Maitland in 1754 described the prison as:

> "a dismal place where the prisoners of all types were sometimes packed so close together and the air so corrupted by their stench and nastiness, that it occasions a disease called the jail distemper, of which they die by dozens, and cartloads are carried out and the bodies are thrown into a pit in the churchyard without ceremony" (qtd in Pritchett 9).

The prison was run by corrupt jailers who bargained with prisoners for money or, in the case of women prisoners like Margaret, special "services." The prison even had a room just for this purpose. The plight of women was particularly bad and many had "no alternative but to become prostitutes, or perish with hunger" (qtd in Pritchett 10).

After more than six months in Newgate, Margaret was finally "tried and subsequently convicted in the Hall of Justice of 'Old Bailey', located in the suburbs of the City of London, on 25 Feb 1730" (7). She then appears on a 9 Mar 1730 *Transportation Bond* which means her sentence was transportation to the New World, where she would be sold "to the highest bidder at the plantations" (9). The boat that contained Margaret and 105 other prisoners set sail on 17 Mar 1730. The journey was not easy and the "inhumane conditions … sometimes resulted in the death of a quarter or more of the convicts while enroute to the colonies" (9). Conditions about these ships "were often worse than those at Newgate"—and the voyage would take approximately two months (10). Margaret's sentence in the colonies was for fourteen years—during which time frame she was forbidden to return to Great Britain.

Pritchett describes what it was like when the ship reached its destination:

> "Upon approach to port, the whole

atmosphere aboard ship changed dramatically, with increased tension among the passengers and a flurry of activity by the crew, as the *Patapscoe Merchant* prepared to dock in Baltimore. Captain Lux had dutifully ordered a public notice to be posted which announced his arrival, listed the number and type of prisoners to be sold, and the date and time of the aboard-ship sale. The prisoners were directed to make themselves as presentable as conditions and available clothing would permit. About a week after the ship had landed, the human cargo was awakened early one morning and they were all herded on deck where they were aligned into tight rows. Rum was brought aboard for those planters who were invited to inspect the cargo. One can only imagine the humiliation to which all prisoners were subjected by the prying eyes and probing hands of the planters, but it must have been particularly difficult for the female prisoners" (11).

Unfortunately few details exist about the transfer of Margaret's bond. Tradition tells us that it was purchased by Tobias Phillips, "a second generation planter from old Rappahannock (now Richmond) County, Virginia" (11). He was a successful tobacco planter and "sailed the 100 miles or so up the Chesapeake Bay" to purchase Margaret's bond.

The story goes that Margaret was "a domestic servant on a tobacco plantation at some distance from the Phillips' main house" and lived as Tobias's wife when he stayed there. Margaret did have two children by Tobias: John (b. abt 1731) and Thomas (b. abt 1733).

Margaret's precise death date is unknown. She is not mentioned in Tobias's will, written 10 Sep 1739. However the will does mention Margaret's son Thomas so it seems likely that she was already dead by this time—not surviving to know freedom again.

I descend through Margaret's youngest son, Thomas. Even after Margaret's death, Thomas stayed on the Phillips planation, serving out his mother's bonded term. But in spite of these challenges, Thomas "married, raised a large family, and gave material support and the services of at least one son in the Continental Line" in the war for independence. He was also a pioneer settler in the piedmont regions of Pittsylvania County, VA. In the latter part of his life, Thomas migrated to Wilkes County, NC, "virtually a complete wilderness" at the time (29). He is counted there on a 1787 North Carolina census and again on the 1790 US census (Jackson, NC; Ancestry.com 1790). Thomas was "an active supporter and elder in the Roaring River Baptist Church, on Little Sandy Creek of the east prong of the Roaring River, near present-day Traphill, North Carolina" (29). Thomas died in Wilkes County about 1797 (West, Deaths and Individual). His burial location is unknown but it is possible he was buried in the Roaring River Baptist Church cemetery (31).

Thomas's youngest son, Henry Hardy Lawrence, born 12 Jun 1771, continues my line of descent. Henry had two wives, both of which play into different branches of my family. Winnie Manord is his first wife and I descend through their son James Edward Lawrence. Henry's second wife was Lany Visant and their daughter Lucy Lawrence married Levi Jackson Scoggins (a son of William Delaney Scoggins). Some time between 1820 and 1830, Henry migrated

to Georgia (while several of his siblings had migrated to Jefferson County, TN). He appears on the 1830 US census in Pike County, GA. By 1840 he had settled in Dirt Town Valley in Chattooga County where he purchased 320 acres (35).

Henry died on 8 Apr 1855 and "was buried on his farm in a solitary limestone grave." He had nine children in all, seven of which—at the time of Henry's death—are identified as residents of Chattooga County (35).

James Edward Lawrence was born 9 Aug 1799. He married Louisa Askew on 2 Oct 1825. Census records show they lived out their lives together in Dirt Town Valley (living at the extreme northern end of the valley in the house on the opposite page). Their oldest daughter, Clarissa Lawrence, was born 12 Nov 1827. She was known for her friendly demeanor. G. Woods said of her, "a more cheerful and sympathetic lady can scarcely be found" (Grigsby, transcriptions). Clarissa married William Jack Chapman in 1851 and brings us full circle to the Chapman family.

But as you know by now nothing around here is ever that simple. The Lawrence family ties into the Scoggins family beyond the Lucy Lawrence/Levi Jackson Scoggins connection. Henry Hardy had another son named Malachi. Malachi's daughter Julia Ann married Lindsey Hamilton Scoggins, another son of William! Malachi's son Henry married Catharine Bennett. Their daughter Evaline Clarissa Lawrence married Thomas Newton Scoggins, yet another son of William! See page 131.

Like the Scoggins family, the Lawrences were also heavily involved in the Civil War. This research is in progress. You can find more of these details in my tree on Ancestry.com, which is regularly updated with my latest findings.

Lawrence Chapman Scoggins
b. 20 Mar 1896 d. 8 Apr 1968
married 27 Feb 1921

Ida Mae Rambo
b. 1 May 1900 d. 23 Dec 1981

Lawrence Chapman Scoggins, the namesake of his grandmother's and mother's surnames, was born 20 Mar 1896 in the Green Bush community in West Armuchee, Walker County, Georgia. He grew up in the house pictured on page 136.

Born in the final years of the 19th century, Lawrence was a young man in the World War I era. At the time of his draft card he was 21 years old, tall and slender. He had blue eyes and light brown hair. Interesting details for sure, but nothing actually surprised me like the words "physical disability" (Ancestry.com WWI). I asked my father about this, as he is just old enough to remember Lawrence. Apparently his disability was due to a childhood injury of a badly broken arm. The bone punched through the skin and became infected. When a doctor saw him he discovered a maggot in the infection. The doctor set the break but left the maggot to help clean the wound. After that he was never able to straighten his arm again (R. & M. Scoggins, correspondence). This break was probably the result of the cotton gin accident recounted on page 136.

Lawrence married Ida Mae Rambo on 27 Feb 1921. Ida Mae was born in the first months of the 20th century on 1 May 1900. For the early years of their marriage they lived with Lawrence's parents in West Armuchee. They had their

Right: Ida Mae and Lawrence by their first home in Subligna. This home was torn down around 1940 so this photo is probably from the 1930's. I believe that's Wade on the porch in the background. (Collection of Frances Scoggins)

Lawrence — Ida Mae

- **Margaret**
- **Harold** m. Ethel Dorthelia Holcomb
- **"Dock"** m. Ina Plunkett
- **Frances**

Left: Ida Mae and Lawrence relax on their front porch in Subligna, 1965.

Below: Lawrence as a boy. This was probably taken at his childhood home in Green Bush, c.1910.

(Collection of Frances Scoggins)

first anniversary present one day early on 26 Feb 1922 when Margaret Lillian, their first child, was born. They would have a total of four children:

1. Margaret Lillian (b.26 Feb 1922, d.30 Nov 1995
2. Harold Wallace (b.26 Feb 1924, m.Ethel Dorthelia Holcomb, d.13 Mar 2000)
3. Lawrence "Dock" Chapman (b.8 Oct 1928, m.Ina Plunkett)
4. Frances Druscilla (b.10 Mar 1938)

Lawrence and Ida Mae's first two children, Margaret and Harold, were born in the house where they lived with Lawrence's parents in Green Bush. Later the family moved to Subligna.

Lawrence is unique in my family tree in that he is one of the few men who was not a farmer. He worked in saw-milling. Lawrence's youngest daughter Frances remembers "riding with [her] mother to the sawmill to carry [her dad's] lunch" (F. Scoggins). He also worked with his father at the Scoggins and Sons cotton gin (read more about that beginning pg 135). He continued running

Lawrence Scoggins Home

Lawrence and Ida Mae had two homes of their own during their life. The first home stood near the present day Methodist Church in Subligna. Around 1940 a new home was constructed slightly to the north and built using lumber saw milled by Lawrence himself. The original house, which can be seen in the photo on pg 150, was torn down not long after the new one was built.

Today the 1940 home still stands on parcel number 0083A-00000-011-000 (Chattooga Tax). This "new" home is on the spot where one of the original Subligna homes stood, built by Dr. Sam Hamilton in 1858 (White).

My father made this CAD drawing, remembering how the house looked when he was a boy. Note the two front doors. This is because when the home was built, Ida Mae's parents lived in the home with her and Lawrence. The house had been constructed so that they could come and go on their own.

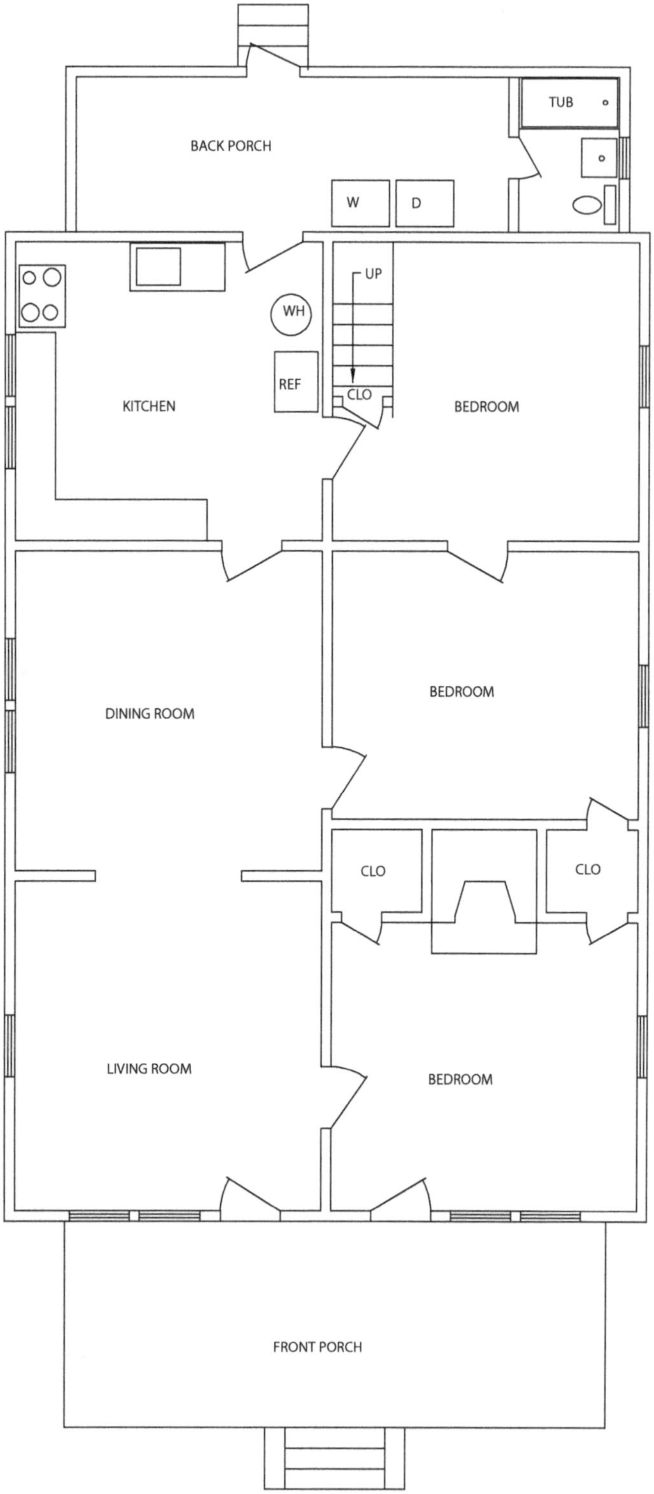

Above: My father took this photo in the early 1970's when he was developing and printing a lot of black and white photography.
(Collection of Michael & Rhonda Scoggins)

Right: Lawrence Scoggins House, Subligna, circa 1940 (drawn by Michael D. Scoggins)

Above: This drawing of the Lawrence Scoggins home was made by my father when he was just a boy. He drew it in school and then gave it to his grandmother. She kept the drawing all her life and it was passed down to her daughter Frances, who recently gave it back to my father. (Collection of Michael & Rhonda Scoggins)

Above: One of only two known photographs of Lawrence inside Scoggins Mercantile. You can see Quaker Oats, Campbell's Soup, and many other items for sale. c.1957. (Collection of Dot Scoggins)

Opposite: Ida Mae, always proud of her flowers, poses in her front yard. 1965. (Collection of Frances Scoggins)

the gin after his father died until cotton was no longer a profitable crop and the farmers stopped growing it.

But to family members today Lawrence is best remembered as the proprietor of Scoggins Mercantile, one of several general stores in Subligna (see pg 171 for more about Subligna).

The Scoggins Mercantile building itself—still in use today as Archie's Market—was built around 1947 by Lawrence and his nephew Leland Coulter Scoggins. Leland was a partner in the store at that point but was drafted into the Korean war about 1950 and "was forced to sell his crops, including ninety acres of cotton in the field, and his interest in the Subligna General Store, which he and his uncle, Lawrence Scoggins, had built and operated" (Chattooga Heritage 311).

But Lawrence is first listed as a retail merchant on the 1930 census—almost two decades before the reference above. It is unclear where the store was operated at that time—possibly in an older building near the same site. But it does seem Lawrence was working as a merchant from at least the late 1920's

Lawrence sold many things at Scoggins Mercantile. His grandson Michael remembers "he sold flour in sacks that were made from a yard of cloth. When I was young Mama

Dateline Georgia: Front Porch Sitting
The Atlanta Constitution, c.1977

SUBLIGNA—One of the many pleasures of this traveling job is to conduct an informal front porch sitting. With no fixed destination, talk wanders up and down memory lanes. So it was with Mrs. Lawrence C. Scoggins.

Actually, I had come to the front porch to talk about the old "Scoggins Home," up the valley in West Armuchee, the upstairs of which yet gives off the mellow glow of heart pine.

I considered the size of the old home, the huge rooms and the high ceilings. I had visited earlier in the day and asked, "How did you heat that place in the 1920's?"

Mrs. Scoggins laughed. "Not very well! Back then it had double chimneys, fireplaces on each side but it was still cold in winter. Seems like we didn't notice the cold so much back then. I surely did notice this past winter. Guess that happens when you're 77."

The late Lawrence Scoggins was a sawmiller, not a farmer. Mrs. Scoggins recalled, "I cooked many a sawmill dinner when we lived out there in the country.

"You'd cook it on a Comfort (wood-burning) range and you'd put it in a bucket. I'd fix two big pans of 'cat head' biscuits. They'd be eight biscuits in each pan. 'Course, back then we didn't fix sandwiches because we didn't have loaf bread, just corn bread and biscuits. In summer I'd get corn and cook it."

"Any dessert in a sawmill dinner?"

Mrs. Scoggins laughed at the memory. "Yes there was! I'd butter some of the biscuits and put sugar on 'em. They liked that."

"I guess a sawmiller got pretty hungry?"

"Well, they never brought none back."

Sometimes Mrs. Scoggins had to drive the family Model-T into the wilderness. She explained, "It set so high off of the ground that you could pretty well drive over most of the stumps."

The early 1920's was the cranking era, according to Mrs. Scoggins. "We had this deep well at the old house. You'd have to crank forever to get a bucket of water. If you weren't thirsty when you started, you'd be when the bucket finally come up. And you had to crank that T-Model. I sure did crank it!"

The coming of the car sort of liberated Mrs. Scoggins who wasn't the least bit bashful about taking over the controls, the gas and spark levers on the steering wheel and the three-pedal floorboard.

She looked from her front porch on the hill down to the pavement. "I'd get the kids in that Model-T and drive all of the way to Rome. That was a pretty long trip then. I remember once I had a puncture three times before I got there. I fixed all three of 'em. Had my puncture kit. Everybody carried one in their car then. I guess it was a half day's trip to Rome then."

Mrs. Lawrence Scoggins paused in her talking during our front porch sitting. I thought she seemed sad when she made her final comment: "Way they drive now, it don't take long."

made Eric and I shirts out of flour sack." Other items for sale were Coca-Cola, Neihi, and Royal Crown colas. Prince Albert tobacco and Bruton snuff were also popular items (M. Scoggins, interview).

The store was a place for community just as much as commerce. "The men like[d] to come and sit around the warm stove and talk," says Frances. As sunset approached, Frances and her mother would sit on their front porch across the road and wait for Lawrence to come home (F. Scoggins).

Ida Mae took care of things at home while Lawrence was out saw-milling or running the store. See the above article to learn about her sawmill dinners. Ida Mae was fond of flowers and made sure the Scoggins home was surrounded with them. Frances remembers of her mother, "[She] loved working outside with the beautiful flowers that she grew" (F. Scoggins). There are a number of family photos of Ida Mae posing with her botanical collection.

The family sometimes took vacations together. Frances recalls trips to the Smokies where they "always went to see the play *Unto These Hills*." They also took trips to Florida. "Daddy and I walked through a tobacco plant," Frances remembers. "Silver Springs was enjoyable seeing all the fish under glass. Harold stayed in the store while we were away" (F. Scoggins).

Lawrence died of emphysema 8 Apr 1968. "Harold helped him into the car," says Frances. "He said he wouldn't be back. I remember Margaret and I sitting in the living room when Harold, Dot, [and] Mother came [home]." They knew right away what had happened.

Ida Mae lived for thirteen more years. In Dec 1981 she went into the hospital in Summerville. She was there for 12 days with heart problems and high blood pressure. She died two days before Christmas on 23 Dec 1981 and was laid to rest on Christmas day. Both Ida Mae and Lawrence are buried in Subligna Cemetery.

RAMBO and PECK families

Peter Gunnarson RAMBO
b.1611 in Sweden
d.1698 in Pennsylvania

↓

Peter
b.17 Jun 1653 in Pennsylvania
d.12 Dec 1729 in Pennsylvania

↓

Swan (Sven)
b.19 Oct 1677 in Pennsylvania
d.7 Nov 1730 in Pennsylvania

↓

Swan
b.1720 in Pennsylvania
d.1800 in South Carolina

↓

cont. to the right with Jesse

RAMBO

The Rambo family is one of the few lines in my tree that is not of British descent. My primary source for learning about the Rambo line is the work of Beverly Nelson Rambo and Ronald S. Beatty.

Peter Gunnarson Rambo, my 9th great grandfather, is the original immigrant in this family line. He was born about 1 Jun 1612 in Hisingen, near Gothenburg, Sweden. He came to the "new world" as a colonist for the New Sweden Company aboard the *Kalmar Nyckel*. He arrived in New Sweden on 17 Apr 1640. Peter first lived at Christina near the fort (in present day Delaware) and worked as a farm hand. There he cultivated tobacco for the Swedish West Indies Company. By the end of 1644 Peter had become a freeman. He "settled on a plantation near Cobbs Creek in Kingsessing, located in present day West Philadelphia" (Rambo/Beatty). By 1669, Peter Gunnarson and his family had relocated "to Passyunk on the east side of the Schuylkill River opposite Aronameck" (Rambo/Beatty).

On 7 Apr 1647 Peter married Brita Mattzdoter from Wasa, Sweden. Together they had 8 children (4 daughters and 4 sons, although one daughter died at 8 years old). I descend through their son Peter.

Peter was very involved in life in the colony, even known by William Penn. He "served on the court under Swedish, Dutch, and English rule for 29 years" and he appears in many court records throughout the years. Through his dealings with the Indians he also "learned enough of the language to serve as interpreter" (Rambo/Beatty).

The Rambos were Lutheran and Peter "was one of the founders of one of the first Swedish churches in America, located at Wicaco, a short distance south of Penn's Landing in Philadelphia" (Rambo/Beatty). The Gloria Dei church presently sits on that site. Construction of the building that stands today began after Peter's death in 1698 and was completed in

Above: A reproduction of The Kalmar Nyckel sails the waters of the Delaware, Oct 2011.

Right: The Gloria Dei church in Philadelphia was constructed in 1700. The original building was from 1677. Oct 2011.

(Photos by Jordan M. Scoggins)

1700. No one knows for sure where Peter is buried although many claim the "new" church building from 1698 was constructed over his grave. However, there is no evidence to prove this legend.

Peter was 86 years old at the time of his death, making him one of the last of the original Swedish settlers.

Peter and Brita's son Peter (b. 17 Jun 1653, d. 12 Dec 1729) was also an active member of the Gloria Dei church. He served as warden for a number of years. He married Magdalena Skute on 12 Nov 1676 (Rambo/Beatty).

Peter and Magdalena's son Swan (or Sven), my 7th great grandfather, was born 19 Oct 1677. He had eight children with his first wife, Ann, and five children with his second wife Barbara. I descend through the oldest child from the second marriage, Swan. Swan was born about 1720. Peter was dead by 1730. By the end of that decade, or early in the next, Barbara migrated southward with Swan (and possibly her other children). She settled in Augusta County, VA. She died around 1748. By 1755 Swan had relocated to Rowan County, NC. By 1770 he had moved to South Carolina, far away from his Pennsylvania homeland. He died there around 1800 (Rambo/Beatty).

Jesse
b. 9 Oct 1778 in South Carolina
d. 16 Dec 1860 in Georgia

Kinchin
b. 5 Feb 1802 in South Carolina
d. 21 May 1882 in Georgia

↓

Ansel
b. 27 Feb 1836 in Georgia
d. 26 May 1905 in Georgia

↓

Wade
b. 10 Dec 1876 in Georgia
d. 9 Nov 1951 in Georgia

my great grandmother Ida Mae, grandfather Harold, father Michael, and then me

The generations get a little murky at this point. There are only three known children of Swan and also some confusion about his wife. Rambo/Beatty acknowledge that in *The Rambo Heritage*, by Simmeon Brooks Rambo and Mary Emma Hamrick, Swan's wife is identified as Jane Pinson while Kinchin Rambo's family Bible identifies her as Elizabeth. Either Swan had two different wives or Jane and Elizabeth are the same person. It is even possible, since Jesse is 21 years younger than his next known sibling, Joseph, that there could be another generation here that has not been traced/documented (Rambo/Beatty).

I descend through the youngest of Swan's known children, Jesse (b.9 Oct 1778).

It is clear that Jesse continued the migration pattern of his father and moved from Barnwell, SC to Gwinnett County, GA in the 1820's (Johnson). He was awarded land lot 97 in the 4th district, 2nd section (in Gwinnett County) in the Cherokee Land Lottery of 1832 (Ancestry.com Cherokee). Jesse remained here for the rest of his life.

In an unattributed article (originally written about 1872) posted on Hennington-Van Horn's *Gayle's Family History*, Jesse is described as "queer and unique in personal appearance."

> "He was about five feet eight inches in height, weighed about one hundred and ten pounds, was erect and fidgety, clad generally in summer in a longtail blue surtout of homespun manufacture, copperas pants with legs stuck in his stockings, with cow leather shoes tanned in his own trough and made by his Negroes, a pair of brass-rimmed spectacles always on, and for many years a high-topped hat of the beegum style given him by Mr. Spence, and a little old blue cotton 'umbrella' carried in his left hand when not stretched over him" (qtd. in Hennington-Van Horn).

Beyond his looks, Jesse was "queer in his talk, queer in his notions, queer in his habits, queer in everything." The writer continues and describes Jesse's "good humor, his anecdotes, his droll sayings and expressions" (qtd. in Hennington-Van Horn). He was "eccentric, strange, and unusual" (B. Rambo 95).

There is a funny story about Jesse:

> "[Jesse] used to say he never bet but once in his life. When he lived in South Carolina, and soon after his marriage, a big, awkward, lightwood-smoked, spraddle footed piney woodsman, without shoes, his copperas breeches reaching half way from his knees to his ankles, marched up to his cabin with a rifle and took a seat in the yard. He soon began to tell of his exploits as a marksman, the number of deer and turkeys he had killed, and that he would never shoot a squirrel except in the eye. Just at this moment, a rooster walked across the yard. The hunter said he could shoot off his comb without otherwise touching it and that he would bet a dollar on it. Mr. Rambo thought it an impossibility, was sure

Jesse's house still stands on present day Old Snelleville Highway in Gwinett County, Georgia. It has been remodeled over the years but one end of the house, pictured above, retains the original siding. Sep 2011. (Photo by Jordan M. Scoggins)

Friendship Primitive Baptist Church was cofounded by Jesse's son Kinchin. Jesse and Mary are buried in the tomb-like graves in this photo, Sep 2011. (Photo by Jordan M. Scoggins)

he could win his money and covered the bet with the first and only money he had ever earned. The man raised his rifle, clucked to the chicken to attract its attention, fired, shaved off its comb as if it had been cut with a knife. Mr. Rambo's dollar was gone. That broke him from gambling" (qtd. in Hennington-Van Horn).

Indeed it must have taught Jesse his lesson as he seems to have fared well over the years despite that "he thought of himself as being poverty-stricken and wailed" (B. Rambo 95). The census records provide a glimpse into his wealth. He may have indeed been poverty stricken in his early years, but by no means was he a poor man later in life. Census records show that in 1810 he did not have any slaves. By 1820 eight slaves were counted in his name. By 1840 the number of slaves more than doubled at 19. In 1860 Jesse still had 18 slaves (Ancestry.com, 1860 Slave). With abolition still a few years away, it would be interesting to learn what happened to Jesse's slaves when he died later that year.

Jesse's house still stands in Gwinnett County on Old Snellville Highway. Pat Johnson, writing in the *Gwinnett Daily News*, had the opportunity to describe the home's construction when it was renovated in the late 1970's. The house was "put together with pegs instead of nails" and "local historians suppose Rambo built his house shortly after coming here" (Johnson). When Jesse lived there the house would have been surrounded by his vast farm—the 1860 census counts him with 540 acres. There must have been at least one or more slave homes on his farm as well. Today the house is surrounded by Atlanta's suburban sprawl with subdivisions and businesses lining the local streets. Jesse's farm is a far cry from when he moved there nearly 200 years ago. What witty saying would come out of his mouth at the sight of that?

Jesse and his wife, Mary Humphrey (b.15 Oct 1780), are buried at Friendship Primitive Baptist Church only a few miles away.

Jesse's only son, Kinchin, was born while Jesse was living in Barnwell County, SC. Kinchin likely made the journey to Georgia with his parents. He married Mary Ann Prior 5 Jul 1824. Immediately they started a family and had 9 children over a span of 25 years.

In 1832, lucky like his father, Kinchin drew a lot in the Georgia Cherokee Land Lottery (number 258, 24th district, second section, Cherokee) (Ancestry.com, Cherokee).

Kinchin was a Primitive Baptist minister. According to transcripts from his diary, he was ordained 20 Apr

Rambo Son of
Kinchin Rambo and
Mary Ann his wife
was born April 26th 1825
Elizabeth Rambo daughter
of Kinchin Rambo and
Mary Ann his wife
was born Feb 26th 1827

Ansel Myer Rambo
Son of Kinchin Rambo
and Mary Ann his wife
was born
Feb. 183

FAMILY RECORD.

BIRTHS.

Mary Ann Rambo, daughter
of Kinchin Rambo and
Mary Ann his wife was
born the 10th of February 1839

Kinchin Lawrence Rambo
Son of Kinchin Rambo and
Mary Ann his wife was
born March 23rd 1841

Sarah Ann Rambo
daughter of Kinchin
Rambo and Mary
Ann his wife was
born January 31-1844

Barbara Ann Rambo
daughter of Kinchin
Rambo & Mary Ann
his wife was born
February 24th 1847

Martha Caroline Rambo
daughter of Kinchin
Rambo & Mary Ann his
wife was born Oct 19th 1850.

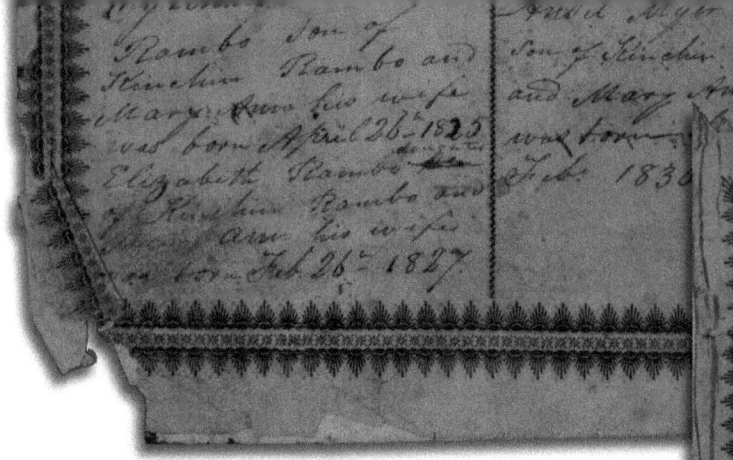

1833. Little more than a month later on 25 May 1833, he helped found Friendship Primitive Baptist Church in Lilburn, GA (Friendship; K. Rambo). Kinchin's diary entries show that he performed marriages, baptisms, ordinations, and other pastoral duties at numerous churches in Gwinnett, DeKalb, Newton, and other counties—-even performing at least one marriage in South Carolina! He was evidently quite the popular minister. In an entry from Jun 1839 he baptized a black man and woman, described as "the property of Major Waters" (K. Rambo). While I know I come from a much different era, I find it surprising that even an upstanding minister of the Christian religion could in good conscience think of other human beings as property. The same general activities are recounted year after year until 1846 when Kinchin writes:

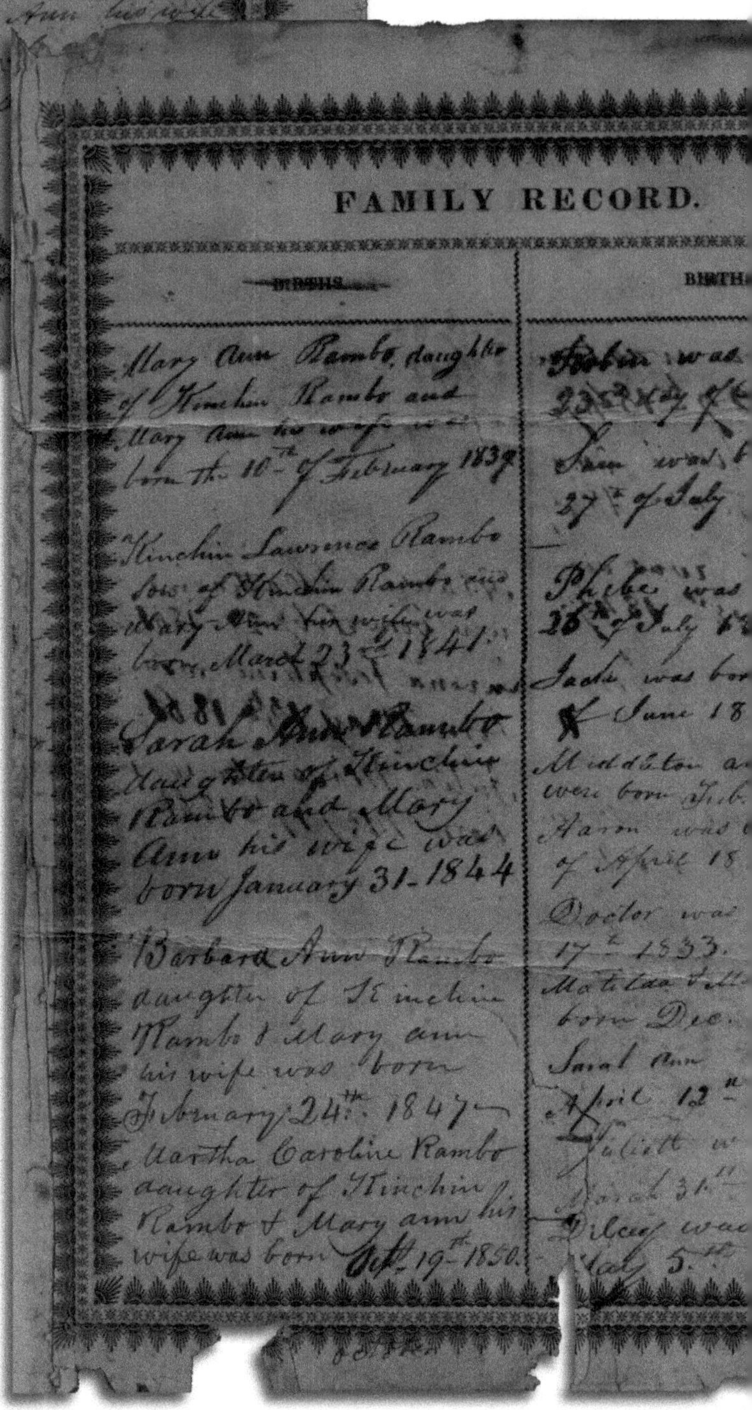

> "I was called to the care of Gilgal Church but did not accept the call. I was also called to the care of Friendship Church again but on account of very serious difficulties in that church, I did not accept the call" (K. Rambo).

There are only a few more entries of a pastoral nature for 1846 and one in 1847. This must have been a time of transition. In Mar 1848, Kinchin and his wife "joined the church at Silver Creek [in Floyd County] by letter" (K. Rambo). This must have been about the time he moved to the farm in Floyd County (off present day Blacks Bluff road). The 1850 slave schedule for Floyd County counts him with 12 slaves (Ancestry.com 1850 Slave).

There are minimal entries through the war years from 1861 to 1865. While the entries simply could be missing (I do not know how complete these diary transcriptions are), I read this as a reflection of the instability of the times. Perhaps it was not safe for him to travel about to perform his duties. As a slave owner he most likely sided with the Confederacy. And too his sons John Humphrey (Co H, TA 22nd Inf Reg, Captain), Henry Van (Co F, GA 65th Inf Reg, First Lieutenant), Ansel Myer (Co H, GA 3rd Cav Reg), and Kinchin Lawrence (Co D, Floyd Legion Inf Reg, GA State Guards) served in the Confederate army (Historical, Soldiers & U.S.; National Park Service). I descend

I obtained these photocopies of Rambo Bible pages from my great aunt Frances. I do not know the origin of the original pages but they appear to have belonged to either Jesse or Kinchin.

through Ansel, my 3rd great grandfather.

Kinchin's diary tells us his pastoral duties picked right back up soon after the war was over. His popularity had not waned, noting in 1866 that he "divided [his] time as well as [he] could with seven or eight churches without accepting the actual pastoral care of any" (K. Rambo).

There are a few notes about life not related to the church. A listing of items purchased at Smith's store in 1874 mentions sundry items such as syrup, tea, sugar, ginger, tobacco, whiskey, and coffee. Also in 1874 he shopped at Harrold's and Hillyer's, buying shoes for his son Ansel. Ansel would have been 39 in 1874 so this must have been a gift (K. Rambo).

The most poetic entry is from 1876:

> "A remarkably warm winter—only two or three little cold snaps—plumb trees in bloom at Christmas and peach trees in February—About the middle of March very cold and windy—particularly the 17th 18th and 19th day and night. The 20th ground covered with snow about 4 inches deep—21st heavy freeze—snow Still on the ground. And peaches nearly all killed for once in March" (K. Rambo).

The last item recorded is from 5 Sep 1880: "I married E. D. Attaway and Sarah A. R. Fuller" (K. Rambo).

Kinchin lived only two more years, dying at 80 years old on 21 May 1882. He had baptized more than 100 souls, married more than 80 couples, and assisted in many ordinations—all in the service of numerous different churches throughout his career. The Rev. Rambo was obviously regarded for his spiritual leadership, a well known public figure and overall "highly esteemed citizen" (Rome).

The Rev. was buried in a family plot on his farm. His wife Mary Ann joined him there 2 Nov 1891. But remarkably enough, Kinchin and Mary Ann's journey in the physical world doesn't end there!

On 29 Oct 2009 I received an e-mail from Erin Kane of Brockington Cultural Resources Consulting. Erin had seen my tree on Ancestry.com and contacted me as a descendant of Kinchin. She informed me of the Georgia DOT project to construct a Rome bypass that cut through an unidentified cemetery. Brockington was hired to perform the historical and genealogical research necessary to identify the graves. Brockington's work revealed the cemetery to be associated with Kinchin's family. The estate had been conveyed to W.G. Foster except for the widow's dower "sixty five feet square for family grave yard with right of way to the public road" (Floyd County Deed Book TT 636). Additional research for death and cemetery records helped support the theory that this was the burial location for Kinchin and Mary Ann (M. Reynolds 7). Including myself and my parents, the identified descendants are scattered across the country in Georgia, Florida, New York, California, and Washington state!

The archaeological excavation revealed five burials. Many interesting details are thoroughly documented in Brockington's official report by Michael Reynolds and Erin Kane. The poorly preserved skeletal remains were used to identify both sex and age of those interred (4). But the most interesting details are the artifacts buried with the remains. There were the usual pieces of casket hardware, including casket handles, thumbscrews, escutcheons, screws, nails, and even fragments of viewing windows from two of the caskets. But the items of most interest to me are "five plain four-hole porcelain buttons, and a hard rubber hair comb with molded raised diamonds on the heading (handle)" found in one grave and a bone hair comb and horse hair bun in another. The archaeologists even uncovered a conifer cone core, "possibly from some form of floral arrangement" (22, 25, 28, 31, 40).

The bodies were reinterred 2 May 2010 at Oaknoll Memorial Gardens in Rome.

I descend through Kinchin's son Ansel Myer. The name is often indexed as Anson though most written records seem to say A.M. I call him Ansel, the traditional name handed down in the family over the years. Ansel was born on 27 Feb 1836 in Georgia, probably in Gwinnett County (as that

Left: I visited the excavation site 12 May 2010 after my father and I had spent the afternoon canoeing near Cave Springs.
(Collection of Michael and Rhonda Scoggins)

Previous page: A view from the cemetery showing the land that was Kinchin's farm and the new bypass under construction. At the bottom is a detail of one of the grave shafts. 12 May 2010.
(Photo by Jordan M. Scoggins)

My parents attended the Rambo reinterrment on 7 May 2010 at Oaknoll Memorial Gardens. My father was a pallbearer at his 3rd great grandfather's funeral! We never would have known about the original graves much less the relocation were it not for my online tree which allowed us to be contacted.
(Collection of Michael and Rhonda Scoggins)

is where his parents were living during that time period). By 1860 he is counted on the Georgia Census Slave Schedule in Floyd County (Jackson, GA). His father is also counted in Floyd County while Jesse, Ansel's grandfather, was counted still in Gwinnett. All owned slaves.

In that same year, Ansel married Sophronia Annie Hardin on 8 Jul. They lived most of rest of their lives together in Floyd County and had six children together.

In Dec 1861 Ansel enrolled in the Confederate army, serving first with the State Troops and later with Co H, 3rd Regiment, GA Cavalry. On 15 Jan 1864 he was captured by Union forces in Sevierville, TN where the Battle of Fair Garden occurred on 27 Jan. He was not released by the Yankees until after Jun 1865 (Ancestry.com, GA Pension & Civil War Prisoner).

After returning home from the war, Ansel worked as a carpenter up until the 1890's. He had become increasingly unable to work and support himself. In 1898, living in Pickens County, he applied for a Confederate pension due to "infirmity and poverty." He suffered from rheumatism and chronic sore leg and had been supported "by [his] children and what [he] could do" over at least the past two years. The physician's report confirmed Ansel was "totally disabled to

Right: These crayon portraits are of Ansel and Sophronia. (Collection of Frances Scoggins)

Above: A tin type of Wade when he was a little boy. (Collection of Frances Scoggins)

perform manual labor of any kind" in 1898. It seems things were getting worse for him. His pension was allowed (Ancestry.com GA Pension).

Sophronia died 14 Apr 1900. She is buried in Smyrna Memorial Cemetery near Atlanta. Ansel died 26 May 1905. He is buried in Old Armuchee Baptist Church Cemetery in Floyd County.

Ansel's youngest child was Wade Hampton Rambo. Born 10 Dec 1876 in Floyd County, Wade is my 2nd great grandfather. He married Fannie Elvira Peck 9 Aug 1899 (Marriage Wade). The next year he was counted on the 1900 census in Smyrna Town, Cobb County, GA working as a carpenter. His father Ansel was living with him at the time. By 1910 Wade was back in Floyd County, living in Texas Valley. His draft registration card from 1918 shows him still working as a carpenter. He was of medium height and slender build with blue eyes and dark brown hair. By 1930 Wade and Fannie were still living in Floyd County. Census records past this date are not yet available. However, in their later years Wade and Fannie lived in Subligna with their daughter Ida Mae and her family.

At the age of 67, Fannie suffered from congestive heart failure. Feeling short of breath she paced around the home where she lived with her daughter Ida Mae and her family. Eventually she sat down on the couch and declared, "I can't go on living like this." And she didn't. Those words on 29 Mar 1950 were her last. There was an open casket viewing in the very living room where she died. Wade was devastated without his wife. The next year, on 9 Nov 1951, he was a patient in Trion Hospital. He died there on 9 Nov 1951 of heart complications—some might say a broken heart. Both Fannie and Wade are buried in Subligna Cemetery.

Hans
BECK
b. abt 1513 in Germany
d. 13 Mar 1593 in Germany

↓

Michael
b. 27 Nov 1567 in Germany
d. 21 Oct 1635 in Germany

↓

Martin
b. 29 Aug 1600 in Germany
d. 8 Nov 1634 in Germany

↓

Michael
b. 3 Oct 1630 in Germany
d. 30 Dec 1703 in Germany

↓

Johann [I]
b. 4 Sep 1678 in Germany
d. 19 Jun 1737 in Germany

↓

cont. next page with Johann [II]

PECK

Fannie Elvira Peck, wife of Wade Hampton Rambo, is my 2nd great grandmother. She was born 4 Nov 1882 and died 29 Mar 1950.

Fannie Elvira represents the 4th generation in a line of women named Fannie. Fannie Elvira's mother is Fannie Emyline Jones. Fannie Emyline's mother is Fannie Abercrombie. Fannie Abercrombie's mother is Fannie Cavender. Fannie Cavender is a daughter of Clemeth Cavender—see the section beginning on page 224 for more on the Cavender family and how they connect to another line in my family.

Tracing Fannie Elvira's paternal line, there is a long history of the Peck family. There are two main Peck families that immigrated to the New World. One group came from England while the other came from Germany. There is no relationship between these two families. Fannie's Peck ancestors are from the German branch and date back to 16th century Ebingen, Germany. At the time the name was Beck. The oldest known ancestor in the line is Hans Beck. I have very little information about these earliest Beck's, but William Greer Peck's book *The Peck Family* is my primary source of information.

Hans Beck (my 13th great grandfather) was born about 1513 in Ebingen, Germany and died there 13 Mar 1593. The next four generations through his son Michael Beck (b. 27 Nov 1567, d. 21 Oct 1635), grandson Martin Beck (b. 29 Aug 1600, d. 8 Nov 1634), great grandson Michael Beck (b. 3 Oct 1630, d. 30 Dec 1703), and 2nd great grandson Johann Jakob Beck (b. 4 Sep 1678, d. 19 Jun 1737) were all born and died in Ebingen as well. Martin's life was particularly short, dying of bubonic plague at only 34 years old. His father Michael died of the same fate. In this period (1634-1635) the bubonic plague is to blame for 604 deaths in Ebingen, over 25% of the population there (W. Peck 4; J. Anderson, Germany).

Johann Jakob Beck [II], born 7 Jul 1723, was

Above: My 2nd great grandmother, Fannie Peck. (Collection of Michael & Rhonda Scoggins)

Opposite: The beach at Dover. When I visited England in May 2005 I had no idea that I had German ancestors, much less that they came to America via Dover! (Photo by Jordan M. Scoggins)

Johann [II]
PECK
b.7 Jul 1723 in Germany
d.1800 in Virginia

↓

Adam [I]
b.13 Feb 1753 in Maryland
d.13 Feb 1817 in Tennessee

↓

Adam [II]
b.14 May 1791 in Tennessee
d.5 Apr 1866 in Georgia

↓

John
b.abt 1818 in Tennessee
d.25 Jan 1908 in Georgia

↓

Adam Wesley
b.23 Apr 1840 in Georgia
d.2 Jun 1909 in Georgia

↓

then John, then Fannie, then Ida Mae,
then Harold, and then me

the last of this Beck line born in Ebingen. He immigrated to the New World on the ship *Lydia*. *Lydia* departed from Rotterdam, stopped over in Dover, England, and arrived in Philadelphia on 27 Sep 1740 (Palantine). Johann is responsible for changing the family name to Peck, "to eliminate the confusion caused by the German pronunciation of Beck to sound like Peck in English" and was known as Jacob in this country. He married Lydia Borden (b. abt 1728 in New Jersey) in 1743 (Yates). They lived in both Maryland and Virginia at different times, ultimately settling near Fincastle, Botetourt County, VA. Both Jacob and Lydia died in 1800 (W. Peck 4; J. Anderson, Germany & Adam).

Johann and Lydia had at least eight known children. Among those children is Adam Peck [I], my 7th great grandfather. Adam was born 13 Feb 1753 in Sharpsburg, Washington County, MD. He married Elizabeth Sharkey on 29 Jun 1777 in Botetourt County, VA. He served as Ensign under Capt. Patrick Lockhart in the Botetourt County Militia in 1781. Later he served with the Virginia Militia from Fincastle, Boutetourt County, VA (Ancestry.com, U.S. Sons; West, Births & Individual; Yates).

Carrying on the pioneer spirit of his father, Adam migrated south into Tennessee in 1788. He settled in Mossy Creek, now called Jefferson City, in Jefferson County. In about 1795 Adam built Mossy Creek's first grist mill while another early settler, Thomas Hume, opened the first store around the same time (Miller).

Adam died 13 Feb 1817 and is buried with Elizabeth in Westview Cemetery.

Adam had a son also named Adam. This Adam [II] was born in 1791 after his parents settled in Mossy Creek. He married Elizabeth Gayle there on 30 Jul 1816 (Ancestry.com, TN). Elizabeth was the widow of Adam's brother Patrick. Patrick had died in the Battle of New Orleans in 1815 and "Adam kept his promise to look after Patrick's wife and their three children by marrying her." Adam and Elizabeth went on to have three children of their own as well (Amerson).

The Adam Peck family remained in Mossy Creek for a time, counted on the census there in 1830. But by 1840 Adam gave in to that pioneer spirit and sought greater things farther south in Lumpkin County, Georgia. As "one of the earliest settlers in [the Lumpkin County] area," Adam was looking for gold. Reportedly he was one of the first to attempt vein mining and his enterprising ambitions made quite a deal of money. He was "a man gifted with intelligence and leadership ability," serving as Lumpkin County surveyor for 20 years, foreman of the Grand Jury in 1858, and school trustee for Wahoo District in 1884 (Amerson).

But Adam did not only serve his local community. As a young man he fought in the Battle of New Orleans in the War of 1812 with his brothers Patrick and Moses. Still living by the time of the Civil War but too old to serve in a regular regiment, Adam joined the Georgia State Guards in Company B, 11th Battalion (Amerson; Historical, Soldiers & U.S.; National Park Service).

Elizabeth died 23 Jul 1874 and is buried in Johnson Cemetery in Russel County, Kentucky. I'm not sure why she is buried in a state where, as far as I can tell, she did not live. Adam lived over a decade longer and died 5 Apr 1886. He is buried in Mount Gilead Baptist Church Cemetery in Lumpkin County.

Adam and Elizabeth's oldest son John Gayle Peck was born in 1819 while they still lived in Mossy Creek. He moved to Lumpkin County with his parents where he married Mary P. Sinyard 7 Mar 1839 (Dodd; Hunting; Marriage John).

John served in the Civil War in the same regiment and company as his father above (Historical, Soldiers & U.S.; National Park Service). He was a miller and built one of the first saw mills in Lumpkin County. In the autumn of 1879 John, "suffered a serious if not fatal accident at his grist mil at Shoal Creek" (qtd. in Amerson). He was making repairs to the water gate and suffered a fall onto the rock below. The accident was apparently quite bad and, as indicated by the reporter above, John was not expected to live. Fortunately, though, he survived and lived more than two more decades. In 1908, still living in Lumpkin County, John died on 25 Jan. He is buried in Mt. Gilead Baptist Church Cemetery.

The oldest child of John and Mary is Adam Wesley Peck. Born 23 Apr 1840, Adam did not possess the pioneer spirit of his namesakes. He lived his entire life in Lumpkin County. He married Nancy Elvira McGee 26 Jan 1859. They had over fifteen children! I descend through their oldest child, John M. Peck. Adam and Nancy are buried in Wahoo Baptist Church Cemetery.

Below: Adam Wesley Peck and Nancy Elvira McGee. (Collection of Frances Scoggins)

Above: Frances Scoggins identified this crayon portrait as her grandmother's mother, Fannie Emyline Jones, wife of John M. Peck.

Right: Tintype of Fannie Emyline Jones.

(Collection of Frances Scoggins)

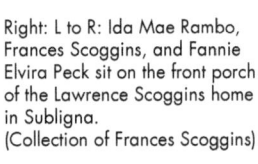

Right: L to R: Ida Mae Rambo, Frances Scoggins, and Fannie Elvira Peck sit on the front porch of the Lawrence Scoggins home in Subligna.
(Collection of Frances Scoggins)

Below: Wade Hampton Rambo relaxing on the front porch.
(Collection of Michael & Rhonda Scoggins)

John was born 4 Dec 1860. He married Fannie Emyline Jones 22 Jan 1882. They had several children together, among them my 2nd great grandmother Fannie Elvira Peck. Fannie Emyline, who had been born 5 May 1860, died at the young age of 31 on 20 Jan 1892. A few years later in 1896 John remarried to Harriet Lenora Rambo. Harriet was the oldest child of Ansel Rambo (see pg 164) which makes her my step 3rd great grandmother through the Peck line, but also my 2nd great grand aunt through the Rambo line!

There's also another interesting connection here through Fannie Emyline. Fannie Emyline was the daughter of Jarrett Jones and Fannie Abercrombie. She was the third out of 11 children. Fannie was the daughter of John Abercrombie and Fannie Cavender. Fannie Cavender was the daughter of Clemeth Cavender. This means that Clemeth Cavender is my 6th great grandfather. But the Cavender family also come into play in another line. See page 224 for more about that. So far little is known about the Jones and Abercrombie lines; further research is required.

Not quite the pioneer like his ancestors, John did seem to have restless feet. He lived in at least four different counties in Georgia as indicated by census records: Pickens in 1900, Floyd in 1910, Douglas in 1920, and Cobb in 1930. He died in Cobb county on 13 Feb 1931.

Back to where we started, Fannie Elvira Peck, born 4 Nov 1882, married Wade Hampton Rambo, tying this all together. The Beck/Peck line from Hans to Fannie Elvira represents 12 generations and over 400 years of history.

SUBLIGNA

Subligna is a small community located in Chattooga County, Georgia. Located at the fork where East Armuchee Road and West Armuchee Road meet, Subligna marks the northern extreme of Dirt Town Valley and leads the way south towards Gore.

One of the early settlers of the area was Dr. William Dunlap Underwood. After coming from Spartanburg, SC to Villanow, GA in 1850 he ultimately settled in Subligna in 1854. Underwood became a prominent figure in the community—and it is for him the area is so named: "Sub" in Latin means "under" and "ligna" in Latin means "wood" and from there you have Subligna (White).

Since it's earliest days Subligna has been home to a variety of business. Dr. Underwood and James Young Foster were the first to open a store in Subligna, probably in the 1850's. Underwood was also the first postmaster and ran the post office inside his store. Another prominent Sublignian was Dr. James Wilson Clements. In 1871 Clements and his brother-in-law W.P. Lower had a shop near the present day convenience store and Clements also owned a blacksmith shop. Dr. Clements was even "the first surgeon in Subligna and served the country during the Civil War" when Subligna was used as a training camp for soldiers. Other shops were run by Tom O'Neal and Obe Broom (White).

The 1930's brought immense change. The Subligna road was paved for the first time and the community was serviced with electricity (Brown).

The Underwood & Foster store was now operated by the White family and known as the White store. Brothers Will, Tom, and Lee White all helped run it. It remained in business until Mar 1973 when it was badly damaged by the tornado and never reopened or rebuilt. Starret Self also operated a store, as did E.B. Self. My father remembers both Self stores and estimates Starret's closed in the 1950's. E.B.'s store operated longer and dad remembers kids from Subligna School would often go there to get hot dogs or hamburgers for their lunch. My grandfather Harold bought the store building in the early 1970's and my father used it as a work shop until it, too, was damaged by the 1973 tornado. It was at this store in 1947 that Harold first met Dot (read about that day on pg 228)!

Of most significance to me, of course, is the Scoggins store. It was known by several different names over the years, first as Scoggins Mercantile, then Scoggins General Merchandise, and later Scoggins Grocery... but everybody called it the Scoggins store. My great grandfather Lawrence Chapman Scoggins (see pg 150) built the current store building with his nephew Leland Coulter Scoggins in the late-1940's (though Lawrence had been a merchant even before then). Leland sold his share when he joined the army in 1950. It's unclear exactly how ownership changed hands after that, but Zenas Holcomb had a share at one point (see photo on pg 207) as did my grandfather Harold (see photo on pg 178) (L. Scoggins). There was a barber chair in the back of the store where G.B. Carpenter and Sid Eakers both worked as barbers. During most of the 70's Harold was the sole owner until about 1979 or '80 when he sold the store to Tim McWilliams. Tim operated the business as Subligna General Store all throughout my childhood. After Tim sold the store it was run by at least a couple of different people, including Harold and Christy Hughes for a time (McCollum). Today it is called Archie's Market and is operated by B.J. and Archie Patel. Read more about Scoggins Mercantile starting on pages 154 and 178.

The Scoggins family also ran a cotton gin. The Scoggins & Sons gin was in use for at least two generations. First operated by James Harvey Scoggins, it was located near the present day pastorium for Subligna Baptist Church. Read more about and see the gin starting on page 135.

One of the oldest churches in Chattooga County is the Methodist Church in Subligna. Originally known as Mt. Zion Methodist Church, according to Aleta White it "was built of logs and stood a short distance from where the present church [built about 1857]

Top: Men lounge on the front porch of White's store. L to R: Jeff White, Tom White, Willie White, Emmett Chapman, Lee White, and an oil salesman from Rome, GA.
(Collection of Delores Grigsby)

Bottom: The Subligna Baptist Church building, 1964.
(Collection of Frances Scoggins)

now stands." Aleta was writing in 1959. Not long after that the wooden church building was replaced with the brick building that stands today. Today the church does not hold regular meetings, only coming together once a year for special homecoming services.

Other Subligna area churches included the Emmaus Primitive Baptist Church which was built in 1857 about a mile up West Armuchee Road on property purchased from Malachi Lawrence. Levi Sanford Scoggins was a charter member of Emmaus. A.C. Ward and his wife Delila Brown (see pg 215) were also members there (Baker). The Cumberland Presbyterian Church was located on the land where my grandfather Harold Scoggins lived (White). Neither Emmaus or Cumberland exist anymore.

Subligna Baptist Church was formed just after the turn of the century in about 1903 with the help of B.F. Hunt (who had also helped start East Armuchee Baptist Church). The congregation originally met in the old Subligna school and finally built their own building, finished in the spring of 1905 (Grigsby, Transcriptions). That building was damaged in the 1973 tornado. For a while the church held services in the pastorium until the church was rebuilt and completed in about 1974 or '75. Additional extensions have been completed over the years.

After the Methodist church had moved into its new home, the old log building became the first school in Subligna and was used until 1876. In that traditional one room school house, "the children sat on slab seats around the room. The teacher occupied the middle of the floor. He held a stick in his hand and when he struck the floor with his stick it meant that children from the smallest to the largest recited or read aloud at the same time" (White).

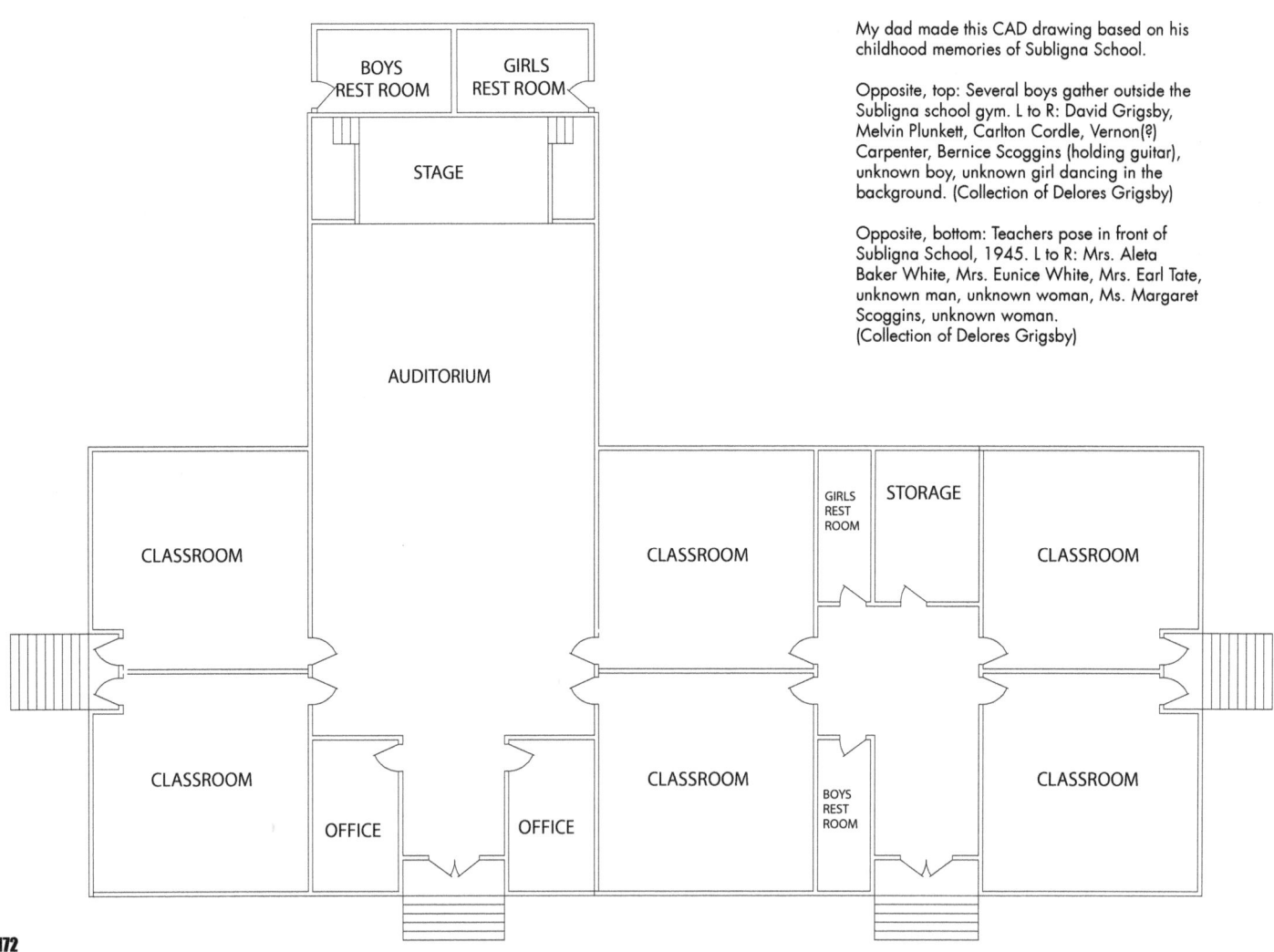

My dad made this CAD drawing based on his childhood memories of Subligna School.

Opposite, top: Several boys gather outside the Subligna school gym. L to R: David Grigsby, Melvin Plunkett, Carlton Cordle, Vernon(?) Carpenter, Bernice Scoggins (holding guitar), unknown boy, unknown girl dancing in the background. (Collection of Delores Grigsby)

Opposite, bottom: Teachers pose in front of Subligna School, 1945. L to R: Mrs. Aleta Baker White, Mrs. Eunice White, Mrs. Earl Tate, unknown man, unknown woman, Ms. Margaret Scoggins, unknown woman.
(Collection of Delores Grigsby)

In 1876 a new school house was built behind what is today the Subligna Community Center. Dr. Clements and Milton White served as trustees. Mr. Irvine was the first principal with General Graves as his assistant. Captain Jackson was the teacher from 1877 to 1883, and Gus Shropshire in 1884. This building was in use until 1923 when the large multi-room building of Subligna School's heyday was erected. Some time after the school was built, a separate gymnasium was constructed. The gym had a stage that was used for performances or other activities. It also had separate rooms that housed a wood shop and the school library.

My father remembers many details about the school:

"The heat was radiators in each classroom and auditorium. There was a coal boiler under the southeast classroom that heated the water for the radiators. There were large windows in each classroom that served for air conditioning. The walls were tongue and grove wood ... There was an electric bell and the button was located in the office. It was rung by hand not automatic" (M. Scoggins, interview).

And unlike modern schools, there was not a lunch room. "We usually ate outside or in the classroom," recalls Mike:

"When I was in the first three or so grades I took my lunch in my Roy Rogers lunch box with milk in the thermos. ... There was a water fountain (not cooler) where we could get a drink and that was where I washed my thermos out." But when he was a little older, Mike would "walk to the [Scoggins Mercantile] store and Daddy would make me a sandwich. ... Some students, especially older ones, would go to E.B. Self's store where Mrs. Self made hamburgers and hot dogs. I remember someone saying that one time she ran out of hamburger meat and made hamburgers out of sausage" (M. Scoggins, interview).

As time moved on small community schools everywhere were consolidated with larger schools that served broader areas. The Subligna high school closed in 1957. The remainder of the school was forced to close its doors about 1960. The students were sent to school over Taylor's Ridge in Summerville, though those who did not want to go went to Armuchee Valley in Walker County. My father remembers, for "the first few years after the elementary [school] closed Mr. Tom White drove a bus he had and took anyone who wanted to go to Armuchee Valley. That was why I went to school up there" (M. Scoggins, interview). Teachers were displaced as well. Mr. Roberson, Mrs. Hunt, and Mrs. Bowman found new positions at Armuchee Valley.

As disappointed as the community was with the loss of their local school, they were determined to not let the building itself fall into disrepair. Harold Scoggins was one of the men involved in finding a new use and in 1962 the school was converted into a work glove factory by the Best Manufacturing Company. Best brought a new industry—and new employment—to the area and operated for over a decade (Street; School Building). My father worked at the Scoggins store during

Harold and Dot Scoggins's home was badly damaged by the tornado. Their back porch was completely blown away. Harold took the opportunity to make the house better than ever before and went to work on it right away (you can see him on the roof in the upper left corner of the photo). Mar 1973. (Collection of Dot Holcomb Scoggins)

this time and recalls, "we would be very busy on Fridays when the mill turned out. We would cash checks and hopefully sell groceries and some who had bought on credit would pay their bills." The mill employed about 50 people, mostly women, including Martha Delle Grigsby Richardson and Delores Jackson Grigsby. Doris Mills was the supervisor.

The gym also found new life. It was deeded to the community and served as a gathering place for local events. Mike recalls:

> "Donkey basketball was held there a few times. The board at that time bought some used skates and skating was held in the gym for many years. Rhonda and I ran the skating for about two years after we were married. We either got five or ten dollars for running skating. We also sold hot dogs and chips and candy to make a little more money. Skating gradually faded away and the gym was not used much. It went into disrepair, was fixed up some and not used much except for the Subligna Reunion until about eight years ago when a new board was elected and money raised and prisoners helped fix it up. It now has a green metal roof and hardwood floors with nice restrooms and a kitchen. They rent it for various events to raise money for the upkeep now" (M. Scoggins, interview).

In 1973 Subligna experienced a severe tornado unlike anyone had ever seen before. The tornado was part of a huge storm system that hit Mississippi, Alabama, Tennessee, and Georgia. The twister hit Subligna around 2:25pm on 16 Mar, a Friday afternoon. First it touched down about on the highway between Gore and Subligna and then "followed the road almost six miles into the community, through it and about two miles past the town." Luckily, no one was seriously injured by the tornado in Subligna. But property damage was extensive with "20 houses severely damaged, two mobile homes destroyed, three stores damaged and one church receiving roof and window damage." Numerous other barns and sheds were damaged or destroyed. Both power and telephone services were out in the entire area and were not fully restored until 3pm the next afternoon. The storm took on sort of legendary status for local residents. Even though it happened several years before I was born, I remember well people talking about "when the tornado hit Subligna." It's the kind of thing people never forgot (At Tornado; Green).

Today there are no schools in Subligna, there are no blacksmiths or cotton gins, and there is only one store. In 1991, Subligna looked to the past and celebrated 125 years of history with an all-day gathering. There was "a singing flag, old-time brush arbors, youth choirs, clogging, one-room school demonstrations, drawing for quilts and old-time preaching" (Subligna Celebrates). Subligna Baptist Church is alive and well but the Methodist church has not held regular services for several decades. County water service was even brought to the community in 2010. Dr. Underwood might be surprised at life in Subligna in the 21st century but he would not be disappointed in the community of friends and family that, no matter how small, makes Subligna a pleasant place to be.

Harold Wallace Scoggins
b. 26 Feb 1924 d. 13 Mar 2000
married
Ethel Dorthelia Holcomb
b. 25 Apr 1929

This portrait of Harold was probably taken before he was married. (Collection of Dot Holcomb Scoggins)

Harold Wallace Scoggins was born on Scoggins Lane in the Green Bush community of West Armuchee Valley on 26 Feb 1924. He was the second child of Lawrence Chapman Scoggins and Ida Mae Rambo. He went to school at Subligna and graduated from high school there in 1941. For five weeks that year he took wood work training from the National Defense School. He went on to study at Berry College for a year and a half until 1943. There he studied English, Mathematics, Chemistry, Biology, Bible, Spanish, and Physical Education. He was also president of the local Future Farmers of America chapter (Army discharge).

On 6 Apr 1943 Harold enlisted in the United States Army, entering active service on 13 Apr 1943 at Fort McPherson, Georgia. When they asked him what he wanted to be he said, "Anything but military police." They made him a military police. Harold always thought it was because he was tall and that they wanted MPs to have a presence of authority.

He became a Corporal in the Military Police Platoon of the 66th Infantry Division (known as the Black Panthers) with qualifications as a rifle marksman and carbine marksman (Army discharge). His unit was activated at Camp Blanding, FL on 15 Apr 1943, where they spent three months in training. Around the middle of July the Black Panthers were moved to Camp Joseph T. Robinson for unit exercises and from there eventually transferred to Camp Rucker, Alabama for further specialized training. After a year and a half in training, "sailing orders came in October [1944] and the division moved to Camp Shanks and Camp Hamilton outside New York City to prepare for embarkation." Harold's collection of photographs from his time in the Army include a shot of the Statue of Liberty while visiting New York City (66th).

Departing from New York on 1 Dec 1944, Harold sailed on the *Brittanic*. The transatlantic voyage took 12 days and arrived in England on 12 Dec (66th). There was additional training for combat and Panthermen enjoyed some free time as well, exploring England and its many pubs and sites. The soldiers were warmly received as "liberators and heroes" by the English public who "had gone through a whole lot more war up to that time than [the Panthermen] had" (Wessman 38).

The order to ship out came quickly. The 66th sailed out of Southampton Harbor on Christmas Eve. Half of the men were on the *Leopoldville* with the other half on the *Cheshire* (Wessman 39). The boarding was hasty and there are no accurate records for who sailed on which ship (Sunk). This would be a minor detail except that all did not go well for the ill-fated *Leopoldville*.

That evening the 66th got its first devastating taste of war. The German submarine *U-486* launched a torpedo from about a mile away. The torpedo

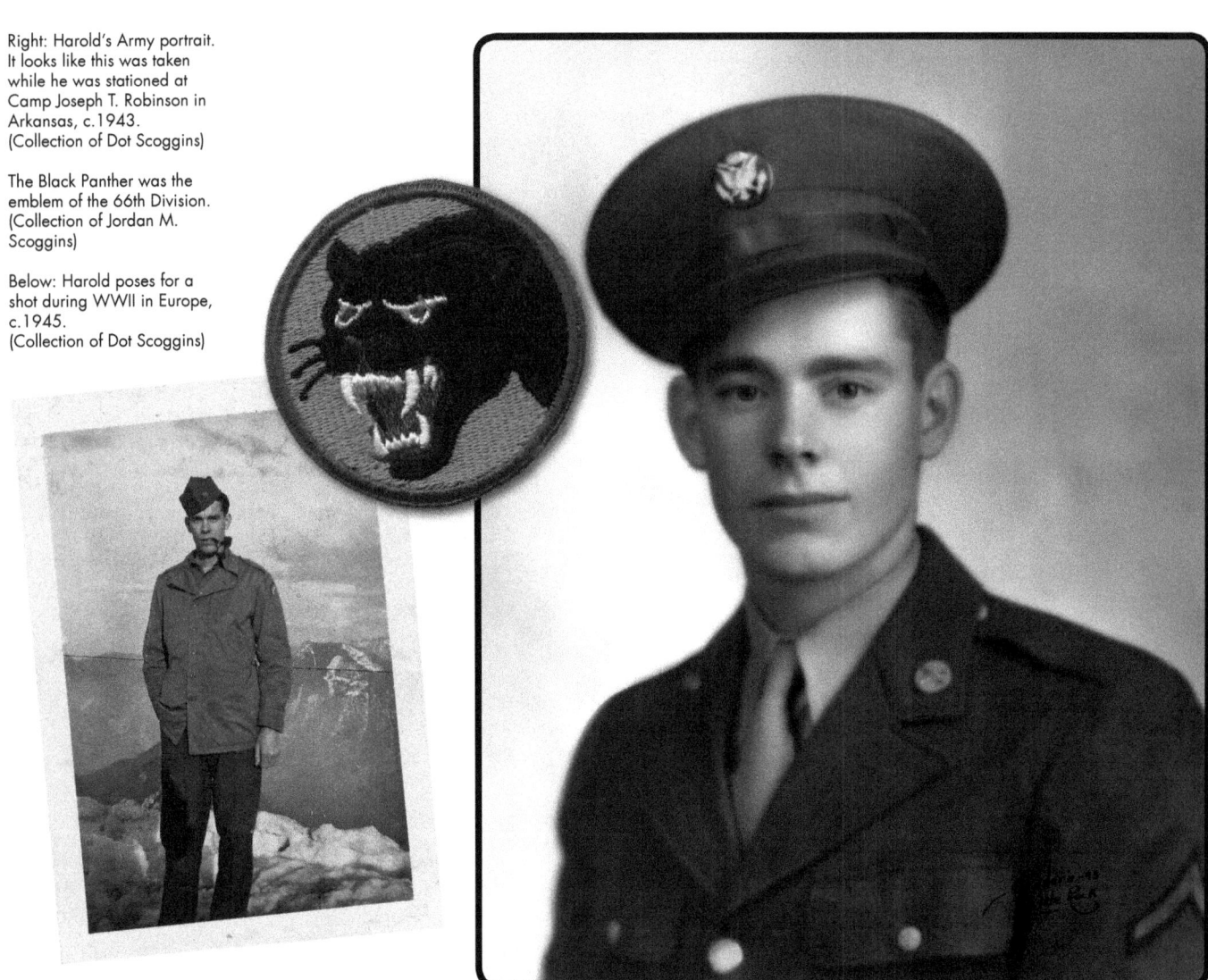

Right: Harold's Army portrait. It looks like this was taken while he was stationed at Camp Joseph T. Robinson in Arkansas, c.1943.
(Collection of Dot Scoggins)

The Black Panther was the emblem of the 66th Division.
(Collection of Jordan M. Scoggins)

Below: Harold poses for a shot during WWII in Europe, c.1945.
(Collection of Dot Scoggins)

struck the *Leopoldville* at 5:50pm. The ship was in sight of their destination, Cherbourg, France. Rescue attempts ensued and some men survived, but approximately 763 soldiers died that night. It was one of the worst American army disasters of WWII—and as a result it was kept hidden. Officials did not want the American public to learn about the enemy's success. Survivors were forbidden to talk about the tragedy, and the families of dead solders were told their loved ones were missing in action and that they did not know what happened. It was almost 50 years before families learned the truth (Maynard 18; Sunk; Wessman 40).

It's a 50/50 chance whether or not Harold was aboard the *Leopoldville* and survived as "there was no order as to what ship the men were being loaded [on to]. Men from the same company would be separated, some loaded on the *Leopoldville* and some on the *Cheshire*" (Maynard 14). It was luck of the draw, it seems, as "many times it was finger pointing by officers standing between lines of men" that determined what ship you boarded.

If Harold was on the Leopoldville, it was likely such a traumatic event that, paired with orders to never speak of that day, he never spoke of it to the family. If he was instead on the Cheshire he still never spoke of his lucky draw. Had I only known about this before Harold died maybe we could have learned more.

After the division arrived in France, command was set up at Châteaubriant for combat in the Saint-Nazaire and Lorient pockets as part of the Northern France campaign (Army Almanac; Order of

Battle). The 94th Division had been stationed there and the 66th were sent to relieve the 94th, who would move on to combat in the Battle of the Bulge (Maynard 18).

While the 66th was in this area, Harold wrote home in a V-mail dated 19 Jan 1945 to his sister Frances back in Subligna. It was a short and sweet note and didn't hint at all at what he was experiencing in the war. This is the only known surviving correspondence from his time in the service.

Panthermen fought in France for several months. Finally, in May of 1945, the German forces surrendered to the 66th Division. The Division had liberated "856 sq. miles of French territory and an estimated 186,000 French civilians" (Maynard 49). As a Military Police, Harold no doubt played his part.

But within just a few days the 66th Division were headed to their next command post. Traveling through Lemans, Rembouillet, and Verdun, France they arrived in Koblenz, Germany—the new command post—on 23 May. The Division's job was "To occupy and control the city of Koblenz and the surrounding area," which consisted of "over one million people in [a] 2,400-mile sector" (Maynard 50). But the assignment was quickly changed and on 27 May they were headed to Marseille in France. Near Marseille they "[built] and [operated] two large staging areas on desert like flats of baron [sic] land" (Maynard 51). The 66th Division was based at these camps, St. Victoret and Arles, until the close of WWII in

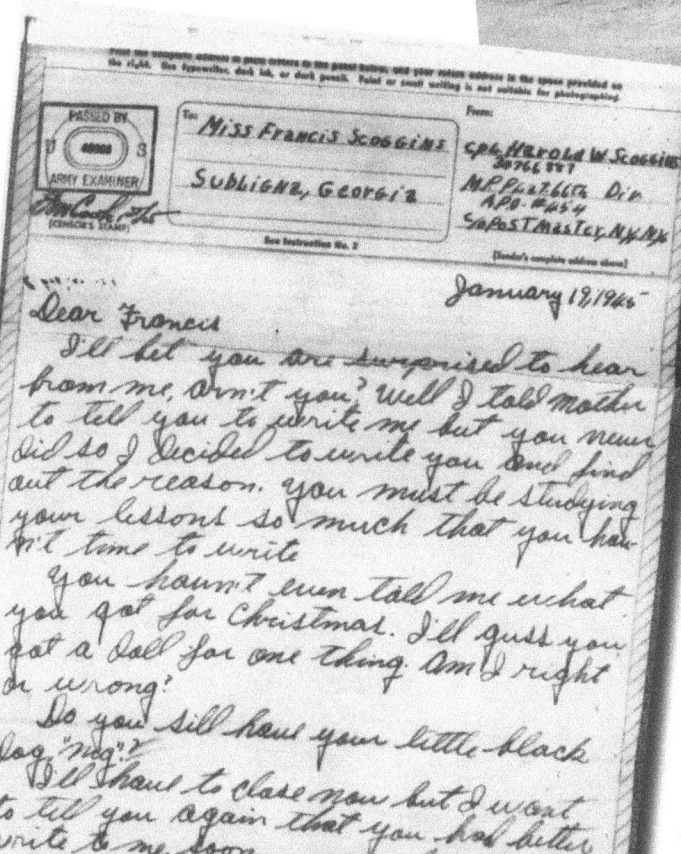

Left: The V-mail Harold sent to his little sister, Frances, in Jan 1945. (Collection of Frances Scoggins)

Above, top: Harold in uniform poses with Frances. The shadow of the person taking the photo is probably his mother, Ida Mae. Notice the Black Panther patch on Harold's shoulder. Above, bottom: Harold and a man who is believed to be his buddy Bernard Barton (of Crystal Spring, PA) have a relaxing moment while in Europe. Harold and Bernard remained friends for many years. (Collection of Dot Scoggins)

The pin is an MP pin though not one that belonged to Harold. (Photo from eBay.com)

September 1945.

At this point, "the 66th Division slowly began to break-up" (Maynard 55) and a soldier's Adjust Service Rating (ASR) determined his fate. Panthermen with enough "points" were able to come back to the states for immediate discharge. Other soldiers with moderately high points were assigned to a different division and remained in Europe for occupation duty in Germany and Austria. Those with median scores came back to the states for redeployment in the Pacific if needed. And those with the lowest points were reassigned directly to the Pacific (Maynard 55-57).

Harold fell into the second category as did many of his fellow Panthermen. He was assigned to occupation duty in Germany and Austria. His discharge papers do not state which division he was reassigned to but it was likely the 42nd Rainbow Division—which occupied Austria—as this is where many of the 66th ended up. Harold's WWII photo collection reveals that he spent time in Zell am See, Austria—a city where the 42nd was stationed (Army discharge).

Harold departed back to the US on 26 Mar 1946, arriving on 3 Apr. He was discharged from the US Army on 8 Apr 1946 at Fort McPherson, GA. He spent almost three years in the Army with 1 year, 7 months, and 23 days of continental service plus 1 year, 4 months, and 3 days of foreign service (Army discharge). He was not wounded in action, though 1,947 men from the 66th were casualties—either killed, wounded, missing, or captured (Order of Battle). While almost 2,000 casualties may seem like a lot, this was not bad considering the entire 66th was made up of 40,000 men (Wessman 10).

As described on his discharge papers, Harold's duties in Europe included the following:

> "Patrolled streets in towns and cautioned enlisted personnel regarding dress and behavior. Visited cafes and other public places to settle brawls and arguments. Requested passes and furloughs from soldiers. Assisted in directing traffic in cities and towns occupied by the U.S. Army. Accosted civilians in restricted areas and requested credentials or other forms of identification. Was authorized to make civilian arrests of persons suspected of participating in "black market" sales of scarce items and others who were offenders against the Military Government. Suppressed members of collective gatherings and any supposed rioting or sabotage. Supplemented the strength of the civilian authorities in all instances" (Army discharge).

The total pay for Harold's service came to $300 (Army discharge). He received National Service insurance, already effective at the time of his discharge, for a premium of $6.50 a month (Army discharge). Harold was awarded the following decorations and citations: Good Conduct Medal, World War II Victory Medal, American Service Medal, European-African-Middle Eastern Service Medal with 1 Bronze Star (Army discharge).

After the war, Harold came back home to live with his parents. He had left Subligna still a boy but came back an adult as only a man who returns from war can be. He worked along with his father in saw milling and cotton ginning. But his primary occupation throughout most of his life was working at and later owning Scoggins Mercantile (read about the beginning of Scoggins Mercantile on pg 154). Harold was the second generation to operate the store. Even my father, the third generation, worked there from 1966 to

1968. In later years when he was teaching school, dad would sometimes work there for a week or so during the summer so that his parents could take a vacation. Identified by his handwriting, one of the surviving store ledgers shows that Mike worked there from 17 to 22 Jul 1978. "We sold everything from groceries to feed to hardware to plumbing to boots and gasoline," dad remembers (R. & M. Scoggins, correspondence). The gas was supplied by Standard Oil of LaFayette. The store also sold Aristocrat Ice Cream and all of your standard groceries.

In 1946 he met Dot Scoggins who he married on 8 Feb 1947. Read more about their courtship starting on page 228.

For about three months they lived with Harold's parents in Subligna but soon moved into their own home just down the road. This is the house they would stay in for the rest of their lives. It was an older home, built in 1904 (parcel number 00078-00000-001-00D) but over the years Harold and Dot would make it their own, taking on renovation projects one at a time. The first thing Harold did was replace the old, cracked ceilings. He also ripped out the wall between the living room and the central hall to open up that space and make it bigger. Closing off the rear part of that central hallway created a room with much needed closet space and space for laundry machines. Around 1953 or so Harold finally added a bathroom. My father was old enough that he remembers using the outhouse before they had the bathroom.

The renovations made the home more suited to modern living. Dot remembers, "he worked on the house from the time we moved in … 'til he got where he couldn't work." Dot also revealed Harold was the creative force: "He always had the ideas in his head what he wanted to do. I just let him alone because I didn't have sense enough … to have those ideas." And Harold made use of everything he could to make the home better. In the early 1960's when the old Subligna School building was being converted into a factory, Harold salvaged some of the tongue and groove wood that covered the classroom walls. He used the recycled wood in the attic of the house to spruce up that space. The attic was unfinished but my father and uncle Eric loved to hang out there when they were kids.

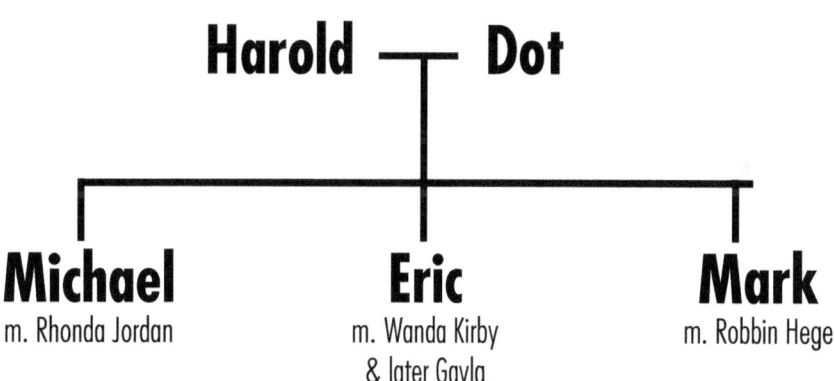

Above: The whole family poses for a portrait, 1962.

Opposite: Harold standing in front of Scoggins General Merchandise, probably mid to late 1950's and the Harold Scoggins home, 1964.

(Collection of Dot Holcomb Scoggins)

Harold and Dot Scoggins
late 1960's

Michael David Scoggins
1966

Eric Keith Scoggins
about 1968

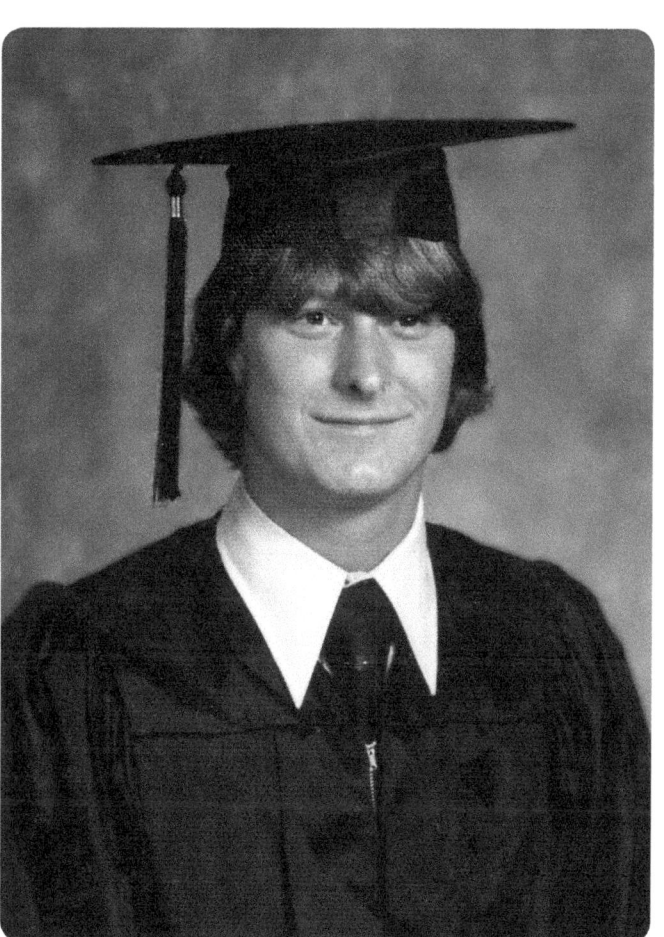
Mark Kevin Scoggins
about 1977

The home was badly damaged in the tornado of 1973 (see pg 174) and friend Glenn Orr tried to convince Harold to tear the house down and use it as an opportunity to start with something new. But Harold didn't want to do that. "The foundation was good," Dot recalls. So "he just went to fixing [all the damage from the storm]" (dot audio tape). Even by the time when I was growing up I remember Papa always working on the house. He added a sun room to the south side of the house, made improvements to the bathroom, and built a large outbuilding to house his tools and trinkets.

Barely a year after Harold and Dot were married, Dot gave birth to their first son. They had a total of three children:

1. Michael David (b.16 Feb 1948, m. Rhonda Verlyn Jordan)
2. Eric Keith (b.17 Apr 1950, m. Wanda Kirby first, later divorced and married Gayla Rhudy)
3. Mark Kevin (b.6 Mar 1959, m. Robin Hege)

Michael was born at Kitchen's Clinic in LaFayette, Eric was also born in LaFayette, and Mark was born in Rome.

In the early years Dot was a housewife, raising the kids and keeping house. Harold supported his family by continuing his father's business. He operated Scoggins Mercantile in Subligna. At some point the name was changed to Scoggins General Merchandise. Running a store was hard work. Harold worked six days a week from about seven in the morning until dark (R. & M. Scoggins, correspondence).

Harold and Dot kept a garden and grew vegetables for themselves. Dot would can vegetables, and when they eventually had a freezer she would freeze them. Sometimes they raised chickens, and even kept laying hens at one point. Harold once even raised pigs which provided plenty of meat for the family. Michael remembers, "Daddy had an electric meat cutter which we used to slice the pig bellies into bacon" (R. & M. Scoggins, correspondence).

Harold made sure his boys had things to entertain them. "Daddy made us a goat cart that we would hook to Eric's goat and ride but we always had a hard time making it go where we wanted it to go," Michael remembers. "Also after daddy replaced the engine on his walk behind garden tractor he had us a go cart made to put the old engine on. We would ride it all over the yard. I slung Eric off the back of the go cart one time and he broke his arm" (R. & M. Scoggins, correspondence).

Dot made sure the boys always celebrated their birthday. Every year she made a cake for their birthdays, putting her confectionery skills to good use. This became a long held family tradition that she would continue with all of her grandchildren as well.

Gradually Harold and Dot's children grew up and started their lives as adults. Michael married Rhonda and they moved out on their own in 1967. Eric followed not long after in 1969. Mark was younger than his brothers and didn't marry until 1980.

It was around this time that Harold sold the Scoggins store. He wasn't retiring though. He bought a van which he used to distribute inventory to stores that sold nuts and bolts in bins. Harold

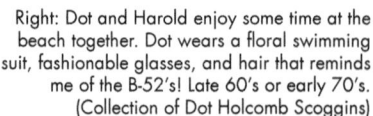

Right: Dot and Harold enjoy some time at the beach together. Dot wears a floral swimming suit, fashionable glasses, and hair that reminds me of the B-52's! Late 60's or early 70's. (Collection of Dot Holcomb Scoggins)

Left: Dot and Harold standing with one of the trucks Harold drove.

Below: Harold could be quite the practical joker. Here he's wearing Dot's bathing suit. His friend Hub Dover stands with him. Dot, Mary Reece and Louise Dover look on. Mark is blowing up a float. Florida, 1966.

(Collection of Dot Holcomb Scoggins)

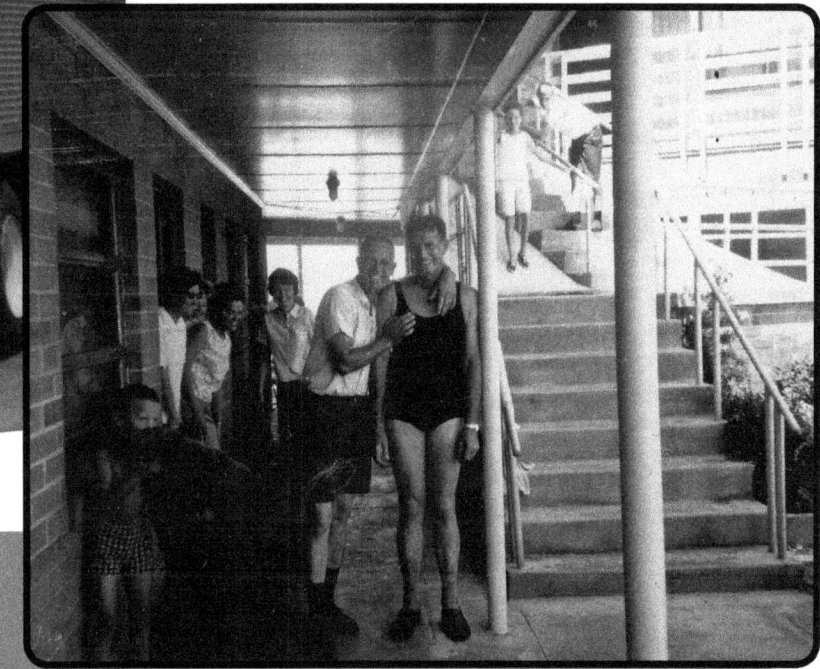

had spent most of his life running the Scoggins store. This new line of work put him on the distribution side of the retail industry and didn't tie him down at home like the store had always done. Dot even joined Harold on the road in the van many times, making work trips into fun road trips. The van was the perfect symbol of freedom for the now-empty-nesters.

He also bought and drove a tractor trailer truck. His first job was for a company that hauled pots and pans across the country. Occasionally the company would discard lightly damaged pans and Harold would bring them home. My parents still cook with some of these pans to this day! Later on Harold and his brother Doc both drove for a company that delivered diesel fuel and food supplies for the railroad. And at one point his driving partner was a man that lived on Lookout Mountain. The schedule was pretty good with this job. He would leave on a trip late Sunday night or early Monday morning and return home no later than that Wednesday, yet he was paid for a full week. My father said to his dad:

"With that kind of time off you should have no problem getting all your work done at home!"

Harold looked at Mike, "You will never get everything done."

Many years later after my own father retired he recounted this story to me, expressing his own frustration at how right Harold really was!

But Harold always made time for fun too—especially when it came to his family. While raising his own children, he took the family on vacations whenever he could get away from the store. "We camped on the beach in Florida when we were very young but mostly [we] stayed in cabins on the bay [at Panama City]," my father recalls. Once or twice we went to Pennsylvania and Washington, D.C. Daddy had an army buddy [Bernard Barton] that lived in Pennsylvania" (M. Scoggins, interview).

In their later years, Harold and Dot made it a tradition to take their grandchildren on a special trip every year. My sister Julie and cousin Keith were about the same age so it started with them. Opryland, Six Flags. Where else? By the time Erica and I were old enough, Grandmother and Papa started taking us on our own trips. The first trip I remember was Rock City. Lake Winnepesauka, though, became the staple throughout the years. Eventually they took us all to Six Flags and the last trip I remember was to Disney World in 1993. These annual trips were a great way for Harold and Dot to spend time with their grandchildren and also helped build the relationships between the cousins. A fantastic time was had by all.

The extended family at large also shared many good times together. We spent every Christmas Eve at Harold and Dot's house, celebrating the holiday with food, gifts, and lots of love. Every holiday was an excuse for a family gathering. And every birthday too!

Harold always enjoyed teasing and playing with his grandchildren. My sister, Julie, remembers how he would tickle us grand-kids and not stop until we exclaimed, "Calf rope!" To this day I don't know what "calf rope" meant exactly—though we all certainly said it many times!

Harold had a number of surgeries over the years, including prostate, carotid artery, and back surgeries. He even had two open heart surgeries—once in 1994 and once in 1999. I can remember visiting him in the hospital as he recovered from one of his surgeries. The hospital had a rule that children under a certain age were not allowed to visit patients. Erica and I were too young so our parents had to sneak us in. The two of us devised a plan to hide behind the curtains if a nurse were to come into the room. I don't remember if we had to execute this plan or not, but I do remember being there and being excited about our top secret visitation!

Above: Invitation for Harold and Dot's golden wedding anniversary celebration in 1997.

Right: Harold and Dot make a toast at their anniversary celebration.

(Collection of Michael & Rhonda Scoggins)

A little known fact about Harold's health is that he had psoriasis. This skin disease runs in my Scoggins line. Harold's father, Lawrence, had it and Harold's son Mike—my father—does as well. I, too, inherited this condition. Dad doesn't remember Harold ever having particularly bad patches. Unfortunately it has been much worse for dad and myself. Harold was also color blind–a trait that I also inherited (though in this case, mine is not as severe as his).

In 1997, Harold and Dot celebrated their golden anniversary. The family hosted a reception in the fellowship hall at Subligna Baptist Church. Many friends and family came to celebrate 50 years of marriage.

At age 76, on 13 Mar 2000, Harold died at Redmond Hospital in Rome, GA. The funeral home visitation was at Erwin-Petitt in Penville and funeral services were held at Subligna Baptist Church. He is buried in Subligna Cemetery.

HOLCOMB

HAWKINS • WARD
KEOWN • CAVENDER

William
b. abt 1795 in South Carolina
d. 18 Mar 1859 in Georgia

↓

Marion
b. abt 1832 in Georgia
d. 2 Mar 1864 in Arkansas

↓

Wm. Jackson
b. 28 Feb 1861 in Arkansas
d. 8 Jun 1933 in Georgia

↓

Zenas
b. 24 May 1903 in Georgia
d. 29 May 1985 in Georgia

↓

Dot
b. 25 Apr 1929 in Georgia

↓

my father Michael and then me

William is the oldest known Holcomb ancestor. I represent the sixth generation to descend from him. The Holcomb line has proven more difficult to trace than any other but has also been one of the most rewarding.

Holcomb Heritage
The Holcomb Family Origins

The Holcomb line of my family has proven the most elusive and mysterious. Therefore in many ways it has been the most interesting to explore as I have had to work the hardest to uncover information. When I set out to write this book, my family had no knowledge farther back than my 2nd great grandfather, William Jackson Holcomb. There was a vague recollection by some of the family that the Holcombs had something to do with Arkansas, but no details had survived the generations. I became determined to uncover the story in this line, setting me on the most unique portion of *Jordan's Journey*.

I still do not know the actual origin of my Holcomb line in this country. More than likely, though, they came from England. J. Montgomery Seaver wrote about the Holcomb family origins in his 1925 book *The Holcomb(e) Genealogy*. Seaver claims that about "98 percent of the American Holcomb(e)s lived in Devonshire, England" (iii). I have not found any connections between my line and those in Seaver's book. And as his title illustrates, the surname has been spelled in multiple ways, including Holcomb, Halcomb, Holcombe, Halcombe, Halcom, and Holcom. In this book I have standardized upon Holcomb, the spelling used by my grandmother.

Another Holcomb resource, *The Holcombes, Nation Builders* by Hannah Elizabeth Weir McPherson, has proven more useful. It is a dense and sprawling text, somewhat difficult to navigate and read. Unfortunately, though, I take its lineages with a grain of salt as some of the information presented easily conflicts with modern research. The book presents the following as a possible lineage for the early Holcombs in my line. Please note that this line is not documented and proven and is merely a jumping off point for further research at this point (page numbers as well as the book's own unique identifier for each individual are included):

- William Holcombe (D, pg 314)
- Richard Holcombe II (D-3, pg 327)
- Joseph Holcombe (D-3-5, pg 576)
- Thomas Holcombe (D-3-5-4, pg 599)
- William Holcomb (D-3-5-4-5, pg 610)

McPherson herself fully acknowledges "probable error as to some or many" of the children of the above Thomas (599). The proper documentation to prove William—my 4th great grandfather—is the son of Thomas simply may not exist, thus the difficulty I and McPherson encounter in this line.

Genealogical research, though, is a lifelong endeavor. I will continue my Holcomb search and aim to break through this proverbial brick wall. Even if that never happens I have already uncovered enough information to make a strong connection to my Holcomb heritage.

Right: me poring through *The Holcombes, Nationl Builders* in the Milstein Division, NYPL, Dec 2011. (Photo by Andrew P. Jones)

William Holcomb
b. abt 1795 d. 18 Mar 1859
married
Rachel Isom
b. abt 1795 d. aft 1870

William "Billy" Holcomb is my 4th great grandfather and the farthest back Holcomb ancestor that I have traced with certainty. The main record for William is the 1850 census. Born in South Carolina about 1795, he was then living in Dirt Town in Chattooga County, GA. Living with him are his wife Rachel and sons James and Marion.

I have also found an 1840 census that appears to be the same William. The 1840 census gives much less detailed information than 1850 but by breaking things down I feel fairly confident this is the same William. He's living in what is described as District 962. This is probably Dirt Town as I recognize Henry Lawrence (from the Lawrence family, see page 148) who in 1850 appears on the Dirt Town census along with William.

Nine people are living in William's household in 1840—significantly more than in 1850. However given his birth year it is no surprise that he would have had several children no longer living with him by 1850. The breakdown of the household members (all "free white persons") in 1840 is as follows:

Males - 5 thru 9:	2
Males - 10 thru 14:	2
Males - 15 thru 19:	2
Males - 40 thru 49:	1
Females - Under 5:	1
Females - 40 thru 49:	1

This indicates William and Rachel had at least seven children (6 boys, 1 girl). We know from the 1850 census that James was born about 1829 and Marion was born about 1832. Since census ages are only an estimate or guess (and therefore must be used as a guide, not written law), James and Marion probably account for the two males age 5 thru 9. This leaves 4 sons and one daughter unaccounted for.

Looking at the 1850 census, when only Marion and James were at home with their parents, I've investigated other Holcombs living in Dirt Town. The following are present:

- James Monroe Holcomb (b. abt 1822)
- Dennis Holcomb (b. abt 1825) with wife Mary Ann (his name is transcribed as Devins on Ancestry.com)
- William Holcomb (b. abt 1827) with wife Elizabeth and son George C.
- John Holcomb (b. abt 1825) with wife Malinda and daughter Ann S.
- John Holcomb (b. abt 1825) living with the Hugh M. Mills family.

I will break down each of these here.

It seems unlikely that James Monroe is a child of William since in 1850 a son named James is still living with William. James Monroe did, however, have a brother named William as evidenced through James Monroe's Civil War claim papers filed in the late 1870's (Southern claim). It seems more likely James Monroe is William's (b. abt 1795) brother. However this does not seem to fit either as William the brother of James Monroe is described as serving the Union in the Civil War, going "behind the Federal lines and was engaged by the government authorities at Chattanooga, TN" (Southern claim). My ancestor William died in 1859. So, unfortunately, I cannot say with any certainty how/if James Monroe Holcomb is related.

Dennis Holcomb is the right age to fit into the "10 thru 14" category from the 1840 census. In 1850 he is living next door to William and Rebecca. Living with him is his wife Mary Ann and his 10 year old "Sister Holcomb". This sister fits into the right category to be the one female under 5 years on the 1840 census. In 1860 Dennis is counted in White, Pike County, AR. His mother, Rachel, is living with him as well.

William Holcomb (b. abt 1827) is the other son in the "10 thru 14" category from 1840. He married Elizabeth Reynolds on 10 Sep 1846 (Marriage William). Like his older brother Dennis, William and Elizabeth also migrated to Pike County, Arkansas, where they are counted in Caney Fork in 1860.

I have been unable to find any additional information on John Holcomb, married to Malinda. He could fit into the "15 thru 19" category on the 1840 census but, so far, there just isn't any more information to go on.

Finally, the other John Holcomb is the most difficult to track here. He appears to be single. Identified as a farmer living with the Mills family, he is presumably either hired help or a boarder. He would also fall into the "15 thru 19" category from the 1840 census.

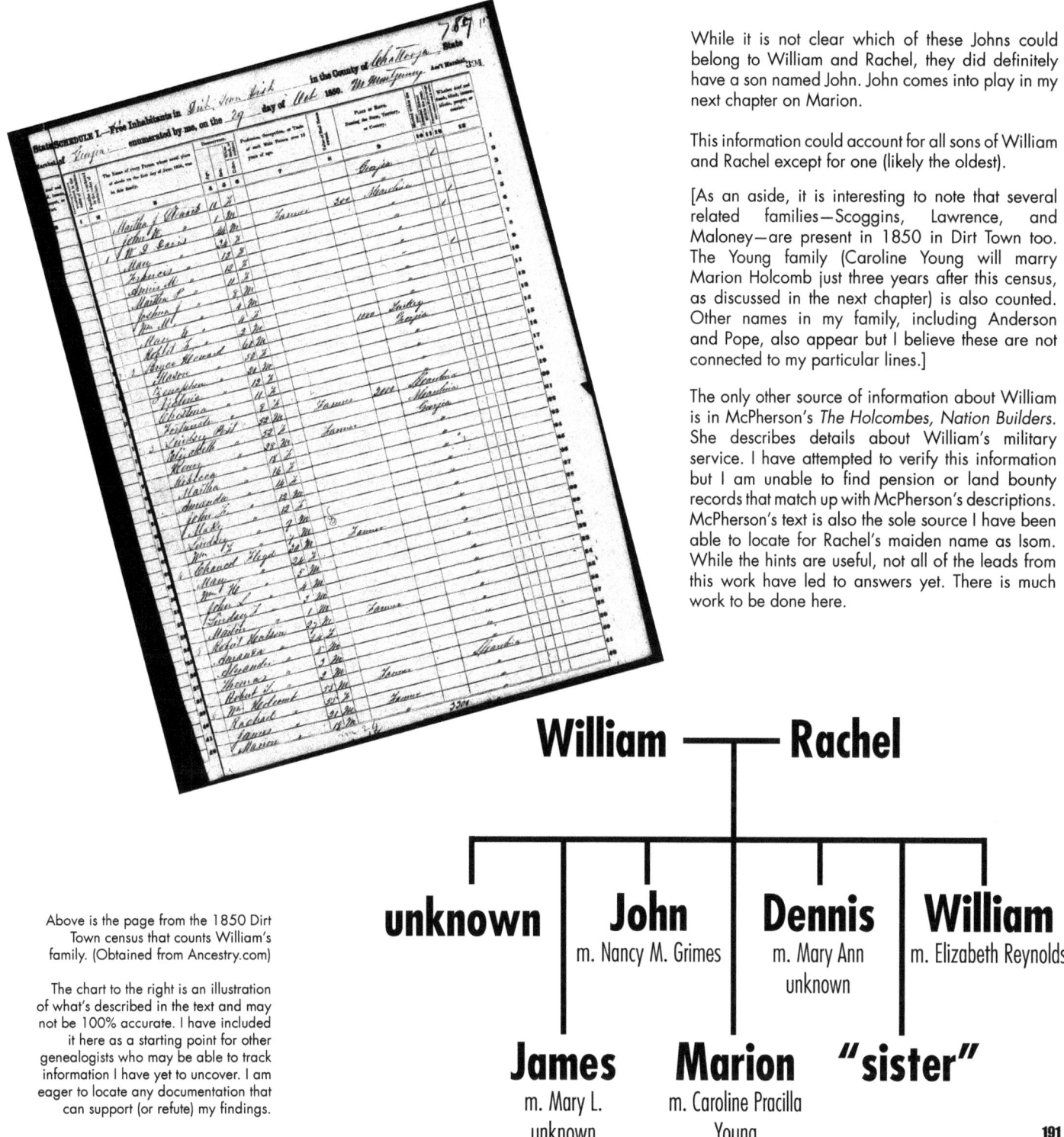

While it is not clear which of these Johns could belong to William and Rachel, they did definitely have a son named John. John comes into play in my next chapter on Marion.

This information could account for all sons of William and Rachel except for one (likely the oldest).

[As an aside, it is interesting to note that several related families—Scoggins, Lawrence, and Maloney—are present in 1850 in Dirt Town too. The Young family (Caroline Young will marry Marion Holcomb just three years after this census, as discussed in the next chapter) is also counted. Other names in my family, including Anderson and Pope, also appear but I believe these are not connected to my particular lines.]

The only other source of information about William is in McPherson's *The Holcombes, Nation Builders*. She describes details about William's military service. I have attempted to verify this information but I am unable to find pension or land bounty records that match up with McPherson's descriptions. McPherson's text is also the sole source I have been able to locate for Rachel's maiden name as Isom. While the hints are useful, not all of the leads from this work have led to answers yet. There is much work to be done here.

Above is the page from the 1850 Dirt Town census that counts William's family. (Obtained from Ancestry.com)

The chart to the right is an illustration of what's described in the text and may not be 100% accurate. I have included it here as a starting point for other genealogists who may be able to track information I have yet to uncover. I am eager to locate any documentation that can support (or refute) my findings.

William — Rachel

- **unknown**
  - **James** m. Mary L. unknown
- **John** m. Nancy M. Grimes
  - **Marion** m. Caroline Pracilla Young
- **Dennis** m. Mary Ann unknown
  - **"sister"**
- **William** m. Elizabeth Reynolds

191

Francis Marion Holcomb
b. abt 1832 d. 2 Mar 1864
married
Caroline Pracilla Young
b. Jun 1836 d. 23 May 1904

Francis Marion Holcomb was born about 1832. He grew up in Dirt Town Valley in Chattooga County, no more than a few miles away from the family of his future wife, Caroline Pracilla Young. This story of his life is reconstructed primarily from his pension files and all quotes and other information are from that source unless otherwise specified (Widow's Application).

Marion, as he was commonly called, was a farmer. He was "a big stout looking man," who spent time working for James W. Selman, a farmer in the local community near Crystal Springs. Marion was also a skilled deer hunter.

Marion and Caroline were married on 4 Aug 1853 by Justice of the Peace Rody Quinn (Marriage Marion). The wedding took place at Caroline's mother's home at the Chattooga/Floyd county line near Crystal Springs. In 1898, Sarah C. Moore remembered, "I couldn't forget [their wedding]. We had a fine time. I think we danced all night … [and] mighty warm weather, I know that." It must have been a fine celebration, full of music and merriment.

Caroline gave birth to seven children with Marion. The names of only four of these children are known, and only two of them survived past childhood. The first known child was Nancy Jane, born about 1855.

Marion and Caroline remained in Dirt Town Valley near Crystal Springs until about 1857. They moved to Arkansas with Marion's brothers Dennis, John, and William. Traveling by covered wagon to the Arkansas frontier, Caroline gave birth to their second known child, Mary Ann, as they passed through Alabama. According to Caroline's recollections, while in Arkansas they moved around quite a bit. They first lived with Marion's brother Dennis for about a year. They lived on Red Bluff Road in Dallas County for a while and also on Mr. Allen's place for a time. They also lived in Caney Fork in Pike County where they were counted on the census in 1860.

John Holcomb, Marion's brother, was counted on that 1860 census as well, listed next door to each other. William, too, was counted nearby. John's wife Nancy Grimes deposed in Caroline's widows pension case that from 1859 to 1861 Marion and Caroline lived in the same house with her and John, first in Dallas County and then "a while in this county, about 3 miles from here ['here' being Pike City]." Nancy also stated her present post office was Pike City. She went on to say she lived only "a mile or two apart" from Caroline while Marion was in the Confederate army.

Unfortunately, local records in Arkansas do not provide additional information. The Pike County Courthouse burned in 1895. All records were destroyed, leaving no trace of land deeds or other county records that might shed light upon Marion or his brothers (Pike 15). Gregory A. Boyd's *Family Maps of Pike County, Arkansas*, however, does provide a bit of insight. Land patents are recorded for John in Caney Fork. John was counted in Caney Fork from the first census in 1860 through the rest of

We discovered Caroline's name from census records but Marion's identity was a complete mystery. This record from the Chattooga County courthouse was the vital first link to discovering his identity and unraveling his story.

Above: I took this photo in the area of Caney Fork where John Holcomb's patent was located. The dense forest holds mysteries as hidden as Marion's identify was to me. Sep 2011.
(Photo by Jordan M. Scoggins)

his life (he died in 1899). His patent was not granted until 1875—so it's not proof positive that he was living on the same land in 1870 and 1860 though it is most likely the case. The lots assigned to him do match Nancy's description and are about three miles from Pike City.

Martin V. Osborn's statements further support the above. Martin, who lived in Caney Fork, stated that from 1858 to 1860 he lived a quarter of a mile from Marion. John H. Wood, also of Caney Fork, said he lived about 2 miles from Marion for a year or two and was "well acquainted with [Marion] and [they] visited back and forth." A Caney Fork land patent indeed was granted to John H. Wood in 1859 with another in 1860, and three for Martin V. Osborn in 1860—all located about the distances from John Holcomb's patents as described above (Boyd 179-80). All this aligns with Nancy's description.

Since Marion's pension documentation clearly states that Marion and Caroline lived with John Holcomb circa 1860, John's Caney Fork land patent is the best guess for the location of Marion and Caroline's home during the general period surrounding 1860.

I visited Caney Fork in Sep 2011 to get a feel for where Marion lived. While Marion and his family certainly resided there in 1860, it's also clear they moved about and lived in other places as well. But geographically speaking, Caney Fork is the closest connection I have to Marion. The dense forests and dirt roads that cover the area feel wild and free. It's hard not to expect an encounter with a 19th century farmer. Deer dot the landscape, perhaps descendants of the same deer hunted by Marion. In Marion's time, "you could see 50 or 100 deer before breakfast."

Caroline gave birth to their first known son, William Jackson Holcomb, on 28 Feb 1861. Judging by family names he was named after Marion's father, William, and Caroline's uncle Jackson Young.

That spring Marion and Caroline went to Desha County. But they only remained there for the season. While living in Desha County Marion fell ill with chills and fever. Showing no signs of improvement the family made their way back to Pike County as soon as the crop could be gathered.

While passing through Arkadelphia, Marion met a doctor who sold him $2.50 worth of medicine. The medicine finally helped Marion get well. In the pension files, Caroline explained that Marion's mother (Rachel) and sister were the only two people who witnessed this. Presumably this means Rachel and the unknown sister had been living with them in Desha.

It took them 14 days to get from Desha County to Pike County. Today that distance wouldn't take much more than 3 hours. When they finally made it to Pike County, they lived with John Holcomb's family again until the next spring. By this time the Civil War was well under way but, thus far, had not impacted the Holcombs' life. That would change soon after the first Confederate conscription act on 16 Apr 1862 (Faust).

Marion and Caroline moved yet again, this time to James Bush's place. Shortly after that Marion's Confederate service began on 4 Jul 1862. The service records do not reflect whether Marion was actually conscripted or went willingly. Though if it was the latter, it had likely become all too clear that conscription was unavoidable and thus motivated a volunteer enlistment. What is sure is that Marion was through and through "a United States man"

Left: Another view on the land of John's Caney Fork patent. Sep 2011. (Photo by Jordan M. Scoggins)

who did not support the Rebel cause. He served as a butcher in Co K of the 24th AR Infantry. His superior hunting skills made him perfect for the job—and also kept him out of certainly more dangerous combat engagement (Service records Holcomb CSA).

That fall the regiment camped at White Sulphur Springs near Pine Bluff, Arkansas. Many of the men, including Marion, came down with measles. It settled in Marion's lungs and he developed a hacking cough. Accounts indicate that although he became healthy again, the cough stayed with him probably the rest of his life.

Back home while Marion was away both of his daughters, Mary Ann and Nancy Jane, died on 15 Nov and 5 Dec 1862 respectively. Marion was not able to come home and tend to his grieving wife and infant son. Caroline told the story, "All [of Marion's company] was captured except about 40 men and my husband was one of the 40 men. My husband and those who were not captured came home and were not in the CSA again." These prisoners were taken at the Battle of Arkansas Post on 11 Jan 1863. Service records show Marion absent from 31 Oct to 31 Dec 1862 (Service records Holcomb CSA).

Marion did not return home until the next spring. In his pension files, several people who knew him said he stayed out in the woods for a time. This was a known practice by area men who were avoiding the CSA (Cosby 21). Jeptha J. Wisner, a fellow Caney Fork resident and hunting buddy of Marion's, had been conscripted around the same time as Marion entered the service. Jeptha deserted the CSA and described hiding out in the woods for an entire year before finally volunteering his service to the Union (Soldier's Certificate Wisner). John H. Wood said "[Marion] got away at the Battle of Arkansas Post" which matches what Caroline described, and several other soldiers also indicated this was the case. If this is so, it's unclear why the service record from Oct to Dec is marked "absent" for Marion—possibly he was out hunting for his job as butcher. Either way, he certainly left the CSA and spent time in the woods in order to avoid further conscription.

Allen Sogan was a fellow butcher with Marion who came back to Marion's house with him after they left the CSA. Allen told a story of he and Marion being captured by an Army company from Texas. "They thought we were deserters," said Allen, "and we were locked up at Arkadelphia for 3 or 4 weeks and they turned [us] loose. I didn't see [Marion] after that until I saw him at Little Rock [when we were in the Union army]." Marion told his friends about his time as a prisoner. Martin V. Osborn recalled, "I heard him tell how he had to whip several men from Texas because they run [sic] down Arkansas while he was in the Confederate army, so he must have been alright." Like a game of Telephone, Martin's account is a slight variation of how Allen remembered it.

When Marion returned home in the spring of 1863, he was no doubt happy to be with his wife. He worked the farm for the season but come autumn, just a few weeks before Christmas, Marion joined the army again. Being "a United States man" all along, he finally aligned himself with the Union. He enlisted in Co B of the 4th Arkansas Cavalry on 17 Nov 1863 (Service records Francis M. Halcomb USA, 37). His brother John followed, enlisting in Company L of the same regiment on 20 Dec 1863 (Historical, Soldiers & U.S.; National Park Service). Numerous others from the area also joined the regiment (see pg 201).

Marion is listed on a hospital muster roll in Jan and Feb of 1864, no doubt in poor health and suffering (Service records Francis M. Halcomb, 59). Henry Widener, a neighbor in Caney Fork, saw him during this time and described him as "very weak." Back at home pregnant Caroline was great with child. She gave birth to James Marion Holcomb—probably named after Marion's brother James (who remained in Georgia) and, of course, Marion himself—on 4 Feb 1864. A month later, still in the hospital in Little Rock, Marion died on 2 Mar 1864. Cause of death: pneumonia (Service records Francis M. Halcomb USA, 37). His body is interred in the Little Rock National Cemetery (Knight 66).

Left: In Sep 2011, my parents and I traveled from Georgia to Arkansas in our own "covered wagon" in search of Marion and Caroline. We had a much easier trip than them, I'm sure! (Photo by Jordan M. Scoggins)

Above: Me at Marion's grave in the Little Rock National Cemetery, Sep 2011. (Photo by Michael Scoggins)

After Marion's death, Caroline resided in Clark County. First she lived on William Allen's place about a year, then John Widener's place about a year, and finally on Mr. Baker's place for a short while. Sampson Vickery, who had served in the army with Marion and knew Caroline, said "she was in very slim circumstances—had nothing to support her."

Soon enough danger from the war had subsided and Caroline planned her return to Georgia. Traveling with her were her mother-in-law, sister-in-law, and her two surviving children. They prepared to leave in the autumn of 1865. James D. Johnson, another man who had served with Marion, helped Caroline prepare for the migration. He provided her with a team of horses in exchange for a yoke of steers. A man named James Adams wanted to marry the now single Caroline, "but it seemed she wanted to go to her folks and wouldn't stay." Adams went as far as accompanying Caroline on part of the journey to Georgia in an attempt to get her to remain in Arkansas. But she pressed on to her homeland.

With the long journey far behind her, by the 1870 census Caroline and her sons are found in Texas Valley, Floyd County (an area just over the county line from where Marion and Caroline had been counted back in 1850). She is counted a few doors down from Safrona Young—the widow of Wiley Young, Caroline's older brother from that 1850 census—and her five children. Living next door to Safrona is the household of Mary L. Holcomb, widow of Marion's brother James, with 5 children and the 74 year old Rachel Holcomb, Marion's mother who had returned from Arkansas.

Known in her community as "Widow Holcomb," Caroline struggled to support her young children. James W. Selman, the farmer who had employed Marion at one time before they left for Arkansas, paid Caroline to pick cotton, even providing her a place to live on his farm part of the time. No doubt it was the generosity of her community that helped Caroline when she was in need. She had legal custody of both boys until they reached 16 years of age. William Jackson turned 16 in 1877; James Marion followed in 1880. Both were counted at home in Dirt Town with Caroline still in 1880. William Jackson married in 1881 and James Marion in 1888.

On 17 Mar 1894, Caroline signed an agreement for an attorney to work on her behalf in the claim of a widow's pension for her late husband's military service. The proceedings for this claim went on for many years and involved numerous depositions from people in both Georgia and Arkansas that knew Marion and Caroline. Most of the questioning revolved around Marion's health in an effort to determine whether he was ill before joining the army or if his death was a result of his service. These depositions were very detailed and are the sole reason I have been able to reconstruct the story of Marion and Caroline.

In a 27 Jun 1898 deposition Caroline was asked, "Why did you not apply for pension until recently?"

She responded, "the southern people here were so opposed to US soldiers and pensioners that I was afraid that I would not be able to get work to support my children if I tried to get a pension." Indeed, Southerners were deeply impacted by the difficult Reconstruction years and long held a deep distrust for anyone associated with the North. Those scars were so deep you can still witness the effects today.

By 1900 Caroline is in Texas Valley again living with James, now with a family of his own. She was growing old and, no doubt, weary of the ongoing pension claim. On 9 Oct 1901, after over seven years of deliberation, the claim was rejected. Caroline didn't give up the fight though. The case was reopened with new evidence and denied three more times.

Unfortunately, Caroline died 23 May 1904 and, after a ten year process, never saw the claim come to fruition. The location of her burial is unknown.

But Caroline's death was not the end of the pension claim. On 29 Apr 1905, the Department of the Interior issued a decision to repeal the case, stating that it had not sufficiently been proved that Marion was indeed ill before his service in the Union. "The testimony tends to show that a cough existed," wrote the Assistant Secretary, "but it is not sufficient to establish the fact that a *severe* [emphasis added] cough existed. Furthermore, pneumonia is an acute infectious disease and occurs in the robust as well as in the debilitated, in those that are free from disease of lungs as well as those who are afflicted with disease of lungs … The fatal pneumonia, in the judgement of the Department, was the result of the soldier's military service, and whether due in part to preexisting disease of the lungs, was certainly the controlling factor in death cause."

The decision had been reversed and William and James were granted the pension.

Having lived into the 20th century, I do not know why Caroline was completely forgotten in family history. Perhaps because she lived with her son James at the end of her life, maybe William's family did not know her as well. While most of William's children were born before Caroline died, I descend through his son Zenas who was born only a year before she died. Zenas would therefore have had no memory of his Grandmother Caroline. Were it not for the pension file I would know virtually nothing about her or about Marion. I wasn't even able to confirm Marion's military service until I found the pension records. It's amazing how a simple family lineage can become completely lost within such a short span of time.

James and his wife Sara (as well as their children Sara, Ella, Virgil, James, and Raymond) are buried in Old Armuchee Baptist Church Cemetery. William and his wife Amanda are buried in Pleasant Grove Baptist Church Cemetery. The two young daughters who had died in Arkansas are most likely buried in one of the many unmarked graves in Wood Cemetery where John Holcomb's family is laid to rest.

Marion's journey took him to a frontier, Caroline's journey propelled her back home, and over 150 years later *Jordan's Journey* crosses the generations in search of answers about my family's past. I have grown closer to Marion and Caroline than any other distant ancestors in my tree. Their story is unique and their hardships numerous. I have only but a glimpse into their world but I admire the adventurous spirit and bold determination with which they faced life.

When I visited Marion's grave in Little Rock, it was an emotional moment for me. "Here you are, Marion. Here you are, finally. I've been searching for you for so long." A tear streamed down my cheek.

I looked at his grave and saw my own face (Marion was about my age now when he died). If this were the end—if my entire life were to flash before me now—how would I feel? My 3rd great grandfather didn't get the chance to grow old. He didn't get to see the outcome of the war he became so entangled in. He didn't get to see his children become men and lead lives of their own. As I stood there, Marion's tombstone represented so much lost potential.

But it also represented hope: hope for everything I have ahead of me in life and all that I have to look forward to.

And as the wind rustled through the trees I could almost hear him say, "Don't worry, son. You've given me a voice again. Thank you for telling my story."

I hope I've made him proud.

CANEY FORK

Caney Fork is a former township in Pike County, Arkansas located to the northeast of present day Murfreesboro. The general area is found along Shawmut Road within the broader boundaries of Highway 27 on the west, the Pike/Clarke county line on the east, Highway 8 on the north, and Pike City on the south. The easiest way to reach the area is from Highway 27 about eight miles down Shawmut Road. Caney Fork is but a remote memory to the people of today, as this former hamlet is scarcely even mentioned in the official *Early History of Pike County, Arkansas*.

The land patent records documented in Gregory A. Boyd's *Family Maps of Pike County, Arkansas* show the general area was first settled by Europeans in the mid to late 1850's. The earliest land patents were issued in 1859 to Jefferson T. Wood and his son John H. Wood. Both Wood households are counted among the 43 households on the first census of Caney Fork in 1860. Five other men who were also listed on that census were granted patents in 1860 (John Carpenter, Martin V. Osborn, William E. Osborn, James W. Phillips, and James E. Pritchard). Nancy H. Campbell's patent was granted in 1861. John Holcomb does not appear with a patent until 1875 (though he was counted there in 1860 with two of his brothers and their families and again in 1870—his brothers now gone). A large number of households counted in 1860 are never listed as receiving land patents and likewise many patents were granted to individuals that are not listed in the original Caney Fork census. Therefore the above families provide the best representation of those who lived and remained involved in Caney Fork since its earliest days (Boyd 178-80).

When these settlers first arrived in the late 1850's, Caney Fork was a virtual wilderness with minimal to no roads. Covered in virgin forests, the first families would have cleared fields for farming in order to sustain themselves. They were true pioneers, living off the land with no need for "modern" conveniences. Indians certainly had lived in the area at some point, as arrow heads and other artifacts have been unearthed. It is unclear, however, how many Indians (if any) lived there when European settlers moved in. Wood family oral history speaks of an old Indian man and woman that lived near John Henry Wood, though no one is described as Indian on Caney Fork censuses.

The Apr 1990 (Vol I, No 2) issue of the *Pike County Archives and History Society Newsletter* contains a piece on the Henry S. Sparks (1804-1864) family which helps paint a picture of pioneer life in Caney Fork:

"The 1850 Census finds Henry S. Sparks and his family living in Cherokee County, Alabama. Shortly after 1850 Henry S. Sparks, his wife "Marthy" and several of his children moved to Arkansas. They are listed in the 1860 Pike County, Caney Fork Township, Arkansas Census; their Post Office listed as Redland, Arkansas. It is very interesting to read the Caney Fork Township Census records. Many of the families who settled in Caney Fork Township probably traveled with the Sparks and Osburn families when they removed to Arkansas. One must keep in mind that one family rarely traveled alone in our early history but moved along in a caravan. For many families the trip only took a few weeks but more often than not it would take several years because the caravan would stop to make a crop for the trek across country. It was not unusual for all the families to be related, either by marriage or blood" (Focus).

Henry Sparks was born in Georgia, where his oldest child was also born, with the remaining children born in Alabama. This general Georgia-to-Arkansas-by-way-of-Alabama migration pattern was followed by a number of other Caney Fork settlers. The 1860 census records show the Campbell, Holcomb, Osborn, and Wisner families also came from Georgia, with the Phillips family coming from Tennessee and the Pritchard family originating in Kentucky & Indiana. John Carpenter was born in Kentucky but his wife and children (the oldest born about 1846) were all born in Arkansas, indicating he had moved to the state at an early age. The common element of most of the families originating in Georgia is children who were born in Alabama—the Campbell, Holcomb, Sparks, and Wisner families all seem to have spent time in that "Sweet Home" state. The Holcombs came from Dirt Town Valley in Chattooga County, Georgia. The precise Georgian origins of the Sparks, Campbell, Osborn, and Wisner families is a worthwhile topic for further research and might provide new understanding for how these families came together in Caney Fork.

Boyd identifies three historical "towns" that were located within Caney Fork township: Wright, Elk, and Anderson. These places are pretty much lost to history and almost no details of their existence are known.

Above: The Self farm on Shawmut Rd in Antoine just before you get to Caney Fork, Sep 2011.
Opposite: The William Wright home place on Shawmut Rd in Caney Fork, Sep 2011.
(Photos by Jordan M. Scoggins)

John Henry Wood in 1901 and Henry Widener in 1904 each list Elk as his post office on affidavits in Francis Marion Holcomb's widow's pension file (Widow's Application). According to Wood family tradition, the Elk post office was on Jefferson Wood's place. There was also a school in Caney Fork led by John Henry Wood. Called Piney Grove School, Wood family history tells us it was located on Henry Widener's land.

Another community in Caney Fork was known as Mountain Home. On 24 Dec 1886, William D. Wood and his wife Mary C. Wright sold a portion of their land in Caney Fork to the Christians and Citizens Church of Mountain Home. The deed specifies four acres were sold for thirty dollars. One acre was to be used for the church building and three acres were for burial grounds (Deed Wood). The burial ground is the site today known as Wood Cemetery. The church building no longer stands; no known photographs or records survive. A page from John Henry Wood's Bible records his marriage to Mary Jane Sparks on 13 Apr 1856—both listed as being "of Mountain Home" (though not to be confused with the North Central Arkansas town of Mountain Home in Baxter County, incorporated in 1888) (Wood Bible).

It is unclear exactly when Mountain Home—as well as Wright, Elk, and Anderson—existed in the common vernacular other than the limited sources described above. Since our analysis of census records indicate the area was rather sparsely populated it seems unusual for up to four distinct places to have existed. Perhaps different names were used during different periods, with multiple names referring to the same general place. The lack of documentation and written history on the area makes it impossible to say.

Of all the early settlers in 1860 there were a total of 230 people living in 44 families (an average of 5.2 people per family). None of the heads of these families, except for John Bobbit, were actually born in Arkansas, indicating just how much of a frontier the area actually was. Most everyone was born in the southeastern states with the largest numbers originating from Georgia (39 people), Tennessee (12 people), and Alabama (8 people). One person, J.H. Cook, was born in Germany, but his wife was born in Georgia. Farming was the way of life. C.J.C. Campbell is the only man listed with another occupation; he is counted as a mechanic. Ages ranged from 2 months to 69 years, but with the average age being 18 it was a very young population, with 51% of the population 14 years or younger! The next 16% spans ages 15 to 24 and only 33% of the population was 25 or older. Out of that 33%, 41 were men, a large number of whom served in the Civil War.

Unlike much of the south, the men of Caney Fork did not unanimously stand for the Confederacy. Faced with the decision of choosing sides, sometimes "irregular bands of men would join together and take part in battles where needed, but after the war's end they would receive no official recognition as legitimate soldiers" (Cosby 21). And if they did not go willingly, they were often forced by conscription:

> "Reluctant men and boys were threatened by ... bands of soldiers and some were killed. A number of farmers hid out in the woods to avoid conscription and their wives would bring food out to them. Legend states that some hid out for two years or more before deciding to enlist" (Cosby 21).

Meanwhile, back at home, "all the farm and house chores still had to be done [by the women], despite their lack of able-bodied men. Fields and gardens had to be plowed, sown, cultivated and harvested. The livestock had to be fed and tended and firewood had to be split. This was in addition to the usual house chores of cooking, cleaning, washing and ironing, sewing, doctoring the sick and tending the children" (Cosby 27). Even beyond the burden of assuming roles previously held by men, the women and children had to deal with a kind of terrorism as well:

> "Bands of 'Jay Hawkers' roamed the countryside terrorizing the people and stealing livestock, food and anything else they could lay their hands on. Deserting soldiers were another problem. These men hid in the woods and were desparate [sic] for food and clothing" (Cosby 22).

The situation added even more fear to the already difficult struggle for survival. This gives us a glimpse into terrors beyond the bloody battlefields and organized campaigns most of us associate with the Civil War. But it didn't stop there, treading into far darker territory for some:

> "On one occasion, three men were killed, probably by soldiers or Jay Hawkers, and their bodies were left near Elizabeth Horn McCauley's house. The names of these three victims were not known. Elizabeth, her sister Isley Horn and another woman dug a large single grave

at Red Land Cemetery. The women then wrapped the bodies in a wagon sheet and buried them together in the grave" (Cosby 28).

It's a grim scene to imagine. Though the Horn family did not live in Caney Fork—they lived in Caney Valley, just to the north over the ridge—several of the Horn men fought for the Union along with those from Caney Fork. Bythel, Joseph, and Elijah Horn—along with their brother-in-law Joel Keen—all served in Company B of the 4th Arkansas Cavalry.

Men from Caney Fork who served in the 4th Arkansas Cavalry include (Historical, Soldiers):

- John Carpenter, Pvt, Co B,D
- John Hawkins, Pvt, Co H,B
- John Holcomb, Pvt, Co L
- Francis M. Holcomb, Pvt, Co B
- Martin V. Osborn, Corp, Co B
- Wm. E. Osborn, QM Sgt, Co L
- Samuel Parker, Cosy Sgt, Co H
- William Parker, Pvt, Co H
- John W. Phillips, Pvt, Vance's Co
- John Sparks, Pvt, Co B
- Jeptha J. Wisner, Pvt, Co B
- John Henry Wood, Pvt, Co B
- Samuel Woodall, Pvt, Co B

Many of Caney Fork's men were originally conscripted into the Confederate army. After serving their time (or deserting) they later joined up with the Union cause which they supported—such is the case for Francis Marion Holcomb (above) who then lost his life while serving the Union. John Carpenter also did not survive. These men literally gave their life in support of unpopular ideals in their broader region.

Further investigation into Caney Fork's involvement in the Civil War is needed, and while exact numbers of men who served from the township are as yet unclear, it's easy to see just how impacted the community was. With only 53 men age 18 and older living in Caney Fork in 1860 even just the soldiers named above is no small percentage. Today a number of Caney Fork soldiers are memorialized in Wood Cemetery with an arrangement of commemorative stones that have been placed there by Joyce Wood (widow of a descendant of Jefferson T. Wood).

In the years after the Civil War, families continued to settle in Caney Fork. William M. Wright—born in South Carolina—resided in Dalton, Georgia in 1860 and 1870 (and he had served the Confederacy in Georgia's 39th Infantry Regiment) (Historical, Soldiers). In the 1870's he migrated westward. By the 1880 census in Caney Fork, William's family was counted there and had already become aligned with the long resident Wood family: Wright's daughter Mary is still living with her parents but her husband William Wood is there too. The William Calley family—from California, Georgia—settled in the area in the early 1880's. Shortly thereafter William's son Noten married Emily Frances Holcomb, daughter of

Opposite page: September sky in Caney Fork. Above: The Civil War memorial in Wood Cemetery.

John Holcomb. And William's daughter Annie married Elias Jackson Wood (a son of Jefferson T. Wood). Around 1901 another of the Calley siblings, William, married his second wife—Emily's sister Sarah Malinda Holcomb.

But the allied families in Caney Fork go beyond the Wood, Wright, Calley, and Holcomb connections. Jefferson T. Wood's wife was Susannah Carpenter, sister of early settler John Carpenter. John Henry Wood married Margaret Jane Sparks, daughter of Henry S. Sparks and Martha Osborn. [Note that while there are other Osborns in Caney Fork, we have yet to document Martha's relationship to the others.] And even later William Alfred Wood (grandson of John Henry Wood) married Dossie Lou Calley—daughter of Emily Frances Holcomb. Emily is a daughter of the early settler John Holcomb. All together these allied Wood/Carpenter/Sparks/Wright/Calley/Holcomb lines account for many of the early settlers of Caney Fork.

By 1870 Caney Fork had a slightly smaller population than in 1860 with 38 households. Many of the same families are present, with some new folks no longer there and other new folks mixed in. This appears to have been the status quo on through 1880. In general the population declined over the years, bottoming out at 17 families in 1920—a fraction of Caney Fork's 1860 heyday. By contrast, Pike County's population as a whole grew from 639 families in 1860 to 2,634 families in 1920 (Minnesota).

While Caney Fork's population did grow slightly (to 26 households) in 1930, and Pike County's total population was at 11,782, census records are not available past that year. But the trend is obvious: Caney Fork's prime was long behind her. Pike County's population as a whole in 1940 remained about the same (at 11,786). But by 1960 the county population had fallen to 7,864. After 1970, little more than 100 years since it had first appeared as a township, Caney Fork's days were officially over and it was annexed to Antoine and Clarke townships (Minnesota; Allen 169).

Today there remains no infrastructure throughout the area that was Caney Fork except for the roughest gravel roads. The area is not inhabited and there is scarce a sign that it ever was. The land is used now for timber (and hunting). There is no electricity, nor even cell phone service in most of the area. Caney Fork no longer appears on maps; has no home places, towns or communities; and exists only as a fading memory.

William Jackson Holcomb
b. 28 Feb 1861 d. 8 Jun 1933
married
Amanda Murphy
b. 10 Jun 1864 d. 10 Mar 1955

William Jackson Holcomb must have had a difficult childhood. His father died when William was less than 10 years old (see previous chapter on Marion). From that time on he was the oldest male in the house. While it's always tragic for a child to lose his parent, it must have been particularly difficult in rural 19th century America to step up and be the "man of the house" compared to today. I imagine that William had to take on a number of very adult roles in keeping up the farm in his father's absence. The 1880, 1900, and 1910 censuses all indicate that William could not read or write. It may be that the need to work on the farm to support his family eclipsed his chances at an education. I imagine he could scarce afford the time away from daily farm work to attend school regularly. Interestingly enough, the 1920 census says he *can* read and write. This could be an error by the census taker or perhaps he took initiative to become literate in his older age.

In 1881 William married Amanda Murphy. The Murphy family lived in Dirt Town Valley next door to the Holcomb's on the 1880 census. William and Amanda had an astonishing 13 children from 1883 to 1909:

1. Bulah Dorthelia (b.13 May 1883, m.Thomas Walter Pledger, d.9 Aug 1970)
2. Effie R. (b.1 Nov 1885, m.Chelsey Gaines, d.19 Feb 1960)
3. Willie (b.9 Jun 1888, d.?)
4. Henry F. (b.5 Jul 1890, m.Emma Christian, d.14 Apr 1977)
5. George Seaborn (b.30 May 1892, m.Edna Mildred Owings, d.29 Mar 1969)
6. Thomas Deed (b.7 Apr 1894, m.Mary Mathursia Ballinger, d.18 Dec 1956)
7. Annie (b.19 Aug 1896, d.?)
8. Maude M. (b.13 Aug 1898, m.Fleming White Shropshire, d.23 Jul 1988)
9. Myrtis Holcomb (b.25 Nov 1900, m. 1st Joseph A. Drummond, 2nd Henry Wilson, d.12 Feb 1997/8)
10. Zenas Eugene (b.24 May 1903, m.Ruby Mayoma Hawkins, d.29 May 1985)
11. Lawrence (b.26 Apr 1905, m.Mabel Bryan, d.21 Jun 1964)
12. Lottie (b.26 Jan 1908, m.Thornton Bowman, d.23 Oct 1963)
13. Mattie Cecil (b.15 Dec 1909, m.Ennis Clifford Buford, d.21 Feb 1993)

Left: Amanda Murphy and William Jackson Holcomb, probably around 1910. (Collection of Michael & Rhonda Scoggins)

Right: Amanda Murphy and William Jackson Holcomb. (Collection of Dot Holcomb Scoggins)

In stark contrast to the previous Holcomb generation, it appears that all 13 of these children resided in Georgia their entire lives.

Although I never knew William or Amanda myself, I do remember the house where they lived. Something physical that belonged to or was used by an ancestor that died long before I was born always helps me visualize some aspect of that person and allows me to feel more connected.

The story of William's death was recounted to me by Joey Holcomb. It was a summer morning just like any other in 1933. Everybody was up and ready for a day's work in the cotton field. As they started out, William said, "I don't feel so good this morning. I'm gonna hold back. Y'all go ahead." He was having a dizzy spell. "Y'all go ahead and I'll meet you out there in a little while" (Holcomb).

They went to the fields and William went to the front porch and sat down, trying to catch hold of himself. He never made it out to the field that day. And when the others came back for lunch they found William sitting there on the porch, propped up in the chair, back leaning against the wall… dead.

This story has been handed down through the family. Joey, a great grandson of William, grew up in the same house where William lived and died. William died 8 Jun 1933.

Amanda, however, lived over 20 years longer than William. Joey's sister Becky has fond memories of her great grandmother, as Becky lived in the house with Amanda. Becky told me she remembers Amanda would go out into the fields of broom sage, pick what she needed, and sit down right there in the field and put together a broom. She would do all this in her long dress. Afterwards she would bring the broom back to the house and use it to sweep and clean. She also remembers the delicious cornbread Amanda made every day.

But the best memories of Amanda are best told in Becky's own words:

"I was just a little bitty girl. Grandmother, she always made sure her hair was fixed every morning. She got up and brushed and then combed her hair. It was real long. And she did it up in a ball and pinned it and everything. She would take a comb then, a big comb, and get all the hair up out of the floor. And then she would only come over on our side of the house, you know we had that big hall. So she would come on then after she got her hair combed and all. She came and she would sit down in what they called a straight chair, which was a cane bottom. And she'd sit there right by the TV and I was watching little cartoons like Howdy Doody … and Great Grandmother Holcomb would sit there and watch it with me. And

William & Amanda's Home

The house stood on Dirt Town (now Farmersville) Road in Chattooga County. The tax records for the land parcel (00079-00000-023-00A, now owned by my cousin Joey Holcomb) state that it was built in 1913. William would have been 52 at the time. Family stories say the house was built by a black man though no one knows how it came to be the Holcomb home place. The house had a metal roof, pine floors, and pine walls. In 2011 the house was in bad shape and in the process of being torn down (Chattooga Tax).

This plan of the house was drawn by my father and reflects the layout of the house as he knew it when he was a boy.

Left: The remains of the old Holcomb home place as it stood in Sep 2011. The other side of the house had already been demolished. (Photo by Jordan M. Scoggins)

Below: Amanda Murphy blows out candles on a birthday cake taken at the same spot as my photo above. One of her daughters is behind her, then next is Jewell Arthur (wife of Gene Holcomb). The others are unidentified. Early to mid-1950's. (Collection of Dot Holcomb Scoggins)

she would lean over and watch the TV. They always said, 'Good morning, how are you?' She would say, 'Good morning, I'm fine, and how are you?' I would tell her, 'Grandmother, they can't hear you, they can't see you.' She said, 'I know they can [see me]. He looked right at me and spoke to me.' She was a sweetheart, she really was" (D. Scoggins, Holcomb).

Amanda Murphy died 10 Mar 1955. Both Amanda and William are buried in Pleasant Grove Baptist Church cemetery.

Zenas Eugene Holcomb
b. 24 May 1903 d. 29 May 1985
married
Ruby Mayoma Hawkins
b. 6 Nov 1907 d. 14 Dec 1993

Above: Zenas doing what he loved most.

Opposite: Zenas worked in the Scoggins store in the late 60's/early 70's. This photo is from 1968. See more about the store on pg 171.

(Collection of Dot Holcomb Scoggins)

Zenas was born in 1903. He married Ruby Mayoma Hawkins on 6 Jan 1924 (Marriage Z.E.). Both Ruby and Zenas grew up in Dirt Town so probably knew each other at a relatively young age. Ruby had gone to school at Johnston School which was located near the northern end of Dirt Town Road (now Farmersville Road). I don't know for sure but I would guess Zenas went to this school as well.

Zenas had grown up in a very large family (he had 12 siblings), but he and Ruby had only four children (and only three survived):

1. William Eugene "Gene" (b.29 Sep 1924, m. Jewell Arthur, d.23 Dec 2008)
2. Ethel Dorthelia "Dot" (b.25 Apr 1929, m. Harold Scoggins)
3. Ruby Elizabeth (b. & d. 21 May 1939)
4. Frances Elaine Holcomb (b.21 Jun 1943, m. Jerell Teems)

The pair wasted no time, as Gene was born not quite nine months after the marriage. Gene went to school at Gore and graduated from high school there in 1943. He served in the Navy in World War II. His son Joey proudly displays his Navy portrait and other Navy memorabilia in memory of his father. Joey even has a Japanese sword Gene brought back from Japan during the war.

Dot was five years younger than Gene, born in 1929. She was the youngest child for 10 years. Her little sister to be in 1939 was Ruby Elizabeth and unfortunately did not survive. Elaine was born 4 years later, 14 years younger than Dot and 19 years younger than Gene. Since I don't know the date Gene went into the military it is possible he never even met his youngest sister until after he returned from the war.

Zenas and Ruby lived on Dirt Town Road. The house still stands today (parcel number 00079-00000-023-000) (Chattooga Tax). Built in 1929, it's a one story home with a metal roof, pine floors and walls. Originally the building had a wood exterior (it was replaced with white asbestos siding in the early 50's). There were several out buildings that made up the home place: a barn, a corn crib, a smokehouse/shed, and an outhouse (originally there was no bathroom inside). There was even an old blacksmith shop. No one alive remembers Zenas ever using the shop so it probably pre-dates his time and even the house. They never had a well and relied upon the spring at the nearby pond for water (R. & M. Scoggins, correspondence). There was no electricity until the late 1940's. The house was expanded several times over the years. First they added a second bedroom. In the early 50's they added a second room for Ruby's mother to live in. Julia had lived just down the road but after her husband died, she eventually decided she didn't want to live alone anymore. They added a room to the house for her complete with its own front door entrance. Finally, they eventually added a bathroom to the house—previously they had only had an outhouse—complete with a concrete block shower stall made by Harold Scoggins (D. Scoggins, Holcomb; R. Scoggins, correspondence).

Around 1973, Zenas and Ruby built a new house just up the road from their original home. It also still stands (parcel number 00079-00000-024-000). It must have felt luxurious to them at the time with new

carpet and tile flooring, radiant heat, and a brick exterior (Chattooga Tax). This is the home where I remember visiting my Great Grandmother Holcomb often as a child.

My father has fond memories of his grandparents:

"When we were young Eric and I would spend a week with grandmother and grandpa Holcomb. We would play from morning until dark. We always came home with chiggers all over us. One time Daddy even gave us a can of insect repellent to spray on us each day. It helped with the chiggers" (R. & M. Scoggins, correspondence).

Zenas loved baseball and always listened to baseball games on the radio. He also loved to fish, an interest he shared with my dad:

"Grandpa worked at the rug mill in Summerville then. This was before they built Lake Weis in Alabama and many Saturdays Grandpa and other men would go fishing at Scottsboro Lake in Alabama. They would leave about 4:00am in order to get there at daybreak and fish all day. They would come home after dark and clean fish outside. Grandmother would then cook some fish.

"I always wanted to go with Grandpa but I was too young then. During the day when they were gone fishing Grandmother would take me to the pond to fish. I know she didn't have the time but she took me anyway because she knew I liked to fish.

"When I was around ten Grandpa started taking me fishing a lot. We would go to different creeks or ponds and catch bream, bass, suckers and sometimes red eyed trout. He even picked me up early from school one day to go fishing. He would not take [my brother] Eric fishing because he talked and played and scared the fish. Eric didn't like to fish much.

"Grandpa liked fishing so much that after he built the pond he would come home from work and grab his fishing rod and go to the pond and catch a bass or two almost every day. He would clean them and if they didn't eat them then Grandmother would freeze them for later. She really knew how to cook fish. I guess she cooked them in lard.

"One Saturday Grandpa took me fishing to Scottsboro Lake with Si Owens, a friend of his who still lives at Gore. Grandpa always fished hard. It started raining and we kept fishing. I had a brand new cap I had bought for 15 cents I think and I didn't want it to get wet and ruined so I took it off and put it under my jacket to keep it dry. Grandpa had on a red leather hunting cap and after it started raining hard there was red streaks running down his face. Si and I laughed at him but he didn't care, he just wanted to fish. Even years later when I would see Si he would laugh about Grandpa's red face and me putting my cap under my jacket. I don't remember if we caught many fish or not.

"Once we were fishing in a lake somewhere on a boat. I held my rod back over my shoulder to throw the hook and bait into the lake and Grandpa yelled. I had hooked him in the ear with my hook. After getting the hook out he laughed and we continued fishing" (R. & M. Scoggins, correspondence).

My dad's stories about Zenas's love of fishing paint an image of a laid back man who was content to be quiet with nature. I imagine in a boat on the water, fishing rod in hand, was where Zenas was most at peace. Given the hours he sank into the hobby it was probably a meditative time for him, a time to be quiet and commune with the world around him. And when he took my father, that quiet time translated into a bonding experience beyond what words describe. Even to this day my father is a man of few words. It took me a long time to understand why my father's words to me were few and far between. But through exploring the past I have come to realize his silence is not an indication of disapproval—it's just his personality. This is probably one reason he and Grandpa Holcomb got along so well, just them and their fishing rods. Fishing provided the space—the permission, if you will—to sit together in silence and enjoy each other's company.

In 1967 my parents got hitched and the merging of the families this book is about began! Ruby was aware of the two families coming together, as my mother remembers:

"When we first married, [Ruby] would always tell me that she had family in Whitfield since she knew I was familiar with that [county] because I had family from there" (R. & M. Scoggins, correspondence).

Ruby was referring to her grandfather Andrew Clement Ward who lived the earliest part of his life in East Armuchee—where both I and my mother grew up. During the later part of Andrew's life—what Ruby would remember from her childhood—Andrew lived in Whitfield County.

The merging of the two families that my parent's marriage represents seems to have been a natural fit:

"I always felt welcomed by the Holcomb family. I even went with Mike there on Christmas Eve for their family gathering before we married. [Ruby] always enjoyed our visits when we took you and Julie. When Julie was born, I think she thought that her name was Julia [as in Ruby's mother, Julia Estella Ward—but my sister's first name was not chosen for anyone in particular]" (R. & M. Scoggins, correspondence).

Opposite, top: Dot with her second son, Eric, 1952.

Opposite, bottom: Elaine with her first son Jeff, 1962.

Left: The only known formal portrait of Zenas and Ruby,.

Below: Gene.

(Collection of Dot Holcomb Scoggins)

Zenas — Ruby

Gene
m. Jewell Arthur

Dot
m. Harold Scoggins

Elaine
m. Jerel Teems

In his later years, Zenas suffered from a number of health problems. He had some strokes and this caused him to be confined to a hospital bed which stayed in the living room of his and Ruby's home. He had surgery at Georgia Baptist Hospital in Atlanta and later at a hospital in Rome. My mother remembers once when they visited Zenas at the hospital in Rome in the early 1980's:

> "He would ask Mike to give him a cigarette, but he wasn't supposed to smoke. Some men rolled their own cigarettes [back then]. He told Mike to cut a piece off of a washcloth and Mike took his knife and did it. Grandpa started to roll it like a cigarette. Harold asked Mike, "Why did you cut that wash cloth?" Mike said, "Because Grandpa told me to" (R. & M. Scoggins, correspondence).

Zenas died on 29 May 1985, five days after his 82nd birthday. I was only 6 years old at the time so I don't remember Grandpa Holcomb that well. I can recall him sitting in the hospital bed where he stayed in their living room and that's about it. I do have a vivid memory from when Zenas died though. I remember the funeral home visitation and waiting in line with my parents to view the body. Ruby must have been there in front of us. There was an emotional display as she leaned into the casket and kissed her dead husband. I was only six years old and I had never seen anyone touch a dead body before. For that matter I may have never seen a dead body period. It must have been my first encounter with human death and it sort of freaked me out. I don't know if I said anything to my mother at the time or if my reaction was completely internal. But I remember it as if it were yesterday.

Ruby lived several years longer than her husband and I have pleasant memories of spending time at her house. She had a small bag of toys and trinkets, things like old thread spools and little wooden bowling pins, that I always looked forward to playing with. She kept them in a plastic bag in a wooden magazine holder that sat near the front door at one end of the couch. I would always go dig out the bag and spread the trinkets across the floor. Looking back they were such simple nothings, but at the time they entertained me so.

Most significantly, though, Grandmother Holcomb—as we all called her—had a dog. He was a small black dog with a bobbed tail. His name was Rounder because he always "made his rounds" around the neighborhood. I looked forward to playing with Rounder whenever we would visit.

The summer after Zenas died Ruby decided to go spend a few weeks with her daughter Elaine, who lived in South Carolina. Ruby asked us to keep Rounder while she was away. I remember keeping him and having so much fun playing with him around the farm. And I remember being so disappointed when we had to carry him back after she returned home.

Over the next few years Ruby's health began to decline. Eventually Ruby had to move out of her home and into the Oakview nursing home in Summerville. My mother remembers what it was like for Ruby:

"When Grandmother Holcomb got to where she couldn't stay by herself, sitters were hired to stay with her but none would last very long. Grandmother had some strokes after she went to the nursing home. She also fell and broke her hip while there. She also began to lose her memory. Once when we visited her, I was asking her if she knew each of us and when I called her grandmother she said, 'I'm Ruby to you—not grandmother.' I guess her memory was better than we thought at that time. When she died, I don't think she knew anyone. When she broke her hip, the nurses would tie her to her wheelchair to try to keep her from falling again and she could get it undone by herself. We called her Houdini because of that" (R. & M. Scoggins, correspondence).

My parents would take my sister and I to visit Grandmother Holcomb in the nursing home quite often. We would also visit family friend (and neighbor to my parents when they lived near Subligna) Lena Johnston. I remember the nursing home and was always a little creeped out by all the other old people who wanted to touch me and hug me. I guess maybe their own grandchildren, if they had any, didn't visit that often. Or maybe when you're confined to a nursing home day in and day out you're desperate for any kind of outside human contact you can get. There was a sadness to the home, and I felt it was unfortunate for everyone involved.

Before Ruby had moved away to the nursing home, keeping Rounder had become too much of a burden. I proudly adopted him. Rounder became not only my best friend growing up but a constant link back to my great grandmother. Even after Ruby died Rounder would be there with me for many years, an extension of Ruby's presence in my life.

Ruby "Houdini" died 14 Dec 1993. It was hard to escape the grief that Christmas. Rounder died 17 Aug 1997.

Opposite: Zenas poses for a photo with Elaine, c.1943. Ruby & Zenas celebrate their 50th anniversary. L to R: Dot, Elaine, Ruby, Zenas, and Gene. 1974. (Collection of Dot Holcomb Scoggins)

Above, left: A portrait of Ruby, late 1980's or early 1990's. (Collection of Dot Holcomb Scoggins)

Above, right: Rounder was my constant companion growing up. 1992. (Collection of Michael & Rhonda Scoggins)

HAWKINS, WARD, KEOWN and CAVENDER families
(and PURYEAR, HUNT, CLEMENTS, and PARK too)

HAWKINS

The Hawkins and Ward families connect through my great grandmother Ruby Mayoma Hawkins. Her parents were Zechariah Roy Hawkins and Julia Estella Ward (my 2nd great grandparents). They lived on Dirt Town Road in one of the first brick homes built in the area (still standing today on parcel number 00073-00000-040-000) (Chattooga Tax).

Zechariah was the son of Joseph W. Hawkins and Elizabeth Lancaster Wilbanks. Joseph was 34 and Elizabeth was only 16 when they were married in 1879. They were living in Chattooga County, where they remained for the rest of their life.

Zechariah's wife was Julia Estella Ward. They were married around 1902. Both were born and lived in Georgia their entire lives. They are laid to rest in Pleasant Grove Baptist Church cemetery. Through Julia this line connects into the Ward, Keown, and Cavender families. Julia's parents were Andrew Clement Ward and Martha Ann Keown. Martha Ann Keown's mother was Julia Ann Cavender.

WARD

The Ward line, as far back as I have been able to trace, is rooted in Spartenburg, SC. James Ward, born about 1755 in Amherst, VA, appears on the census in Spartenburg in 1790, 1800, 1810, and 1820. He was married to Susannah (Anna) in 1770 and died just prior to 17 Jan 1826 (Hair 57-61).

James's son Nathan Ward was born about 1772. He also married a Susannah (her surname was Trail). Nathan and Susannah were married in 1789.

Tracking Nathan Ward based on census records can be quite confusing. The census records for Spartanburg and Union Counties during this time period show three

Above: Joseph W. Hawkins and wife Elizabeth. Probably late 19th century. (Collection of Karen Willingham)
Opposite: An outbuilding on the Zechariah Hawkins home place, Sep 2011. (Photo by Jordan M. Scoggins)

Joseph
HAWKINS
b.28 Dec 1845 in GA or NC
d.19 Dec 1918 in Georgia

↓

Zechariah
b.23 Sep 1881 in Georgia
d.15 Oct 1947 in Georgia

↓

Ruby
b.6 Nov 1907 in Georgia
d.Dec 1993v in Georgia

↓

my grandmother Ethel Dorthelia, my father Michael and then me

different Nathan Wards. An examination of the ages helps to decipher who is who. Fortunately, Thomas Lee Hair has done substantial research on the Ward family in his book, *The Long Journey: A Family History 1687 to 1991*. Hair's work clarifies my Ward lineage in spite of the confusion presented by the censuses.

Nathan and Susannah lived out their lives in Union County. Nathan last appears on the 1840 census and is presumed dead by 1850. Susannah also likely died during this decade.

Nathan and Susannah had a number of children, all of which have not been traced. Fortunately, the son through whom I descend is documented. Absalom Ward is my 5th great grandfather. He was born 24 Jan 1799 in Union County, SC, and married Nancy Ann Coleman on 27 Sep 1820. Nancy was the daughter of Robert Coleman who was, according to Robert A. Ivey writing in *Union County Heritage*, a Revolutionary War soldier. They were members of the Gilead Baptist Church in Jonesville and resided in Union County until their death (Marby 293-4).

My 4th great grandfather is Alfred C. Ward, born 15 Apr 1822. He was the oldest son of Absalom and Nancy. Alfred married Delila Brown in 1847. Some time after 1850 they migrated to East Armuchee in Walker County, GA. Writes Evelyn Elizabeth Morgan (who married Maxwell Shahan):

> "Alfred … was the only one of that family to leave Union Co., SC. … They came with his wife's parents, William and Nancy Brown. The Brown family settled in Chattooga Co. GA close to Alfred and Delilah in Walker Co. GA a bordering county (Walker Heritage 406)."

Evelyn continues the story with how Alfred and Delila settled on the west side of John's Mountain in East Armuchee. They came from South Carolina in a covered wagon. At one point the wagon turned over going up John's Mountain and out rolled their walnut bureau. The bureau survived but one of the knobs was broken. That bureau survives still today in the home of Evelyn's daughter Judy. Judy was kind enough to share photos of the bureau with me, as well as a photo of Delila Brown herself.

Opposite page: Crayon portrait of the Hawkins family, c.1908. Back row: Julia Estella Ward holding Ruby Mayoma, Zachariah Hawkins. Front row: Viola, Russel, Louella, Roy. (Collection of Dot Scoggins)

Above left: Three generations together, taken in the mid-1940's. L to R: Ruby Mayoma Hawkins, Julia Estella Ward, Ethel Dorthelia Holcomb, and Elaine Holcomb's head at the bottom. (Collection of Dot Scoggins)

Above right: Zechariah Hawkins with wife Julia Estella Ward, c.1920's. (Collection of Michael & Rhonda Scoggins)

Evelyn wrote of the handiwork of the Wards and the "many beautiful handmade quilts and woven coverlids" (Walker Heritage 406).

In the chapter on Micajah Pope (beginning on pg 20) I wrote about the Yankee soldiers coming through Villanow during the Civil War. Like the Popes the Wards too were impacted by the war. Alfred Ward, who was very familiar with the terrain, assisted the troops by leading them through the area. I do not know how he got involved. Perhaps he supported the Union, or perhaps he was drafted into service because of his knowledge. But the story goes that due to being out in the cold and wet weather, Alfred contracted pneumonia and died. He was buried on the Ward homestead on John's Mountain and due to continual rains it was difficult to find solid ground. Delila is buried at East Armuchee Baptist Church.

I will note here that Evelyn's description of Alfred's tombstone in the *Heritage* book seems a bit confused. She describes it as "a tall spire monument." I visited the grave in 2010 and the stone is a large, flat slab. Delila's stone at East Armuchee however *is* a tall spire. Likely the description somehow got reversed, a simple error.

Andrew Clement Ward was the middle child of Alfred and Delila. He was born 24 Jan 1858. Andrew is an interesting figure because of the locations he lived. He grew up in East Armuchee, the same area where my mother and I were raised. There he married his wife Martha Ann Keown (oldest child of Nathaniel Alexander Keown and Julia Ann Cavender). According to the Georgia 1890 Property Tax Digests, some time after 1880 they had relocated to Tunnel Hill in Whitfield County, the general area of my paternal grandfather's family! They appear in Subligna, Chattooga County on the 1900 census. Subligna is where my father was raised. By 1910 Andrew was counted again in Whitfield County Andrew lived there until his death on 17 Feb 1931. Martha Ann died in 1904 and Andrew later married Margaret Elizabeth Carpenter (they did not have children together).

PURYEAR and HUNT

There are also connections to two other Armuchee Valley family lines: the Puryear and Hunt families. The Puryears are mentioned at a few points throughout this book (see the index) in subtle but interesting ways.

Above: portrait of Delilah Brown, wife of Alfred Ward. (Collection of Judy Blackstock)

James
WARD
b.abt 1755 in Virginia
d.17 Jan 1826 in South Carolina

↓

Nathan
b.abt 1772 in Virginia
d.abt 1845 in South Carolina

↓

Absalom
b.24 Jan 1799 in South Carolina
d.9 Jun 1878 in South Carolina

↓

Alfred
b.15 Apr 1822 in South Carolina
d.18 Nov 1869 in Georgia

↓

Andrew
b.Jan 1858 in Georgia
d.17 Feb 1931

↓

my 2nd great grandmother Julia, my great grandmother Ruby, my grandmother Dot, my father Michael and then me

Alfred C. Ward's youngest child, Nancy Elizabeth Ward, married Hamilton Young Puryear.

The Puryear family is also closely aligned with the Hunt family—the Puryear & Hunt store is a prime example (see pg 140). The Hunt family also connects with the Wards. Another of Alfred C. Ward's sons was John Anderson Ward. John's daughter Georgia married Joseph Underwood Hunt. Although Georgia was still alive when I was a child (and lived only a short walk down the road from the house where I grew up), I do not remember her. She was a progressive woman for her era and became the first woman in Walker County to obtain a master's degree.

Georgia's only son was Joseph Louis Hunt. Growing up he was my neighbor and in his later years—right up until his death—he farmed the land owned by my parents. I remember him well growing up. He was true farmer folk and represents the last vestige of a distant era. I spoke to him in May 2010, when I was in the extremely early stages of this book project. He was very interested in the work I was doing and in fact helped me locate the grave of Alfred C. Ward. The lone grave stands on private property nestled in the foothills of John's Mountain. He made the phone calls and helped me find the location and get permission to see the grave. I would not have found it without his help.

I am also related to Louis through his father's line. Louis's grandfather is Benjamin Franklin Hunt (b.21 Oct 1958). B.F. is the famed minister of the Armuchee Valleys (and beyond), having been the first pastor and a charter member of East Armuchee Baptist Church. He was also a founding member of Subligna Baptist Church. B.F.'s mother is Susan Robbs, sister of my 3rd great grandmother Emily Robbs. See pg 65 for my direct line connection to the Robbs.

The last time I spoke with Louis was in Nov 2010. He anticipated my book and urged me, "Jordan, now you finish that book before I'm gone. I want to see that book when it's done."

Louis died 10 May 2011. He didn't get to see this book. For that I am saddened. But I do hope he is somewhere afar looking at it now. Maybe as I write this he's an angel standing by, guiding me through, helping me finish it up before the next character in *Jordan's Journey* joins him.

Below, left: Me at the grave of Alfred C. Ward, Nov 2010. (Photo by Michael D. Scoggins)

Below, right: Delila Brown's tombstone at East Armuchee Cemetery, Jun 2009. (Photo by Jordan M. Scoggins)

James A. KEOWN
b. abt 1744 in Ireland
d. abt 1816 in South Carolina

↓

Alexander
b. 1783 in South Carolina
d. 22 Aug 1822 in South Carolina

↓

James A.
b. 5 Jan 1811 in South Carolina
d. 15 Oct 1887 in Georgia

↓

Nathaniel
b. 29 Dec 1831 in South Carolina
d. 1 Apr 1901 in Georgia

↓

Martha Ann
b. 15 Oct 1853 in Georgia
d. 2 Dec 1904 in Georgia

↓

my 2nd great grandmother Julia, my great grandmother Ruby, my grandmother Dot, my father Michael and then me

KEOWN

The Keown side is traced back to Ireland. James Alexander Keown was born about 1744 in County Down, Ulster Province, Ireland. He would have immigrated some time before 1779 as he is counted on the state census for that year in South Carolina (and again in 1783 and 1790). He was married to Margaret Peggy Daniels and died about 1816.

James's and Margaret's son Alexander was born about 1783. He married Elizabeth Puthuff. Some claim that Elizabeth was Cherokee (or at least half Cherokee). I have seen no documentation to support or deny this claim so it is impossible to say. Perhaps this information was handed down through the generations by oral tradition. Supposedly Elizabeth was adopted and raised by the Lusk family (which she then gave as the middle name to two of her children). But, again, here I have found no actual documentation on this detail.

Alexander died at only 39 years old. Elizabeth never remarried and somewhat unusually for a woman at the time (at least as far as I have

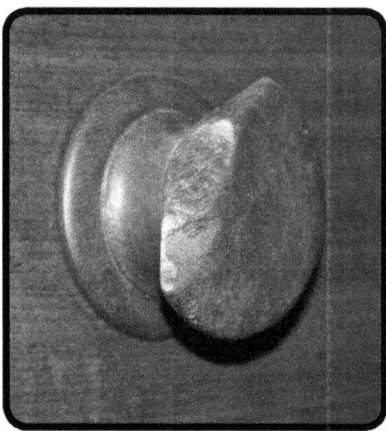

Left: Photos of the chest (with broken knob) used by Delila Brown and Alfred C. Ward (see pg 215). (Collection of Judy Blackstock)

Right: A crayon portrait of Andrew Clement Ward and Martha Ann Keown. (Collection of Dot Scoggins)

Above: The Rufus Richardson family, circa 1895. L to R: Callie, Alice, Rufus [father], Ollie, Minerva Jane Keown [mother], John Newton, W.J. "Buddy" (Collection of Martha Delle Grigsby Richardson)

Opposite: Minerva Jane Keown as an old woman with her great granddaughter Delores Jane Richardson, 1950. (Collection of Martha Delle Grigsby Richardson)

encountered in my family tree) she appears on the 1830 (in Lancaster, South Carolina) and 1840 (in Walton, Georgia) census as the head of the house. By 1850 she had settled in East Armuchee, where at least five of her children were living as well. Elizabeth and her daughter Sarah are living together. Jane Lusk with her married surname Price is listed next door to Elizabeth as a widow with three children. Nathan Lusk is also next door with his family. Isaac Newton too is in East Armuchee with his family. And, finally, James Alexander—my 5th great grandfather—is counted there as well.

Isaac Newton married Sarah Jane Davis. Their oldest child was Minerva Jane Keown. Minerva lived to be 102 years old and is something of a local legend in East Armuchee. Through her I have a connection to the Richardson family as she married James Rufus Richardson (son of John Jefferson Richardson and grandson of Moses Richardson. See pg 147). Rufus and Minerva were charter members of East Armuchee Baptist Church (East Armuchee). Their son Oliver had a son named James Grady who I knew growing up. He was married to Martha Delle Grigsby, a dear woman who I have such fond memories of. Even my mother says that Martha Delle was like a mother to her growing up. Little did mom know there would be a very distant family tie between Martha Delle and my mom's future husband. This proves that the idea of family is not just about similar DNA but also about the people you share your life with. Martha Delle's granddaughter Shannon was one of my friends growing up in East Armuchee. At the time I

Good Neighbor Plan Would End Wars, 100-Year-Old Walker Woman Believes
The Chattanooga Times, 1950

VILLANOW, Ga., Dec. 3—A beloved Walker County greag-great-grandmother, who celebrated her 100th birthday at home here yesterday, has a plan for permanent world peace and individual happiness.

"Folks have quit being good neighbors all over the world," gracious, white-haired Mrs. Minerva Jane Richardson told a large group at her birthday dinner. "That's the reason for so many wars, so much trouble. People don't take time to know each other any more. They're running after something all the time.

"We are living in strange times," Mrs. Richardson said with emphasis, "and there is not much hope unless people change. When you have a lot of friends and are a good neighbor, you can be happy even without much of the world's goods."

Recalling events of her life with amazing clarity, Mrs. Richardson, who can walk with a cane and handles her own correspondence, still frowns at the mention of the Yankees. Of the Union troops in Sherman's march to the sea, she said:

"They came through East Armuchee and took everything we had. We didn't have a thing to eat from Sunday until Tuesday. And to cap the stack one of the buglers found our syrup barrel and filled his bugle full. Then he took our only mirror and when I asked him not to break it, he threw it at me and broke it against the door."

Her husband was the late J.R. Richardson, who fought with the Army of Northern Virginia in the 11th Georgia Regiment, Anderson's Brigade. She is the granddaughter of the late Mr. and Mrs. Newton Keown, pioneer settles of Walker County, who migrated from South Carolina.

"The happiest time of my youth," Mrs. Richardson recalled, "was the 21-day trip by covered wagon to Mississippi. We just lived there a year and came back to East Armuchee because mother was sick."

Asked what her formula for long life included, Mrs. Richardson quipped: "Eat anything you want. I've never used anything stronger than coffee, but now I drink soft drinks because the doctor says it's all right."

Scientific progress has both amazed and frightened Mrs. Richardson, especially in the past few years, she said. She thinks the automobile is "fine when you drive slow," but the airplane is "too fast unless you have to get to some of your folks who are sick."

Mrs. Richardson lived in the same house for more than 60 years, and moved to the home of her son, J. Ollie Richardson, in the valley four years ago, after the death of a bachelor son, John. She has 21 grandchildren, 29 great-grandchildren and five great-great-grandchildren.

Most of the grandchildren were among some 250 persons who have visited her since Sunday.

Mrs. Richardson lived with her daughter, Mrs. John Hames, in East Lake, Chattanooga, for approximately one year. She soon tired of city life and preferred to return to her birthplace in the fertile East Armuchee Valley.

never even knew she was a distant cousin!

And just as complicated as those strands of DNA, Martha Delle's father is William Rice Grigsby, whose father is William David Grigsby, whose father is John Grigsby, who married Eleander Chapman. (Phew, not only does my brain hurt writing about this but I kind of feel out of breath!) Eleander's brother is William Jack Chapman who married Clarissa Lawrence. William Jack and Clarissa are my third great grandparents on my paternal grandfather's side (they are the parents of Drucilla Chapman, see pg 146), where all these connections to the Ward and Keown families are through my paternal grandmother's side!

Finally, stepping back just a bit to James Alexander Keown again, we can bring this full circle. James's son Nathaniel Alexander married Julia Ann Cavender on 15 Aug 1854. They were both charter members of East Armuchee Baptist Church (East Armuchee).

Nathaniel served the Confederacy, enlisting in Co C, GA 60th Infantry Regiment, on 3 May 1862 in LaFayette, GA. During his service he was in and out of the hospital several times, first admitted to hospital on 5 Jul. He was again admitted, this time at the CSA Post Hospital in Dalton, GA, on 15 Oct with chronic rheumatism. He was fighting again by Dec at the latest and was wounded at Fredericksburg on 13 Dec. He was sent to Chimborazo Hospital in Richmond, 21 years old at the time. In Jan and Feb of 1863 he is marked as being home sick on furlough but is counted present again by the Mar/Apr roll. The regiment fought again at Fredericksburg on 3 May where Nathaniel was again wounded. Not his lucky city, needless to say. He was sent to Howard's Grove Hospital in Richmond and later transferred to the hospital at Camp Winder. By Sep/Oct he is marked present again but in Nov/Dec he is absent—though this time not due to injury. Starting 5 Dec, Nathaniel was detailed as a shoemaker for the CSA in Richmond. He was paid $3 a day for his work and is counted in this role through at least Aug 1864. My guess is that his rheumatism made fighting difficult and a job as shoemaker was something he could be more productive at. The Rebels, after all, couldn't all run around barefoot (Service Records Keown).

In spite of his numerous hospital visits, Nathaniel did survive the war. He outlived his wife Julia who died 28 Feb 1884. Nathaniel remarried to Pricellia Clementine Maloney, having one child. He died 1 Apr 1901.

Nathaniel and Pricellia are both buried in Macedonia Cemetery in Villanow. Julia Ann's grave is recorded in *Walker County Georgia Cemeteries* in the Old Ben Hill Pope Cemetery (named so because it was located on the farm owned by Ben Hill—a great grandfather on my mom's side. See pg 43). The cemetery was surveyed by Evelyn Morgan and Georgia Ward in Fall 1967. The graves are up on a hill just down the road from where I grew up. I remember hiking there on more than one occasion as a child—but I never knew who exactly was buried there. My father and I visited the cemetery in 2011 and could not locate Julia Ann's tombstone. We could only find remnants of two Kinsey graves. In the middle of the woods and badly overgrown, the cemetery is all but lost to the ages. One of the two visible markers is even overturned. I am grateful for Evelyn and Georgia's work to document who is laid to rest there.

Nathaniel and Julia's oldest child Martha Ann Keown brings us to the Ward family—where this all started!—with her husband Andrew Clement.

But… you guessed it: there's more! If you've learned nothing else, know that nothing is ever simple. James Alexander also had a daughter named Mary Ann Amanda Keown. Mary Ann was the widow of T.B. Williams who died in the Civil War, serving in the same company and regiment as her second husband (Historical, Soldiers & U.S.; National Park Service). Through this second husband, Madison Green Clement, Mary Ann connects into one of the family lines on my maternal grandmother's side of the family from the first half of this book. It was also a second marriage for Madison and I descend through his first wife. This makes Mary Ann my step 3rd great grandmother on my mother's side as well as my 4th great grand aunt on my father's side! See page 58 for details on the Clement family line.

Above: My father at the Old Ben Hill Pope Cemetery, Nov 2011.

Opposite: Detail of the Villanow store, May 2010

(Photos by Jordan M. Scoggins)

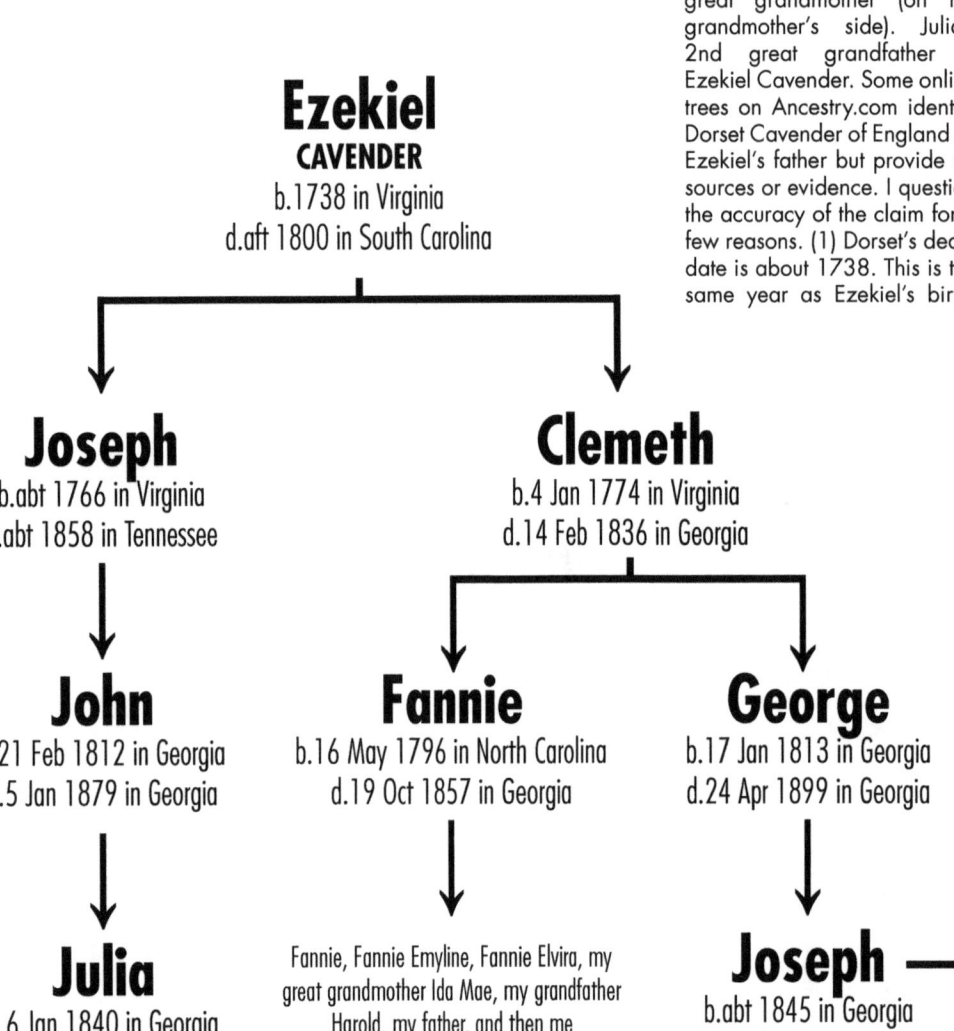

CAVENDER

The Cavender line comes into play a couple of different ways.

Julia Ann Cavender is my 4th great grandmother (on my grandmother's side). Julia's 2nd great grandfather is Ezekiel Cavender. Some online trees on Ancestry.com identify Dorset Cavender of England as Ezekiel's father but provide no sources or evidence. I question the accuracy of the claim for a few reasons. (1) Dorset's death date is about 1738. This is the same year as Ezekiel's birth. This is obviously not impossible but does present cause for question. (2) Supposedly Dorset died in Maryland and Ezekiel was born in Virginia. Again, this is not impossible but raises suspicion given the proposed dates. Therefore I present Dorset as a cautious option here, a possible guess on the origins of my Cavender ancestors. If Dorset is not the person specifically the Cavenders still likely originate from England. Hopefully more light can be shed upon these origins one day.

Ezekiel is counted on the 1800 census in Pendleton District, SC. He appears to have died some time after that but before the 1810 census. Although there is an 1810 census for an Ezekiel Cavender in Pendleton District, there is no one on the census that falls into the proper age category. Either Ezekiel was still alive and his age was recorded incorrectly or this could be a son (though I have seen no evidence that he has a son named Ezekiel). A mystery!

Ezekiel's son Joseph W., born 1766 in Virginia, married Miriam Henry. They ended up in Maury County, TN. They had many children but Julia Ann descends through Joseph's son John H. John was born 12 Feb 1812. His 1860 and 1870 census records state he was born in Georgia, but the U.S. Federal Mortality Schedule in Walker County says he was born in Kentucky! He married Francis Dyer in 1837 (also listed as born in Kentucky in the 1860, 1870, and 1880 census while the 1900 census states she was born in Virginia). The 1840 census finds them in Paulding County, GA. This is probably where Julia Ann was born as she was born 6 Jan 1840.

By 1850 the Cavenders had settled in East Armuchee, as evidenced by John's slave schedule for that year (Ancestry.com, 1850 Slave). This is where he remained and raised his family. They would have arrived in the area during the period when the last of the Cherokees were being removed. John and his brother Wade "enlisted in Captain Farris's Company of the Georgia Highland Militia, and helped the army permanently remove the Indians from their mountainous North Georgia homes"). Not all aspects of family history are something to be proud of.

John died of paralysis on 5 Jan 1879. Francis lived at least two more decades, still in East Armuchee on the 1900 census living with her daughter Winnie.

Another connection comes in on my grandfather's line. Fannie Cavender, my 5th great grandmother on that side, is a daughter of Clemeth Cavender. Clemeth is the brother of Joseph (b.1766). These two brothers are both my 6th great grandfather on two different family lines. This also

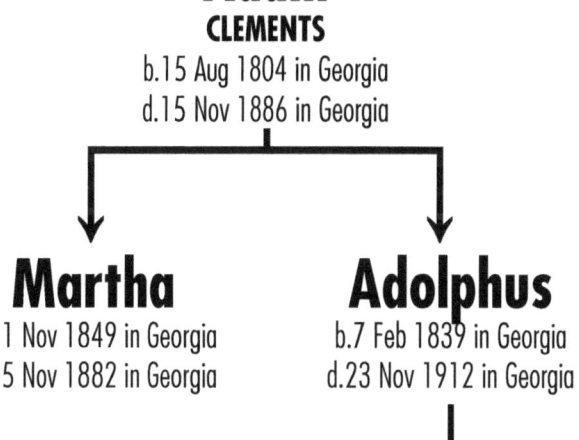

Above: Making my way through the field to the Cavender Cemetery, May 2010. (Photo by Michael D. Scoggins)

Adam
CLEMENTS
b.15 Aug 1804 in Georgia
d.15 Nov 1886 in Georgia

Martha
b.11 Nov 1849 in Georgia
d.15 Nov 1882 in Georgia

Adolphus
b.7 Feb 1839 in Georgia
d.23 Nov 1912 in Georgia

Charles who married Mary Ethel Clement, daughter of J.C. Clement (see page 58 for more about that family)

makes their father Ezekiel my 7th great grandfather in two different ways!

The most recent Cavenders in my lines, Julia Ann (my 4th great grandmother) and Fannie (my 5th great grandmother), are first cousins once removed to each other.

Even though the blood connection is on my father's side of the family, The Cavenders are a prominent family in Villanow history—a history that I long associate with my mother's side but it is just as much my father's heritage as well.

The most well known Cavender in Villanow is Joseph Warren Cavender (b.1845). Joseph descends through his father George Washington Cavender, brother of Fannie and son of Clemeth. Through Fannie, Joseph is my first cousin six times removed. Through Julia Ann, Joseph is also my second cousin six times removed.

J.W. is most commonly known as the merchant who ran the Villanow store longer than anyone else in its history (Williams). In a 6 Apr 1893 piece from the Walker County Messenger, J.W. is referred to as "the Mayor of our prosperous little city" of Villanow. Speaking of Cavender's store, the writer said J.W. "knows just what the people want and is ever ready to accommodate all who apply to him" (Grigsby, Transcriptions). Read more about the store starting on page 32. During the Civil War J.W. served as a Sergeant in Cos F and B of Georgia's Phillips's Legion (National Park Service). J.W. and his wife, Martha Almina Clements, are buried in the Cavender Cemetery just north of Villanow.

CLEMENTS and PARK

The Clements and Park families are closely allied with my direct family line. Though I do not descend from anyone in either family I have included them here because there are distant and interesting connections on both sides of my family.

On my father's side the Cavender family is the connection. Joseph W. Cavender (b.abt 1845) married Martha Almina Clements in 1869. On both the 1870 and 1880 census Joseph and Martha are living with Martha's parents, Adam Clements and Mary Wilson Hill Park.

On 2 Nov 1892 Martha gave birth to her second son, Joseph. Probably due to complications from that birth she died 15 Nov 1882 at only 33 years of age. The infant Joseph died not a month later on

9 Dec. Martha was buried in a family cemetery just north of Villanow, standing close by to present day ruins of the old Adolphus (her brother) home. This may have been the house where Martha and Joseph lived with her parents and Adolphus moved in after Martha's death. This is difficult to trace since Adam died in 1886 and Mary died in 1892 and the 1890 census is not available. The last home Adolphus lived in was located on the present day Edwards Sod Farm off highway 136 just west of Villanow. The house still stands today and according to the Walker County Tax Assessor web site that home, standing on parcel number 0561 009, was built in 1873 (I believe Adolphus was not the original owner) (Walker Tax).

Another child of Adam and Mary is James Wilson Clements. Though born in Villanow, J.W. became more associated with Subligna in Chattooga County later in life. There he practiced medicine for many years and in the 1930's was "the oldest active physician in Georgia" (Baker 693). The oldest child of Adam and Mary, Julius Park Clements, was also a physician (Baker 693; Fleming).

This family group even connects into my mother's family in a distant manner. Adolphus's son Charles

Above: The Adolphus Clements family, c.1885, just north of Villanow. L to R: Charlie, Nancy Elvira Phillips, Claudius, Mary, Adolphus, and Ella holding baby Nonnie. (Collection of Charles Clements)

Opposite, top: A portrait of Adolphus Clements. (Collection of Charles Clements)

Opposite, bottom: The ruins of the Adolphus Clements house (above) only steps away from the Cavender Cemetery (previous page), Feb 2011. (Photo by Jordan M. Scoggins)

married Mary Ethel Clement, daughter of J.C. Clement (the Clement and Clements lines are not related; see page 58 about the Clement line). I visited Charles and Mary's son Charles (b.1926) in Feb 2011. He shared several family photos with me, including an image of Adolphus's family in front of the house near the family cemetery already mentioned.

There is one more distant connection through Martha Almina Clement's mother Mary Wilson Hill Park. Mary was the daughter of James Park and Martha Yandell. James descends from the Revolutionary War veteran Moses Park (b.28 Nov 1738, d.10 May 1828) (Ancestry.com, U.S. Sons). Mary's brother Thomas Yandell Park had a son named Bryant Robert. Bryant had a son Bryant Lawson. Finally Bryant Lawson's son is Robert Park. Robert married June Elizabeth Pope... a familiar surname for sure! June, daughter of Santa Orville Pope and Battie Lee Smith, is the granddaughter of Ben Hill Pope (see his chapter on pg 43). June is my 1st cousin once removed on my mom's side of the family. The relationship to Robert is extremely distant on my father's side (coming only through marriages in the Park, Clements, and Cavender lines) but is pretty wild to contemplate none-the-less!

Ethel Dorthelia Holcomb
b. 25 Apr 1929
married
Harold Wallace Scoggins
b. 26 Feb 1924 d. 13 Mar 2000

Ethel Dorthelia Holcomb, known as simply "Dot" to her friends and family, was born at home on 25 Apr 1929. She grew up on Dirt Town Road which was indeed dirt (it was not paved until the early 1950's).

Dot rode the school bus every day to Gore. Some of her teachers at Gore were Mr. & Mrs. Pankersley, Ms. Weesner, Mr. Hyatt, and Ms. Byrd. Her favorite subjects were English/spelling and Home Ec. She also played on the basketball team. When I asked Dot about this in 2011 her voice lit up at the mention of basketball, "Oh, I loved to play basketball. I was a forward. And we had a good time–we won most of the games!" The school also had a softball team in the summertime which Dot also enjoyed. She graduated from Gore in 1946. The next year Dot would meet Harold for the first time. In 2009 she recorded to tape the story about their courtship. This is my retelling of that story:

Summer, 1947. Harold was taking a break from the summer heat on the steps of E.B. Self's store in Subligna when two girls came by. It was Frankie Dawson and a young woman he didn't know. The unknown lady caught his eye.

"Well hello," Frankie greeted Harold.

"Hey there, Frankie."

"This is my friend Dot."

"Nice to meet you, Dot. I'm Harold."

"Nice to meet you." She had never seen him before.

"What have you young ladies been up to?"

"Oh we just came from the funeral at the Methodist church. It's so hot out so we thought we'd come get a cold drink," Frankie explained.

The three made conversation. But Frankie and Dot grew thirsty and soon went in to buy the drinks they had come for and left.

***

A few days later, Dot was at home tending to her chores as usual. She brought in wood for the stove while her parents were out at the crib shucking corn. A log truck drove up and parked at the foot of the hill. It was Harold. He had been thinking about Dot ever since the day he met her at Self's store. After finishing work with his father at the sawmill that day he decided to finally call

Above, top: An elementary school portrait of Dot (Collection of Dot Holcomb Scoggins)
Above, bottom: Dot dresses up for a high school event. (Collection of Joey Holcomb)

Right: Dot's high school junior year portrait, 1945. (Collection of Dot Holcomb Scoggins)

on Dot that afternoon. He got out of the truck and started up the hill to the house.

"Daddy's down at the crib shucking corn," Dot shouted from the door, mistaking Harold for someone there to see her father.

But Harold made his way on up to the house. "I didn't come to see daddy," he replied. "I came to see you."

Dot blushed. She chatted with Harold for a while and eventually he asked her for a date.

"Well, I don't guess they'll let me go," Dot flirted.

"But you haven't asked them, now have you?"

Dot played hard-to-get and repeated herself.

"But you haven't asked them," Harold persisted.

Finally she gave in and started down the hill. Harold followed.

"Harold wants me to go somewhere with him tonight," she announced through the cracks in the crib.

"Well, are ya gon go?" her mother replied.

Taken aback that her parents hadn't challenged her, Dot almost didn't know what to say. Harold tried not to giggle at this grown woman—out of high school and of age to make her own decisions—who still went to her parents as if she were a little girl. Though he was pleased when she said yes.

Harold went home to clean up from a day at the sawmill. Dot cleaned up from her chores. And that night they went on their first date.

* * *

Next morning when Dot got up, her mama asked, "Well, how'd ya like him?"

"Oh, he's all right but he's too old for me."

Dot had only just graduated high school but Harold had been in college for a while and he had been in the war for three years. So to Dot the age difference seemed much more than it really was. She couldn't quite envision a future with him, and didn't even know if she would ever see him again.

But a few nights later she did see him. Harold came back to ask her for another date. And, of course, she went. They went to Harold's friends, Betty and Glenn Orr.

There were many more dates after that. More often than not they ended up at Betty and Glynn's every time. Usually they would all eat dinner together. Sometimes they'd make sandwiches and sometimes they'd go to the store and pick something up to eat. But they just about always ate over there.

One time when they were heading to Betty and Glynn's it was pouring rain outside. Harold pulled the car up but they would have to make a dash for the house and probably still get wet.

"Think you can make it?" he said.

Dot may be a farm girl but she always looks pretty for the camera, mid 1940's.
(Collection of Dot Holcomb Scoggins)

"Boy I don't know. Look at those huge puddles out there! It's like we're parked in the middle of a lake. If I fall in one of those puddles it'll just ruin my dress!"

Harold didn't hear her. He was already out of the car, heading around to Dot's side. He threw open the door and swept her into his arms.

Dot stiffened. Not because she didn't like it—she did—but they had only been dating a short time. His arms had never been around her like that before.

Harold struggled to move through the sheets of water, trying to keep her dry. "Now limber up a little bit or I'm gonna drop you," he laughed. Harold's laughter helped and Dot relaxed a bit. She could just see herself falling out of his arms, splashing into the puddles dress and all.

But Harold made it. He got her into the house. She wasn't completely dry—that would have been impossible—but she was dry enough. And she liked the feeling of Harold's arms around her.

***

Autumn rolled around and Harold and Dot had been dating two or three months. They had spent most dates hanging out at Betty and Glenn's, always having a good time just being together. One night as Harold was driving Dot home he asked the question.

"What would you say if I asked you to marry me?"

"Well, you've talked about me being so young all the time... I guess that's what I'd say: I'm too young to get married!"

And though it wasn't a traditional proposal, the intent was set.

***

They planned a small church wedding for 8 Feb after the new year. Harold wanted to get married at church but Dot didn't have a lot of money to do things up nice. In fact, she had just had her teeth fixed recently and owed 16 dollars towards her dental work. She didn't have any cash to spend on a fancy wedding. But that didn't matter. They would wear normal Sunday clothes and not even splurge for a bouquet of flowers. Even so Harold wanted to make sure it was special. He got together with Aleta White—one of the local teachers at Subligna school—and made candle holders. They used dowel rods cut about four feet high with Coke bottle lids on the top to hold tapers. The simple, do-it-yourself candles helped make an understated but memorable ceremony.

The church glowed with Coca-Cola candlelight as Dot's brother Gene walked her down the aisle. Harold stood at the front of the church waiting for his bride. When she got to him Harold reached for her hand and it was like holding a chunk of ice. It was so cold that day the gas had frozen up in the church. But it didn't matter. The couple had all the warmth they needed as their hearts were joined. Frances Padget and Harold's older sister, Margaret Scoggins, were Dot's attendants. Dot's parents weren't there that day. She didn't think they would come so she just didn't ask them. Preacher Beavis performed the service.

After the wedding they went across the road to Harold's parents. It wasn't a formal reception but Mrs. Scoggins baked a couple of cakes for the bride and groom and their wedding party and a few other friends. It was an intimate gathering.

As the celebration came to a close and Harold and Dot prepared to head off for their honeymoon, Preacher Beavis whispered to Dot, "I'm gonna put you in the car because these boys have got some things they're gonna do to you if we don't get you in the car."

They quietly shuffled out the door. Preacher Beavis put Dot's suitcase in the back seat then helped her into the passenger seat. Out of nowhere Harold's cousin Don appeared and jumped in the drivers seat while Helen Owens and Wheeler Manis hopped in the back seat.

"Floor it!" Wheeler said.

Don hit the gas and swerved out the driveway before Dot could even realize what was going on.

"What on earth are y'all doing?" Dot screamed.

"It's your weddin' day, Dot. We're just taking good care of you, that's all!"

"Taking care of me?!"

She looked at Helen in the back seat, hoping for some feminine sympathy. But she just reached into Dot's suitcase and wadded up her clothes, wrinkled them real good and jokingly stuck her tongue out.

In a huff Dot turned back to face the road. She begged again, "Please, just take me back. Take me back right now!" But Don kept driving, Dot kept having a fit, and Helen and Wheeler kept laughing. By the time they got to Gore—they'd taken Dot all the way to the other end of the valley—Dot had just about had it. She was exhausted.

"Well, I guess we'll turn around and go back. But Doc was gonna carry Harold off in the other direction so he's probably not there anyway," Don teased.

But back at the Scoggins home Doc had not been so successful with his end of the joke. By the time Don got back, Dot stumbled out of the car as fast as she could and burst through the front door. Harold and Doc were on the couch. You could see the fumes steaming off Harold in the winter chill.

"Are you all right?" he hugged Dot. "They'd been drinking—I was worried something was going to happen."

"Oh, I'm fine." Dot wasn't going to give the boys any satisfaction. "Those crazy boys trying to mess up our day. They're just jealous is all!"

The newlyweds drove to Chattanooga, where Harold had booked a room for their honeymoon. At long last it would be just the two of them, Mr. & Mrs. Harold Scoggins.

But the next day the phone rang. Harold answered.

"What was that about?" Dot asked.

"It's Doc. He and a bunch of the others are downstairs. They want me to come down."

Above: Dot & Harold pose for photos on their honeymoon, Feb 1947. (Collection of Dot Holcomb Scoggins)

"Oh, Harold, no. Don't go. They're going to take you off like they did me!"

"No they won't. If they know what's good for them they won't even try something like that."

So he went. Dot nervously waited in the room. But he didn't stay but a little bit and was back soon.

"What did they want?"

"They're just tryin' to tease us. I told 'em to let us alone. And I think they will this time."

***

After the honeymoon was over Harold and Dot stayed with his parents for about three months. They spent the time getting together the things they would need to move into a place of their own. Friends had thrown a shower before the wedding and had given them dishes, linens, and silverware. They bought a table and chairs from Jim Hunter, and a used bedroom suite from one of Harold's cousins who lived in Chattanooga. Dot's brother Gene gave them an oil stove. And they had a living room suite Dot had bought before she even knew Harold. Before long they had everything they needed. That summer they moved into their home, ready to start a life together and begin a family.

Dot became a homemaker, keeping house and raising children as was the custom in those days. Read more about her life with Harold starting on page 179.

But she always maintained her own identity, too. One of Dot's biggest interests was beauty and fashion. Though she grew up on a farm, in photos she appears far more cultured than your run of the mill country girl. She was always interested in makeup when she was young but could not afford it often. But she developed an interest in hair by playing with her mama's hair all the time. In the late 50's she would do permanents for friends. Some time in the early 1960's she finally fulfilled her dream and went to beauty school. She took an accelerated course over a period of about six months at a beauty school in Rome. After she graduated she opened her own beauty shop (which Harold built for her) in Subligna across the road from the Scoggins store. As a teenager, June Pope worked for her as a shampoo girl. Dot operated her business there—open every Wed through Sat—until about the mid 1970's. After that she ran a less formal version of the shop from the enclosed back porch of her home. Even by the time I came along she was still doing hair. She gave me my first

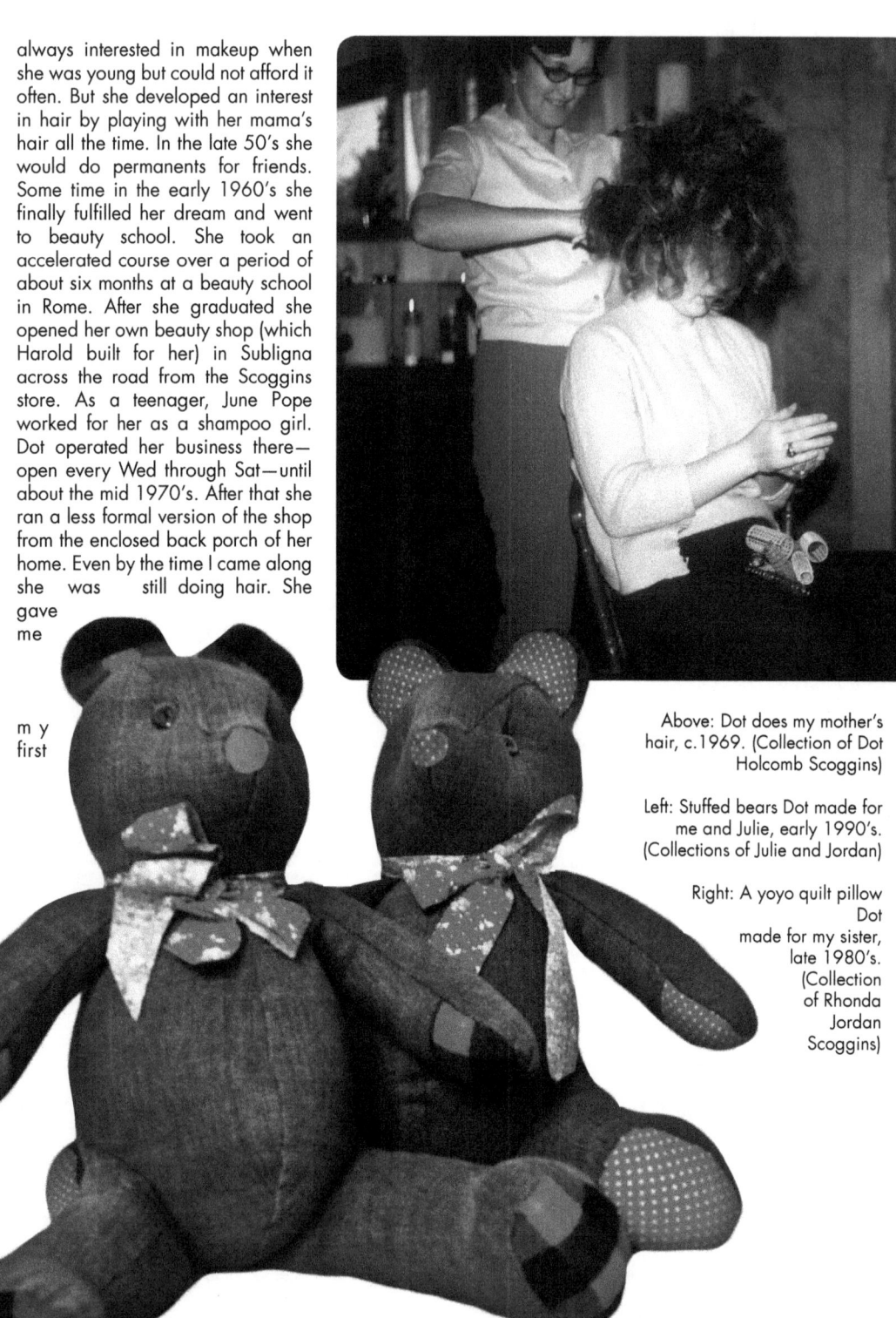

Above: Dot does my mother's hair, c.1969. (Collection of Dot Holcomb Scoggins)

Left: Stuffed bears Dot made for me and Julie, early 1990's. (Collections of Julie and Jordan)

Right: A yoyo quilt pillow Dot made for my sister, late 1980's. (Collection of Rhonda Jordan Scoggins)

haircut (and many more over the years). Dot was also a Mary Kay consultant, regularly holding open houses, hosting beauty events, and traveling to conventions. It was more a social activity—and a way to keep herself in supply of beauty products!—than a means to support her livelihood (R. & M. Scoggins, correspondence).

She was also a skilled seamstress. Taught by her mother and her Home Ec teachers at school, Dot always enjoyed sewing. She made most of her own clothes after she was married, and made clothes for her kids from the time they were children until they were all grown and had families of their own. She also explored her crafty side, making stuffed animals and other toys for her grandchildren. For Easter one year she made us all stuffed bunnies. Another year she made denim stuffed bears. Those always bring a smile to my face!

And I can't forget her culinary skills. Every birthday and holiday Dot hosted family gatherings, making all sorts of food for us all. Her fried potatoes were a family favorite and I particularly loved the baked potato skins she made in later years. And for the lucky birthday boy or girl there was always a special cake. Her cakes were not your run of the mill birthday cake. Every cake was unique. Some of my favorites are a Spider Man cake (for my 2nd birthday), a Smurf cake (for my 3rd birthday), and a Wonder Woman cake (for my sister's 10th birthday). My sister's 13th birthday cake was decorated like a tree stump with a walkway paved with M&M's that led to the front door of the "house" stump. Several individual size cakes looked like little bunnies gathered around their home. It was the perfect cake to spark a child's imagination. I requested the same cake for my own birthday years later.

The family gatherings were special to all us grand-kids. We always had played games and had fun, and often put on shows for the rest of the family. Unlike my mother's family, where I was the youngest grandchild by over seven years, on dad's side all us grand kids were close enough in age that we created worlds unto ourselves apart from the adults. I miss those days of carefree imagination. And as I travel back in my mind I can't help but wonder why we were all in such a hurry to grow up.

With many years of both smiles and sorrow behind her, Dot too looks back on her early days with fond memories. She has come to realize, "I should've talked to [mama] about [coming to my wedding]. But actually we just didn't talk about it. She didn't ask me anything about things I was doing or nothing. They didn't care for me getting married but it was just like something they didn't talk about."

It's funny how we seem unable to openly communicate with the people we are closest to. It's hard to imagine Grandmother not inviting her own parents to her wedding. That fabled generation gap obviously is not unique to my Generation X (and the Baby Boomers before me). Maybe there is a lesson in Dot's story. Maybe the memory of her youth can teach the rest of us something before we too grow old. Dot expected her parents would not attend her wedding and so she never gave them the chance to show her otherwise. Too often expectations—for ourselves and for others—get in the way. We all have family baggage and probably always will. But we should learn to be more open, talk honestly, accept each other exactly as we are, and never expect anything in return.

I can hear a hint of regret in Grandmother's voice—a regret that her many years only now allow her to admit. "But I believe daddy would've come. In later years I saw how he would do things that I didn't think he would do. And mama too."

Expectations… they'll trip you up every time.

Julie & I are ready for Christmas, Dec 1989.
(Collection of Michael & Rhonda Scoggins)

EPILOGUE

Jordan's apartment, Greenwich Village, NYC
Christmas Day, 2010

The phone rings.
"Hello," I answer.
"Merry Christmas!"
It's my sister calling from Mom and Dad's.
"Merry Christmas to you too! How are you doing?"
"We're good. We just had lunch. Grandmother and Eric are here."
I wish season's greetings to them all, and they back.
"It's snowing here!"
"Oh really? That's funny. It's not snowing here at all."
"How about that? You have to come down to Georgia for a white Christmas, huh?" she laughs.
She asks about my job interview from just a few days earlier. It went well but I am anxious to hear the results. Everyone wishes me luck, all hoping my Christmas wish will come true.

The snow turned out to be a major blizzard. The next day it fell in New York with the rare treat of thundersnow. I had a follow-up interview a few days later and wore a vintage sweater that had once been a gift from my mother to my father. It was a present she gave him the first year they were married, over 40 years ago.

I got the job. The storm brought with it the change I needed in life. It was the best Christmas present I could have hoped for.

On that Christmas day we didn't exchange presents—it's not part of our tradition anymore. 1,000 miles away from each other but, perhaps, closer than ever. I prefer to celebrate life with warm hearts and open arms.

No Papa Jordan. No Papa Julie. Time marches ever onward. And while we must look to the future, while we must evolve, while we must move forward into the light… we must also take time for reflection. We must take time for memory. The knowledge of where we come from helps set our sights all the more clearly on where we are going.

I do not know what the path before me may bring but now more than ever I aim to enjoy the journey.

Bibliography

During the writing of *Jordan's Journey*, I took great care to document the sources for my work. As with any family history and genealogy research, many of the sources I referenced are unpublished. I have described all sources here in order to provide a better understanding of each item's relevance. I am very happy to share any material with other researchers and hope that you will do the same. Please see my contact information in the preface to get in touch. Also note that for census data I have not cited granular details for each person in the book. This would fill a book unto itself. This information (along with many other sources) is attached to my extensive shared tree at Ancestry.com which you can link to at http://bd-studios.com/journey.

"1821 Georgia Land Lottery". *Georgia USGenWeb Archives Project*. Web. Accessed 17 Jun 2011.

"66th: The Story of the 66th Inf Division." Paris: Stars & Stripes, 1945. Web. Accessed via Lone Sentry, 17 Jul 2011.

Adams, K.K., "Massie, Poindexter, Anderson, Williams." *William and Mary Quarterly*, Vol 8, Series 2 (1928): 62-3. Print.

Allen, Desmond W. *Arkansas Township Digest: Minor Civil Divisions, 1820-1990.* Conway, AR: Arkansas Research, 1994. Print.

Amerson, Anne Dismukes. "Peck Family Among Founders of Mt. Olive." *Dahlonega Nugget*. 8 Dec 1994. Print.

Ancestry.com and The Church of Jesus Christ of Latter-day Saints. *1880 United States Federal Census*. Provo, UT, USA: Ancestry.com Operations Inc, 2010. Web.

Ancestry.com. *1820 United States Federal Census.* Provo, UT, USA: Ancestry.com Operations Inc, 2010. Web.

—. *1830 United States Federal Census.* Provo, UT, USA: Ancestry.com Operations Inc, 2010. Web.

—. *1840 United States Federal Census.* Provo, UT, USA: Ancestry.com Operations Inc, 2010. Web.

—. *1850 United States Federal Census.* Provo, UT, USA: Ancestry.com Operations Inc, 2009. Web.

—. *1860 U.S. Federal Census - Slave Schedules.* Provo, UT, USA: Ancestry.com Operations Inc, 2010. Web.

—. *1860 U.S. Federal Census - Slave Schedules.* Provo, UT, USA: Ancestry.com Operations Inc, 2010. Web.

—. *1860 United States Federal Census.* Provo, UT, USA: Ancestry.com Operations Inc, 2009. Web.

—. *1870 United States Federal Census.* Provo, UT, USA: Ancestry.com Operations Inc, 2009. Web.

—. *1900 United States Federal Census.* Provo, UT, USA: Ancestry.com Operations Inc, 2004. Web.

—. *1910 United States Federal Census.* Provo, UT, USA: Ancestry.com Operations Inc, 2006. Web.

—. *1920 United States Federal Census.* Provo, UT, USA: Ancestry.com Operations Inc, 2010. Web.

—. *1930 United States Federal Census.* Provo, UT, USA: Ancestry.com Operations Inc, 2002. Web.

—. *Civil War Prisoner of War Records, 1861-1865.* Provo, UT, USA: Ancestry.com Operations Inc, 2007. Web.

—. *Directory of Deceased American Physicians, 1804-1929.* Provo, Utah: MyFamily.com, Inc., 2004. Web.

—. *Georgia 1890 Property Tax Digests.* Provo, UT, USA: Ancestry.com Operations, Inc., 2011. Web.

—. *Georgia Cherokee Land Lottery, 1832.* Provo, UT, USA: Ancestry.com Operations Inc, 2000. Web.

—. *Georgia, Confederate Pension Applications, 1879-1960.* Provo, UT, USA: Ancestry.com Operations Inc, 2009. Web.

—. *History of Troup County.* Provo, UT: The Generations Network, Inc., 2004. Web.

—. *Tennessee State Marriages, 1780-2002.* Provo, UT, USA: Ancestry.com Operations Inc, 2008. Web.

—. *U.S., Sons of the American Revolution Membership Applications, 1889-1970.* Provo, UT, USA: Ancestry.com Operations, Inc., 2011. Web.

—. *World War I Draft Registration Cards, 1917-1918.* Provo, UT, USA: Ancestry.com Operations Inc, 2005. Web.

Anderson, Jim. "Adam Peck Ancestor of Lumpkin Pecks." *Dahlonega Nugget*. 3 Mar 1983, 1B. Print.

—. "Pecks From Germany." *Dahlonega Nugget*. n.d. [probably early 1983, as this looks like the beginning of the piece continued in the 3 Mar 1983 issue]. Print.

Anderson, T.J. & Frances. *Anderson Records*. Self-published, 2003. Print.

The Army Almanac: A Book of Facts Concerning the Army of the United States. U.S. Government Printing Office, 1950, 546-7. Web. Accessed via Hathi Trust Digital Library, 7 Nov 2011.

Army discharge papers, Harold W. Scoggins, serial no. 34,766,887, Military Polic Platoon, 66th Inf Div. 8 Apr 1946.'

"At Tornado-Lashed Subligna... Clean-up Operation Continues." *Rome News-Tribune*. 19 Mar 1973, 3. Web. Accessed via Google News.

Austin, Jeannette Holland. *Walker County Messenger, 1916-1921.* Riverdale, GA: J.H. Austin, n.d. Print.

Baird, Bob. *Bob's Genealogy Filing Cabinet: Colonial & Southern Genealogies.* Accessed via http://www.genfiles.com/, 2 Aug 2011.

Biographical Souvenir of the State of Texas, Containing Biographical Sketches of the Representative Public, and Many Early Settled Families. Easley, SC: Southern Historical Press, 1978. Print.

Bodie, John Bennett. *Seventeenth Century Isle of Wight County Virginia.* Baltimore, MD: Genealogical Publishing Co, 2003. Print.

Boyd, Gregory A. *Family Maps of Pike County, Arkansas: With Homesteads, Roads, Waterways, Towns, Cemeteries, Railroads, and More.* Norman, OK: Arphax, 2006. Print.

Brazier, Maudine; Janet Burks; Rene Jordan. *Descendants of Richard Jordan I Family Website.* Accessed via http://freepages.genealogy.rootsweb.ancestry.com/~jordanfamily/, 17 Jun 2011.

Brown, David T. "Dirt Town Valley Birthplace Is Still Her Home Place." *Rome News-Tribune.* 23 Aug 1995, 5. Web. Accessed via Google News, 18 Nov 2011.

Burgert, Annette K. *Palatine Origins of Some Pennsylvania Pioneers.* Myerstown, PA: AKB, 2000. 368-70. Print.

Chafe, William H. *The Unfinished Journey: America Since World War II.* New York: Oxford University Press, 1999. Print.

Chattooga County Heritage Book Committee, comp. *The Heritage of Chattooga County Georgia, 1838-2006.* Chattooga County, GA: Chattooga County Heritage Book Committee, 2006. 309-11. Print.

Confederate Muster Rolls, Record Group 022-01-063, Defense Dept., Adjutant General's Office.

Cosby, Karen. *Sweet Remembrance: Caney Valley Childhood Memories of Flora Adella Adams Cosby.* Sims, AR: The Author, 1984. Print.

Davis, Charles L.; Henry H. Bellas. *A Brief History of the North Carolina Troops on the Continental Establishment: In the War of the Revolution: with a Register of Officers of the Same.* Philadelphia, PA: s.n., 1896. Print.

Death Certificate for Drucila Chapman Scoggins, 1 Jun 1922. Certificate #21901 issued from Walker County, Georgia. Death Certificates, Vital Records, Public Health, RG 26-5-95, Georgia Archives.

Deed of sale from W.D. Wood to Mountain Home Church and Cemetery, 24 Dec 1886, Pike County, Arkansas, Deed Book M, 516-17. Clerk's Office, Murfreesboro, Arkansas. This original deed would have burned in the 1895 fire that destroyed the Pike County Courthouse; however land owners took in deeds to be recorded after the fire, preserving records such as this. Digital file obtained from Joyce Wood, Oct 2011.

Deed of transfer from Abraham Anderson to Mary F. Anderson, 14 Jun 1904, Whitfield County, Georgia, Deed Record S, 187-8. Clerk of Court, Dalton, Georgia. Retrieved by Michael & Rhonda Scoggins, Oct 2011.

Dodd, Jordan. *Georgia Marriages to 1850.* Provo, UT, USA: Ancestry.com Operations Inc, 1997. Web.

Dyer, Carrie Ruth Goodson. Carrie's memories transcribed from original handwriting by her youngest son John Green Dyer, written c. late 1980's. Accessed via Ancestry.com, 16 Aug 2011.

East Armuchee Baptist Church History Committee, comp. *East Armuchee Baptist Church, est. 1886: Preserving a Heritage for the 21st Century.* LaFayette, GA: comp. 1998-2004. Print.

Faust, Patricia L. "Conscription (Military Draft) In The Civil War." *Shotgun's Home of the American Civil War.* Web. 16 Nov 2011.

Fleming, Marquis. "Subligna Woman Remembers Work of Dr. J.P. Clements." *Dalton Daily Citizen-News.* n.d.

Friendship Primitive Baptist Church, Lilburn, Georgia. n.d. Web. Accessed via http://www.oldplaces.org/gwinnettga/cemeteries/friendship.html, 17 Jun 2011.

Gale Research. *Passenger and Immigration Lists Index, 1500s-1900s.* Provo, UT, USA: Ancestry.com Operations, Inc, 2010. Web.

Generations Gone By. Web. Accessed via http://www.generationsgoneby.com., 18 Nov 2011.

Goodson, Jacob M. Letter to Carrie Ruth Goodson Dyer, Chickamauga, Georgia, 19 Mar 1930. Accessed via Ancestry.com, 16 Aug 2011.

Goodspeed, Weston A., et al. *History of Tennessee from the Earliest Time to the Present.* Nashville, TN: Goodspeed, 1886. Print.

Green, Cliff. Resaca Girl Injured; Subligna Crumpled." *Rome News-Tribune.* 18 Mar 1973, 1B. Web. Accessed via Google News.

Griffith, Jessie J.B. *Births, Marriages, Deaths, Legal Notices in Walker County, Georgia, for the Years 1892-1896.* Fort Oglethorpe, GA: J&B Price, 1983. Print.

Griggs, Charlotte Jordan. Personal correspondence with Jordan M. Scoggins, 2011.

Grigsby, David & Delores, comp. Papers on local history and information, c.1980's. Obtained from the compiler 2011.

—. Transcriptions from microfilm of *Walker County Messenger* and *Summerville News* as relates to the Armuchee Valley region of Walker County, GA, ranging from 1881 to 1927, compiled c.1980's. Obtained from the compiler 2011.

Guthrey, William M. *Genealogical Chart of the Known Descendants of Micajah Pope 1808-1867: With an Outline of His American Ancestors, 1634-1844.* Collinsville, OK: 1972. Print.

—. Research files on the Pope family, c.1970's. Accessed via Ancestry.com, Sep 2009.

Hair, Thomas L. *The Long Journey, A Family History, 1687-1991.* Spartanburg, SC: Reprint Co, 1992. Print.

Harrell, Bob. "Dateline Georgia: Front Porch Sitting." *Atlanta Constitution*, n.d. [c.1977]: 2B. Print.

Hay, Gertrude M. S. *Roster of Soldiers from North Carolina in the American Revolution.* Durham, NC: Seeman Press, 1932. Print.

Hennington-Van Horn, Gayle. "Family Group Record - Jesse Rambo and Mary Humphrey." *Gayle's Family History.* 28 May 2009. Web. Accessed at http://gayle-family-history.blogspot.com/, 30 Aug 2011.

The Heritage of Lumpkin County, Georgia, 1832-1996. Waynesville, NC: Don Mills, Inc, 1996. Print.

Historical Data Systems, comp. *American Civil War Regiments.* Provo, UT, USA: Ancestry.com Operations Inc, 1999. Web.

—, comp. *American Civil War Soldiers.* Provo, UT, USA: Ancestry.com Operations Inc, 1999. Web.

—, comp. *U.S. Civil War Soldier Records and Profiles.* Provo, UT, USA: Ancestry.com Operations Inc, 2009. Web.

Holcomb, Joey. Video conversation with Michael D. Scoggins about old Holcomb home place, 4 Sep 2011. Digital video.

Humphries, John D. *Georgia Descendants of Nathaniel Pope of Virginia, John Humphries of South Carolina, and Allen Gay of North Carolina.* Atlanta, GA: J.D. Humphries, 1934. Print.

Hunting For Bears, comp. *Georgia Marriages, 1699-1944.* Provo, UT, USA: Ancestry.com Operations Inc, 2004. Web.

Jackson, Ron V., Accelerated Indexing Systems, comp. *Georgia Census, 1790-1890.* Web.

—. *North Carolina Census, 1790-1890.* Provo, UT, USA: Ancestry.com Operations Inc, 1999. Web.

—. *Virginia Census, 1607-1890.* Provo, UT, USA: Ancestry.com Operations Inc, 1999. Web.

Johnson, Pat. "History and Beauty: She Wanted an Old House, Made Livable." *Gwinnett Daily News*, 14 May 1978, Gwinnett Life: Sunday Magazine of Gwinnett Daily News: 20-21C. Microfilm.

Jordan, Mary Pope. Interview by Jordan M. Scoggins, early 1990's. Audio cassette converted to digital.

Knight, Rena M. *Civil War Soldiers Buried in Arkansas National Cemeteries.* Conway, AR: Arkansas Research, 1996. Print.

Landrum, John B. O. *History of Spartanburg County.* Spartanburg, S.C: Genealogical Publishing Co, 2009. Print.

Lowvorn, James L. *The Descendants of Alexander Scogin (1750-1810) and Allied Lines.* Knoxville, TN: Tennessee Valley Pub, 1994. Print.

Lowe, Mary Ann. *Some Descendants of John and Elizabeth Love of Ireland.* Self-published, 1996. Print.

Manis, Mary Earl Jordan. Personal conversation with Jordan M. Scoggins, 17 Jul 2011.

Marby, Mannie Lee, ed. *Union County Heritage.* Winston-Salem, NC: Union County Heritage Committee/Hunter Pub. Co.,

1981. Print.
Marriage license, John G. Peck and Mary Sinyard, 7 Mar 1839, Lumpkin County, Georgia. Probate Office, Dahlonega, Georgia. Retrieved by Michael & Rhonda Scoggins, Aug 2011.
Marriage license, Marion Holcomb and Caroline P. Young, 4 Aug 1853, Chattooga County, Georgia. Probate Office, Summerville, Georgia. Retrieved by Michael, Rhonda, and Jordan Scoggins, Feb 2011.
Marriage license, Wade Rambo and Fannie Peck, 9 Aug 1899, Pickens County, Georgia. Probate Office, Jasper, Georgia. Retrieved by Michael & Rhonda Scoggins, Aug 2011.
Marriage license, William B. Jordan to Isabel Anderson, 14 Oct 1892, Whitfield County, Georgia. Probate Office, Dalton, Georgia. Retrieved by Michael & Rhonda Scoggins, Oct 2011.
Marriage license, William Holcomb and Elizabeth Reynolds, 10 Sep 1846, Chattooga County, Georgia. Probate Office, Summerville, Georgia. Retrieved by Michael, Rhonda, & Jordan Scoggins, Feb 2011.
Marriage license, Z.E. Holcomb to Ruby Hawkins, 3 Jan 1924, Chattooga County, Georgia. Probate Office, Summerville, Georgia. Retrieved by Michael, Rhonda & Jordan Scoggins, Feb 2011.
Maynard, William P.L, III. *Panthers Under the Rainbow: A Search for One of France's Highest Military Decorations.* Xlibris, 2007. Print.
McCollum, Louise. "Sublgna, Settled in 1854, and Still Memorable Place." *Rome News-Tribune.* 4 May 2008, 4D. Web. Retrieved from Google News.
McMurray, Richard M. *Atlanta 1864: Last Chance for the Confederacy.* Lincoln: University of Nebraska Press, 2000. Print.
McPherson, Hannah Elizabeth Weir. *The Holcombes, Nation Builders.* Washington, 1947. Print.
Meyer, Virginia M, and John F. Dorman. *Adventurers of Purse and Person: Virginia 1607-1624/5.* Richmond, VA: Order of First Families of Virginia, 1607-1624/25, 1987. Print.
Miller, Robert, ed. Jefferson City, Tennessee. Web. Accessed at http://www.jeffcitytn.com, 2 Sep 2011.
Minnesota Population Center. *National Historical Geographic Information System: Version 2.0.* Minneapolis: University of Minnesota 2011. Online database: http://www.nhgis.org. Accessed Nov 2011.
Morris, Susan D. Newton County. *The New Georgia Encyclopedia.* Web. Accessed 18 Jul 2011.
Nance, Martin L. *Nance Register: A Book of Genealogy.* Shreveport, LA: 1966. Print.
National Park Service. *U.S. Civil War Soldiers, 1861-1865.* Provo, UT, USA: Ancestry.com Operations Inc, 2007. Web.
Newton County Historical Society, comp. *History of Newton County Georgia.* Covington, GA: Newton County Historical Society, 1988. 317-21. Print.
Newton County, GA. Newton County Tax Assessor. Web. Accessed 18 Jul 2011.
Northwest Georgia Historical and Genealogical Society. *Floyd County, Georgia Cemeteries,* Vols I & II. Rome, Georgia: The Society, 1985. Print.
Nugent, Nell Marion. *Cavaliers and Pioneers: Abstracts of Virginia Land Patents and Grants, 1623-1666,* Volume 1. Baltimore: Genealogical Publishing Company, 1963. Print.
Oake, William R,; Stacy D. Allen. *On the Skirmish Line Behind a Friendly Tree: The Civil War Memoirs of William Royal Oake, 26th Iowa Volunteers.* Helena, MT: Farcountry Press, 2006. Print.
Orr, Rosa. *History of Concord United Methodist Church near near [sic] Villanow, Georgia.* n.l.: Ray E. Roper, 1977. Print.
"The Palatine Project: 1740 Lydia." ProGenealogists. Web. Accessed 31 Aug 2011.
Panther Veterans Organization. *40,000 Black Panthers of the 66th Division.* n.l.: 1946. Print.
Patterson, Michael E. History of Joseph Milton Cavender. Unpublished paper, 1999. Accessed via Ancestry.com.
Peck, William Greer. *The Peck Family.* Atascadero, CA: Wilkins Creative Printing, 1971. Print.
Pension application file no. R5770 & R5773, William Jordan, NC Regt, Revolutionary War; Case Files of Pension and Bounty-Land Warrant Applications Based on Revolutionary War Service; Records of Department of Veterans Affairs, Record Group 15; National Archives Buliding, Washington, D.C. Accessed via Fold3.
Pettigrew, Marion D.; Newton E. Brightwell. *Marks-Barnett Families and Their Kin: Including a Reprint of the 1939 Edition.* Baltimore, MD: Gateway Press, 1981. Print.
Pike County Heritage Club, comp. *Early History of Pike County, Arkansas: The First Hundred Years.* Murfreesboro, AR: Pike County Archives and History Society, 1989. Print.
Pope, Fred. Interview by History Committee at Armuchee Valley Community Center, 5 Feb 2011. Digital video.
Pope, Guy. Video conversation about old Ben Pope home place, 11 Nov 2010. Digital video.
Pope, Jim. Video conversation about old Pope kitchen, 13 Nov 2010. Digiital video.
"The Pope's Kitchen Is Special." *Walker County Messenger.* LaFayette, GA: 7 Sep 1980, 1-2. Print.
Pope, Lizzie Clement. Homecoming speech delivered at East Armuchee Baptist Church. Family papers of Mary Pope Jordan, n.d.
Pritchett, William L. *A Southern Branch of the Lawrence Family,* 2nd edition. Baltimore, MD: Gateway Press, 1994. Print.
Proctor, Redfield, et al, comp. *The War of the Rebellion: A Compilation of the Official Records of the Union and Confederate Armies.* Series I, Vol XXXVIII, Part IV. Washington: G.P.O, 1891. Web. Accessed via Google Books.
Rambo, Beverly Nelson and Ronald S. Beatty. *The Rambo Family Tree.* Web. Accessed at https://sites.google.com/site/rambofamilytree/, 24 Aug 2011.
Rambo, Beverly Nelson. *The Rambo Family Tree: Descendants of Peter Gunnarson Rambo, 1611-1986.* Decorah, IA: Anundsen Pub. Co, 1986. Print.
Rambo, Kinchin. Diary and Church Minutes, 1831-1880. Web. Accessed at http://www.couchgenweb.com/gwinnett/rambo2.htm, 17 Jun 2011.
Receipt for W D [William Delaney, but indexed as Wiley] Scogin transaction with CSA, 1863, document no. 53; Confederate Papers Relating to Citizens or Business Firms (National Archives Microfilm Publication M346, roll 0909); Records of the War Department, Record Group 109; National Archives Building, Washington, DC. Accessed via Fold3.
Receipt for William Robbs transaction with CSA, 5 Sep 1863, document no. 117; Confederate Papers Relating to Citizens or Business Firms (National Archives Microfilm Publication M346, roll 870); Records of the War Department, Record Group 109; National Archives Building, Washington, DC. Accessed via Fold3.
Reciept for L S [Levi Sanford] Scoggin transaction with CSA, 3 Jan 1864, document no. 40; Confederate Papers Relating to Citizens or Business Firms (National Archives Microfilm Publication M346, Roll 0909); Records of the War Department, Record Group 109; National Archives Building, Washington, DC. Accessed via Fold3.
Reynolds, Michael & Erin Kane. Relocation of the Rambo Family Cemetery. Atlanta: Brockington and Associates, Inc., Sep 2010. Print.
Reynolds, Nelda Scoggin. "Alexander "Ellick" Scogin - Revolutionary War Patriot". *Our History, Our Daughters' Patriots.* Captain Molly Corbin Chapter, NSDAR, 2008. Print.
—. Personal correspondence with Jordan M. Scoggins on family history and genealogy, 2010-11.
Sartain, James Alfred. *History of Walker County, Georgia.* Dalton, GA: Showalter, 1932. Print.
Scoggin and Kin Home Page. http://freepages.genealogy.rootsweb.ancestry.com/~scogginandkin/. Web. Accessed 11 Aug 2011.
Scoggin, Merle,; Lou; and Charlotte. Research notes from Jul 1979 shared by Nelda Scoggin Reynolds, Aug 2011.
Scoggins, Dot Holcomb. Audio recording about her courtship with Harold, Nov 2009. Audio cassette converted to digital.
—. Video conversation about her parents home with Michael D. Scoggins, Becky Holcomb, etc, 4 Sep 2011. Digital video.
Scoggins, Francs. Memories written about her parents and general Subligna history, 2011.
Scoggins, Leland Coulter. Informal conversation on general Subligna history with Eric Scoggins, Michael Scoggins, Rhonda Jordan Scoggins, and Frances Scoggins, 4 Dec 2011. Digital audio.
Scoggins, Michael David. Interview (written) with Jordan M. Scoggins, Nov 2011.
Scoggins, Rhonda & Michael. Personal correspondence with Jordan M. Scoggins, 2009-11.
Scoggins, Rhonda Jordan. Interviews with Jordan M. Scoggins, Feb 2011. Digital audio.
"Scogin-Scoggin Family, NC, GA." *Georgia Genealogical Society Quarterly,* Vol 7, Iss 2, Sum 1971, 103-8. Print.
Seaver, Jesse. *The Holcomb(e) Genealogy: A Genealogy, History and Directory.* Philadelphia, PA: American Historical-Genealogical Society, 1925. Print.
Service records for Abraham Anderson, 5th Mtd Inf Reg, TN, USA. Carded Records Showing Military Service of Soldiers Who Fought in Volunteer Organizations During the American Civil War (National Archives Microfilm Publication M395, roll 162). Records of the Adjutant General's Office, Record Group 94, National Archives Building, Washington, D.C. Accessed via Fold3.
Service records for F.M. Holcomb; Company K, 24th AR Inf, CSA. Carded Records Showing Military Service of Soldiers Who Fought in Confederate Organizations (National Archives Microfilm Publication M317, Roll 182). War Department Collection of Confederate Records, Record Group 109; National Archive Building, Washington, D.C. Accessed via Fold3.
Service records for Francis M. Halcomb; Co B, 4th AR Cav, USA. Carded Records Showing Military Service of Soldiers Who Fought in Volunteer Organizations During the American Civil War (National Archives Microfilm Publication M399, Roll 37 & 59). Records of the Adjust General's Office, Record Group 94; National Archives Building, Washington, D.C. Accessed at Fold3.
Service records for Francis Marion Anderson, 1st Mtd Inf Reg, TN, USA. Carded Records Showing Military Service of Soldiers Who Fought in Volunteer Organizations During the American Civil War (National Archives Microfilm Publication M395, roll 126). Records of the Adjutant General's Office, Record Group 94, National Archives Building, Washington, D.C. Accessed via Fold3.
Service records for James W. Jordan, 34th Inf Reg, GA, CSA. Carded Records Showing Military Service of Soldiers Who Fought in Confederate Organizations (National Archives Microfilm Publication M266, Roll 413). War Department Collection of Confederate Records, 1825-1927, Record Group 109, National Archives Building, Washington, D.C. Accessed via Fold3.
Service records for John Grigsby, 23rd Inf Reg, GA, CSA. Carded Records Showing Military Service of Soldiers Who Fought in Confederate Organizations (National Archives Microfilm Publication M266, Roll 350). War Department Collection of Confederate Records, 1825-1927, Record Group 109, National Archives Building, Washington, D.C. Accessed via Fold3.
Service records for Nathan A Keown, 60th Inf Reg, GA, CSA. Carded Records Showing Military Service of Soldiers Who Fought in Confederate Organizations (National Archives Microfilm Publication M266, Roll 550). War Department Collection of Confederate Records, 1825-1927, Record Group 109, National Archives Building, Washington, D.C. Accessed via Fold3.
Skoglund, Kevin. *My Family History.* http://www.kevinskoglund.com/familyhistory/. Web. Accessed 11 Aug 2011.
Soldier's Certificate No. 1,062,994 & Widow's Certificate No. 771,961, Jeptha J. Wisner, Pvt, Co B, 4th AR Inf; Case Files of Pension Applications Based on Service Completed in the Years 1817 to Approximately 1903; Records of Department of Veterans Affairs, Record Group 15; National Archives Building, Washington, D.C. Excerpts obtained from Joyce Wood, Aug 2011.
Soldier's Certificate No. 824,146, Abraham Anderson, Private, Cos H & F, 5th TN Mounted Inf; Case Files of Pension Applications Based on Service Completed in the Years 1817 to Approximately 1903; Records of Department of Veterans Affairs, Record Group 15; National Archives Building, Washington, D.C.
Southern claim file for James M. Holcomb (claim #55016), Barred Claims Files, Records of the U.S. House of Representatives, 1789 - 2011 (National Archives Microfilm Publication M1407), Record Group 233; National Archives Buliding, Washington, D.C. Accessed via Fold3.
Spencer, Ingrid. "Dogtrot House, Poplarville, MS, Waggonner & Ball Architects." *Architectural Record.* Web. Accessed 26 Oct 2011.
Street, Bernard. "Best Glove Corporation Plans Major Expansions." *Rome News-Tribune.* 24 Jan 1963, 3. Web. Accessed via Google News 18 Nov 2011.
"Sunk on Christmas Eve." National Geographic. 2001. Television.
Talley-McRae, Helen. "Brick Store Listed in National Register." 8 May 2009. Georgia Department of Natural Resources. Web.
Valentine, Edward Pleasants. *The Edward Pleasants*

Valentine Papers. Vol IV. Richmond, VA: Valentine Museum, 1927. Print.

Walker County Historical Society, comp. *Walker County, Georgia Cemeteries*. LaFayette, GA: Walker County Historical Society, 1987. Print.

Walker County History Committee, comp. *Walker County Georgia Heritage, 1833-1983*. LaFayette, GA: Walker County History Committee, 1984. Print.

Walker County, GA. Walker County Tax Assessor. Web. Accessed 30 Nov 2011.

Wessman, Siinto S. *66: A Story of World War II*. Baton Rouge, LA: Army & Navy Pub. Co., 1946. Print.

West, Edmund, comp. *Family Data Collection - Births*. Provo, UT, USA: The Generations Network, Inc., 2001. Web.

—. *Family Data Collection - Deaths*. Provo, UT, USA: The Generations Network, Inc., 2001. Web.

—. *Family Data Collection - Individual Records*. Provo, UT, USA: Ancestry.com Operations Inc, 2000. Web.

Whisnant, Raymond. *Whisnant Surname Center*. Web. Accessed 17 Jun 2011.

White, Aleta. "History of Subligna." Unpublished article from 1959, probably written for Subligna School where Aleta was a teacher. Obtained from Frances Scoggins.

Whitfield County, GA. Whitfield County Tax Assessor. Web. Accessed Oct 2011.

Widow's Application No. 589,920 & Minor's Certificate No. 594,848, Francis Marion Holcomb, Pvt, Co B, 4th AR Cav; Case Files of Pension Applications Based on Service Completed in the Years 1817 to Approximately 1903; Records of Department of Veterans Affairs, Record Group 15; National Archives Building, Washington, D.C.

Widow's Certificate No. 31,727, Abraham Anderson, Private, Capt. Howard's Co/Capt. Henry's Co., GA Militia; War of 1812 Pension and Bounty Land Warrant Application Files; Records of Department of Veterans Affairs, Record Group 15; National Archives Building, Washington, D.C. [Accessed via Fold3]

Widow's Pension W.512, Mary Anderson for service of William Anderson; Case Files of Pension and Bounty-Land Warrant Applications Based on Revolutionary War Service (National Archives Microfilm Publication M804); Records of Department of Veterans Affairs, Record Group 15; National Archives Building, Washington, D.C. [Accessed via Fold3]

Will of A.W. Peck, 27 Feb 1909 (probated 2 Mar 1910), Lumpkin County, Georgia. Probate Office, Dahlonega, Georgia. Retrieved by Michael & Rhonda Scoggins in Aug 2011.

Williams, David. "Living History." *Walker County Messenger*, 30 Oct 1991: 6A. Print.

Wood Family Bible record, 1856. John H. Wood and Mary Jane Sparks marriage record page only. Original Bible owned by Billy Armstrong of Waurika, Oklahoma. Photocopy held by Joyce Wood of Nashville, Arkansas. Digital file obtained from Joyce, Oct 2011. Wood family tradition describes this as the wedding Bible of John H. Wood and Mary Jane Sparks, given to the bride and groom as a gift.

Wood, Dawn A. "150-Year-Old Home Harbors Plenty of Local Area History." *Summerville News*. 30 Jun 2005, 2B. Print.

Worthy, Larry. "North Georgia Creek History." *About North Georgia*. Web. Availalbe online at http://ngeorgia.com/history/creekhistory.html. Accessed 1 Aug 2011.

Yates Publishing. *U.S. and International Marriage Records, 1560-1900*. Provo, UT, USA: Ancestry.com Operations Inc, 2004. Web.

Young, William H; Nancy K. Young. *The 1950s*. Westport, CT: Greenwood Press, 2004. Print.

Zainaldin, Jamil S. "Great Depression." *The New Georgia Encyclopedia*. Web. Accessed 12 Mar 2011.

Index

Women are genearlly indexed by their maiden name.

A

Fannie Abercrombie 166, 170, 224
John Abercrombie 170
James Adams 196
William Allen 196
Cora Alverson 136
Mary Victora Alverson 136
Abraham Anderson 100–104
Abraham Marshall Anderson 91, 100–102
Emma Octavia Anderson 92, 101–102
Gideon Anderson 100–101
Isabell Anderson 92–100, 102
Lucy Ann Anderson 20
Richard Anderson [I] 100
Richard Anderson [II] 100
Robert Anderson 100–101
Solomon Anderson 101–102
Thomas Anderson 100
William Anderson [I] 100, 102
William Anderson [II] 100, 102
Armuchee Valley School 35, 108, 173
Jewell Arthur 205, 209
Louisa Askew 149

B

Babbs family 69
Corinthia Addie Bagwell 134
Edmund Baker 127–128
Mary Mathursia Ballinger 202
James F. Barron 127, 129
Lovica Barron 127
Bernard Barton 177, 183
Hans Beck 166
Johann Jakob Beck [I] 166
Martin Beck 166
Michael Beck 166
Catharine Bennett 149
Bethlehem Baptist Church 34
Mary [Boling] 91
Mary Frances Boling 103
William Boling 91
Elizabeth Ann Bomar 20
Spencer Bomar 139
Lydia Borden 167
Irene Bowen 115
Mrs. Bowman 173
E.F. Bowman 34
Thornton Bowman 202
Obe Broom 171
Delila Brown 172, 215
Eula Brown 27
William Brown 215
Harriet Ann Bruce 20–21, 26
William Bruce 92
Mabel Bryan 202
unknown Bryant 135
Lillie Bryant 94, 97
Tom Bryant 135
Ennis Clifford Buford 202

C

Annie Calley 201
Dossie Lou Calley 201
Noten Calley 201
William Calley 201
C.J.C. Campbell 200
Nancy H. Campbell 198
Caney Fork 193–194, 198–201
Tom Cantrell 33
G.B. Carpenter 171
John Carpenter 198, 201
Margaret Elizabeth Carpenter 216
Susannah Carpenter 201
Vernon(?) Carpenter 172
Carrie Green Clement 69
William Catlett 139
Cavender Cemetery 225
Clemeth Cavender 170, 224–226
Dorset Cavender 224
Ezekiel Cavender 224–226
Fannie Cavender 166, 170, 224–226
George Washington Cavender 224, 226
John H. Cavender 224–225
Joseph Cavender 226
Joseph Warren Cavender 32–33, 224–226
Julia Ann Cavender 34, 213, 216, 221–222, 224–226
Winnie Cavender 225
Ann Chapman 146–147
Chapman Cemetery 143–145
Drucilla Chapman 131, 134, 136, 138, 142, 144–145, 148, 221
Eleander Chapman 143, 145–146, 221
Elizabeth Chapman 146
Emmett Chapman 171
Frances Druscilla Chapman 150
John Chapman [I] 142, 146–147
John Chapman [II] 146–147
John Henry Chapman 142–143, 146
Selete E. Chapman 148
William Chapman 142, 146
William Jack Chapman 134, 136, 142–144, 145, 146, 221
Thomas Chelsey Jackson Childs 27
Emma Christian 202
Mary Cleckler 127, 130
Cleghorn family 69
James Wilson Clements 171
Billy Clement 60
Callie Clement 61, 69
Carrie Green Clement 61
Emily Clement 107
George Luther Clement 61, 69
James Clement 64
James Constantine Clement 34, 43, 58–61, 64–65, 69–71, 225, 227
Madison Green Clement 58, 64, 65, 222
Mary Ethel Clement 61, 69–70, 225, 227
Nannie Elizabeth Clement 27, 34, 43–58, 58, 61, 64, 69, 76, 104, 109, 113, 117
Adam Clements 225, 226
Adolphus Clements 225–227
Charles Clements 225, 226, 227
Claude Clements 33
Claudius Clements 226
Ella Clements 226
James Wilson Clements 32, 173, 226
John A. Clements 32
Julius Park Clements 226
Martha Almina Clements 225–226
Mary Clements 226
Nonnie Clements 226
Watson Clement 60
William Madison Clement 61, 69, 107
Laura B. Coker 27
Etta Louisa Cole 92
John Cole 92
Nancy Ann Coleman 215
Robert Coleman 215
Concord Methodist Church 20, 31, 34
Concord School 35
J.H. Cook 200
Carlton Cordle 172
Basil Corey 33
Martha Creasman 92
George Creekman 90
Cumberland Presbyterian Church 172

D

Dalton High School 108
Margaret Peggy Daniels 218
Elizabeth Davis 88
Leona Davis 69
Sarah Jane Davis 220
Spencer B. Davis 90
The Diana 86
Dirt Town 23
Frankie Dobosn 228
Rebecca Dobson 66
Hub Dover 183
Louise Dover 183
Margaret Dowling 127
Joseph A. Drummond 202
Mark Dunn 104
Francis Dyer 225

E

Sid Eakers 171
Spat Eakers 32
East Armuchee Baptist Church 32, 34, 54, 59, 172, 216–217, 220
Rodney & Ebeth Edwards 33
George Eepey 34
Emily Clement 69
Emmaus Primitive Baptist Church 172
Lee L. Evans 91, 93
Mary Jane Evans 90, 92, 93

F

Farmersville Cemetery 133
James Young Foster 171
William Booker Foster 131
Flavius Joseph Fricks 20

Friendship Baptist Church 34
Furnace School 35

G

Chelsey Gaines 202
Elizabeth Gayle 167
Eliza G. Gillespie 127
Georgia Gober 66
Carrie Ruth Goodson 42
Jacob Goodson 37, 42
Jacob Goodson [II] 41
James Goodson 40
Jesse Marsh Goodson 31, 41–42
John Thomas Goodson 41
Martha Ann Goodson 20, 26, 27–31, 37, 40–41, 43
Nancy Goodson 37
Nicholas Goodson 40
Williamson Byrum Goodson 40
The Rev. Zachariah Gordon 37
Green Bush 65, 134, 139–141, 150, 175
Green Bush School 139
Malinda Green 65
Mary Gresham 126
Valerie Anne Griggs 115
Carl "Bubba" Lloyd Griggs, Jr. 115
Carl Lloyd Griggs 98, 104
Glynn Jordan Griggs 115, 118–119
Mark Robert Griggs 115
David Grigsby 172
Helen Elizabeth Grigsby 43–44, 47, 51, 55–56, 104, 145
James D. Grigsby 146
John Grigsby 143, 145–146, 221
Martha Delle Grigsby 145, 174, 220–221
Matthew Grigsby 69
Robert Chapman Grigsby [I] 143, 145
Robert Chapman Grigsby [II] 145
William David Grigsby 145–146, 221
William Rice Grigsby 145, 221
Nancy Grimes 192–193
Isabelle Grimsley 133
Marjorie Dorothy Grogan 43–44, 54

H

Charity Hackney 91, 93
John Harrison Hackney 90, 93
Joseph B. Hackney 90, 93
Hames family 69
George Hames 32, 56
Sophronia Annie Hardin 164
Susie Ella Harlow 148
Elisha Harrison 127
Brian Hart 50
Toney Hart 34
John Hawkins 201
Joseph W. Hawkins 213
Louella Hawkins 215
Roy Hawkins 215
Ruby Mayoma Hawkins 202, 206–211, 213, 215–216, 218, 224, 229
Russel Hawkins 215
Viola Hawkins 215
Zechariah Roy Hawkins 213–215
Smith Haynes 20
Robbin Ellen Hegge 179
Cyrus Montague Herndon 131
Lee Higdon 90
T? Hill 135
Martha Hodgus 20
Annie Holcomb 202
Becky Holcomb 203
Bulah Dorthelia Holcomb 202
Dennis Holcomb 190–192
Effie R. Holcomb 202
Joseph Holcombe 188
Ella Holcomb 197
Emily Frances Holcomb 201
Richard Holcombe 188
Ethel Dorthelia Holcomb 11, 150–151, 171, 175, 179–184, 187, 206, 209–210, 213, 215–216, 218, 224, 228–233, 235
Thomas Holcombe 188
William Holcombe 188
Frances Elaine Holcomb 206, 209–210, 215
Francis Marion Holcomb 187, 190–197, 199, 201
George C. Holcomb 190
George Seaborn Holcomb 202
Henry F. Holcomb 202
James Holcomb 190–191
James Marion Holcomb 195, 197
James Monroe Holcomb 190
Joey Holcomb 203
John Holcomb 190–193, 195, 198, 201
Lawrence Holcomb 202
Lottie Holcomb 202
Mary Ann Holcomb 192, 194
Mary L. Holcomb 196
Mattie Cecil Holcomb 202
Maude M. Holcomb 202
Myrtis Holcomb 202
Nancy Jane Holcomb 192, 194
Raymond Holcomb 197
Ruby Elizabeth Holcomb 206
Sara Holcomb 197
Sarah Malinda Holcomb 201
Thomas Deed Holcomb 202
Virgil Holcomb 197
William Holcomb 187, 188, 190–191, 192, 194
William Holcomb [II] 190
William Eugene Holcomb 205–206, 209–210, 230, 232
William Jackson Holcomb 187–188, 194, 197, 202–205
Willie Holcomb 202
Zenas Eugene Holcomb 171, 187, 202, 206–211
Bythel Horn 201
unknown Horne 135
Elijah Horn 201
Joseph Horn 201
Beulah Belle Huggins 43–44
Harold Hughes 171
Margaret M. Hulsey 20
John D. Humphries 16
Benjamin F. Hunt 140
The Rev. Benjamin Franklin Hunt 31, 172, 217
Jim Hunter 232
John Suttle Hunt 140
Joseph Louis Hunt 140, 217
Joseph Underwood Hunt 217

I

Rachel Isom 190–191, 194, 196

J

Delores Jackson 174
Johnson Cemetery 168
James D. Johnson 196
Mary F. Johnson 131
Johnston School 206
A.M. Jones 103
Ann Jones 142
Fannie Emyline Jones 166, 169–170, 224
Jarrett Jones 170
Lucy Jones 142, 143
Adeline Keziah Jordan 92
Alice [Jordan] 87
Anna Delano Jordan 90
Arminda J. Jordan 90
Burrell Jordan 85, 87–89, 90–93
Carl Earnest Jordan 94–95, 97
Carolyn Jordan 99
Charity Jordan 92
Charles Jordan 91
Charles Malvin Jordan 90
Charlotte Alexa Jordan 56, 58, 78, 94, 98–99, 104–109, 111–113
Christopher Edward Jordan 88–89
Cora Jordan 94–95, 97–99
Delene Jordan 99
Delilah [Jordan] 88
Earl Felix Jordan 11, 43–44, 47, 56, 73, 75, 76, 85–86, 94, 97–99, 101, 103–120
Elizabeth [Jordan] 87
Elizabeth Betsy Jordan 88, 89
Ernestine Jordan 99
Estelle Jordan 94–95, 97–99
Faitha Caroline Jordan 90–91, 93
Faith C. Jordan 92
Gene Jordan 99
George Washington Jordan 92, 101, 103
Hannah [Jordan] 86–87
Henry Alonzo Jordan 92–93
Henry Lee Jordan 94–95, 97
Jack Jordan 99
James Abraham Jordan 94–95, 97–99
James W. Jordan 92
James William Jordan 85, 90, 92–94, 103
John B. Jordan 92
John William Jordan 94–95, 97–99
Joseph Jordan (b.btwn 1694-1719) 86–87
Joseph Jordan (b.1716) 86–87
Keziah [Jordan] 88, 90–92
Keziah Delilah Jordan 90–91
Louisa Frances Jordan 92
Lucy Jordan 87
Mary Earl Jordan 55–56, 78, 98–99, 104–108, 110, 113
Mary Jane Jordan 94–95, 97–99
Mary T. Jordan 90
Miriam Jordan 99
Patsy Jordan 99
Rhonda Verlyn Jordan 11, 15, 40, 54–55, 58, 64–65, 74, 85, 96, 99, 104–109, 111–113, 116–117, 141, 164, 179, 208, 220, 235
Richard Jordan [I] 86–87
Richard Jordan [II] 86–87
Richard Jordan [III] 86–87
Richard Jordan (b.1670) 86–87
Robert Alton Jordan 55, 78, 104–108, 110
Samuel Jordan 86
Sara A. Jordan 92
Sarah Jordan 88–89, 99
Sarah J. Jordan 90
Steve Jordan 92
Susan P. Jordan 90, 93
Thomas Jordan [I] 86–87
Thomas Jordan [II] 86–87
Vivian Jordan 99
William Jordan 85, 87–88
William Jordan [II] 88
William Brownlow Jordan 85, 92–99, 101, 103
Jordan's Journey 86

K

Kalmar Nyckel 156
Nilla Keith 60
Alexander Keown 218
Earlie Keown 66
Keown family 69
Gordon Keown 69
Isaac Newton Keown 220
James Keown 135
James Alexander Keown 218, 220–222
Jane Lusk Keown 220
Martha Ann Keown 213, 216, 218, 222, 224
Martha Jane Keown 66
Mary Ann Amanda Keown 58, 222
Maryann Isabella Keown 20
M. Gordon Keown 33
Minerva Jane Keown 220–221
Nathaniel Alexander Keown 34, 216, 218, 221–222
Nathan Lusk Keown 220
Sarah Keown 220
Stephen Center Key 88
Ella Agnes Kiker 27
Kinsey 222
Roland Kinsey 32
Wanda Kirby 179
Mary Ann Knowles 88

L

LaFayette High School 108
Marie Larmon 55, 104, 113
Clarissa Lawrence 134, 136, 143–144, 146, 149, 221
Evaline Clarissa Lawrence 131, 149
Henry Hardy Lawrence 143, 149, 190
Henry Hardy Lawrence [II] 149
James Edward Lawrence 134, 143, 146, 148–149
John Lawrence 149
Julia Ann Lawrence 130, 133, 149
Lucy Lawrence 130, 149
Malachi Lawrence 133, 146, 149, 172
Malachi Columbus Lawrence 133, 146
Margaret Lawrence 143, 148
Thomas Lawrence 143, 149
Thomas Anderson Lawrence 127, 129
Jesse T. Ledford 92
Little Rock National Cemetery 195–197
Emily Love 31, 34, 42–43, 58–62, 64
Fannie Jewell Love 66
John Love 64
John Love (b.1845) 66
John Robert Love 66
Josephine Love 20, 28, 31, 42
Robert Dobson Love 66
William Jasper Love [I] 34, 62, 63, 64, 66
William Jasper Love [II] 66
W.P. Lower 171
Lydia 167

M

Macedonia Baptist Church 31, 34, 69
Macedonia Cemetery 222
William Harvey Maloney 136
Pricellia Clementine Maloney 222
Robert Harlow Maloney 148
Robert Paul Maloney 135–136, 148
Robert Weston Maloney 148
Samuel B. Maloney 148
Donna Manis 115
Thomas Watson Manis 104
Thomas Watson Manis, Jr. 115
Wheeler Manis 231
Mitchell Manning 33
Manning's Mill 69
Winnie Manord 149
Phebe Ellen Valentine Mathis 131
Elizabeth Mattox 91, 101–102
Brita Mattzdoter 156
John William McAlister 92
Elizabeth Horn McCauley 200
Nancy Elvira McGee 168
Bob McGill 135
unknown McKnight 134
Elizabeth McMullen 102
Mary Jane McRachen 90, 92
McWilliams family 139
James Perry McWilliams 139
R.E. McWilliams 137
Tim McWilliams 134
Viven Inez McWilliams 134
The Merchants Hope 100
George W. Moore 127–128
Sarah C. Moore 192
Watson Millington Moore 128
Evelyn Morgan 222
Otto Morgan 33
Roy Morgan 33
Mt. Gilead Baptist Church Cemetery 168
Mt. Olivett Cemetery 91
Mt. Zion Methodist Church 171
Amanda Murphy 197, 202–205
Nancy C. Murphy 88

N

Mary Neal 134
Reece Neal 140
Samuel Nunis 88–89

O

Oaknoll Memorial Gardens 164
Old Armuchee Baptist Church Cemetery 165, 197
Old Ben Hill Pope Cemetery 222
Tom O'Neal 171
Glenn Orr 182, 229–230
Martha Osborn 201
Martin V. Osborn 193, 195, 198, 201
William E. Osborn 198, 201
Helen Owens 231
Si Owens 207
Edna Mildred Owings 202

P

Frances Padget 230
Ella A. Pangle 94, 97
Bryant Lawson Park 227
Bryant Robert Park 227
Samuel Parker 201
William Parker 201
James Park 227
Mary Wilson Hill Park 226
Moses Park 227
Robert Park 227
Thomas Yandell Park 227
Patel, B.J. 171
Adam Peck [I] 167
Adam Peck [II] 167–168
Adam Wesley Peck 168
Fannie Elvira Peck 165–166, 170, 224
Johann Jakob Beck (Peck) [II] 166–167
John Gayle Peck 168
John M. Peck 168–170
Moses Peck 168
Patrick Peck 167–168
O.H. "Doc" Penland 33

James W. Phillips 198
J.C. Phillips 33
John W. Phillips 201
Nancy Elvira Phillips 226
Tobias Phillips 149
Jane Pinson 158
Pleasant Grove Baptist Church Cemetery 132, 197, 205, 213
Pleasant Hill Methodist Church 139
Pleasant Hill School 139
Thomas Walter Pledger 202
Ina Plunkett 150–151
Melvin Plunkett 172
Pocket School 35
Anita Pope 104
Benjamin Hill Pope 47, 56
Benjamin Hill Pope 15, 27, 43–58, 104, 109, 222, 227
Bobbie Pope 55
Burke Hall Pope 43–45, 47, 56, 60
Daniel Walter Pope 20
David Pope 20
David Felton Pope 27
David Huell Pope 20
Ed Pope 25
Elizabeth Pope 16
Fannie Pope 104
Fred Pope 26
Guy Adam Pope 26, 28, 43–44, 46–47, 54, 56–57, 109
Harriet Ann Pope 20
Henry Pope 14, 15, 18
Henry Morris Pope 20, 23
James Constantine Pope 25–26, 43–45, 47, 51, 55, 56, 60, 80, 104, 109, 145
Jamila Pope 51
Jefferson Austin Pope 20, 22–23
Jim Pope 28, 51, 55–56
Joan Pope 55, 73
John Pope 14–16, 18–19
John D. Pope 20, 27
John H. Pope 19
Juanita Pope 54
June Evelyn Pope 55, 227, 232
Karen Pope 56
Linda Pope 55–56
Luther Hill Pope 43–45, 47, 55, 60
Martha Emily Pope 43–45, 47, 56, 114–115
Mary Elizabeth Pope 20, 27
Mary Evelyn Pope 11, 15, 25, 33, 43–45, 47, 54–58, 60, 64–65, 73–82, 94, 97, 101, 104–120
Micajah Pope 15, 16, 19, 20–26, 32–33, 216
Micajah Felton Pope 15, 20, 26–31, 32, 42–43, 46, 71, 73
Nathaniel Pope 14, 16
Santa Orville Pope 43–45, 47, 55, 56, 227
Sarah Pope 20
Susan Frances Pope 20
Thomas Pope 14, 16
William Pope 14, 16, 18
William Henry Pope 20
Ottis Porch 33
Clement Price 60
Price family 69
Frank Price 69, 71
Mary Ann Prior 159, 161
James E. Pritchard 198
Prospect Baptist Church 139
Puryear family 24, 26
Francis Marion Puryear 140
Hamilton Young Puryear 24, 217
John Puryear 24
Elizabeth Puthuff 218, 220

Q

Rody Quinn 192

R

Dick Rackley 135
Elias B. Rackley 135
Ansel Myer Rambo 157, 160–161, 170
Harriet Lenora Rambo 170
Henry Van Rambo 160
Ida Mae Rambo 134, 150–155, 157, 165, 170, 175, 177, 224, 230
Jesse Rambo 157–159
John Humphrey Rambo 160
Kinchin Rambo 157, 159–161, 164
Kinchin Lawrence Rambo 160
Peter Rambo 156–157
Peter Gunnarson Rambo 156–157
Swan Rambo 156–158
Swan (Sven) Rambo 156–157
Wade Hampton Rambo 157, 165–166, 170
Etta Nola Ramsey 27
Frances Ramsey 146–147
Martha Ramsey 146
Rice Ross Ramsey 146–147
William Ramsey 147
Rebecca Ratcliffe 86
Mary Reece 183
Ewing M. Reed 32
Josiah R. Reeves 127, 128
Elizabeth Reynolds 87
Mary Elizabeth Rhea 20
Richardson family 69
Alice Richardson 220
Callie Richardson 220
Delores Jane Richardson 220
Frances Richardson 145–147
Georgia Mae Richardson 43–45, 47, 56
James Grady Richardson 220
James Rufus Richardson 220
John Jefferson Richardson 220
John Newton Richardson 220
Jones Richardson 34
Matthew Berry Richardson 146–147
Moses Richardson 146, 220
Oliver Richardson 220–221
Shannon Richardson 221
W.J. "Buddy" Richardson 220
Emily Robbs 58, 64, 65, 217
Frances E. Robbs 136
Melton Robbs 140
Susan Robbs 217
William Robbs 64–65, 136
Mr. Roberson 173
Jewie Robinson 94, 97
Elizabeth Reynolds 190–191

S

George Scoggin 125
Nathan Jonathan Scoggin 125
Richard Scoggin 125
Richard George Scoggin 125
Alexander Scoggins 123, 125–126
Andrew Jackson Scoggins 128
Annie Lee Scoggins 134
Bernice Scoggins 172
Clyde Scoggins 134
Cynthia Scoggins 127
Cynthia "Sinia" Scoggins 126
Dennis Scoggins 134
Dionysus Scoggins 129
Don Scoggins 231–232
Elisha Harrison Scoggins 129
Elizabeth Caroline Scoggins 127
Ellen Scoggins 134
Erica Nicole Scoggins 183–184
Eric Keith Scoggins 155, 179, 181–182, 207, 235
Eric Keith Scoggins, Jr. 183
Frances Druscilla Scoggins 136, 145, 155, 170, 177
Fred Scoggins 134–135
Gilliam Scoggins 126
Gilliam Millington Scoggins 128
Gilliam Terrell Scoggins 131
Gillum Scoggins 127–128
Gresham Scoggins 123, 126–128
Harold Wallace Scoggins 11, 123, 142, 150–151, 157, 171–172, 175, 209–210, 224, 228–232, 235
Harriet C. Scoggins 131
Hester Scoggins 133
James Franklin Scoggins 128
James Harrison Scoggins 129, 137, 138
James Harvey Scoggins 123, 131, 134–135, 139, 171
James J. Scoggins 129
J. Davis Scoggins 126
Jesse Scoggins 134–135
Joe Ben Scoggins 134–135
John Scoggins 131
John Watson Scoggins 127, 129
John Weston Scoggins 128, 131, 133
Jordan Michael Scoggins 10–11, 15–16, 21, 40, 79, 82, 85, 115, 120, 123, 125, 142–143, 145, 157, 164, 187–188, 196, 213, 216–218, 224–225, 234–235
Julie Marie Scoggins 40, 58, 81, 103, 113, 115, 183, 184, 234–235
Lawrence Chapman Scoggins 123, 134–136, 142, 150–155, 170–171, 175
Lawrence "Doc" Chapman Scoggins 150–151
Lee Roy Scoggins 134, 136
Leland Coulter Scoggins 135, 138, 154, 171
Leland Coulter Scoggins, Jr. 144
Leonard Pritchett Scoggins 133
Levi Jackson Scoggins 128, 130, 132, 149
Levi Sanford Scoggins 127, 129, 137, 172
Levi Smith Scoggins 129
Lindsey Hamilton Scoggins 128, 130, 133, 149
Margaret Lillian Scoggins 150–151, 172, 230
Mark Kevin Scoggins 179, 181–183
Martha Ann Scoggins 131
Mary Jane Scoggins 130
Michael David Scoggins 11, 25, 59, 104, 123, 141–142, 145, 154, 157, 164, 173–174, 179–180, 182–183, 187, 195, 207–208, 210, 213, 216, 218, 222, 224, 235
Millington Scoggins 126
Moses Gresham Scoggins 128, 131
Rhoda Scoggins 126–127
Sarah "Sallie" Scoggins 126
Sinia Ann Scoggins 127
Smith Scoggins 131
Thomas Newton Scoggins 128, 131, 149
Wiley Scoggins 126
Wiley Gresham Scoggins 127, 129
William A. Scoggins 129
William Delaney Scoggins 123, 127, 128, 130–133, 149
William Delaney Scoggins [II] 130
William Pitte Scoggins 128
Winney Emily Scoggins 131
Zillian A. Scoggins 127
Thomas Scoggin 125
E.B. Self 171, 173, 228
Starret Self 171
James W. Selman 192, 197
Elizabeth Ann Sewell 127, 130–131, 148
Sarah E. Sewell 148
Craig Shahan 66
David Shahan 32
David A. Shahan 66
David C. Shahan 66
Howard Shahan 66
James Alexander Shahan [I] 66
James Alexander Shahan [II] 66
James Harvey Shahan 32
John Shahan 66
Minta Shahan 66
Elizabeth Sharkey 167
Artemus Shattuck 139
William Shattuck 139
J.A. Shields 33
Shiloh Baptist Church 139
Wesley Short 41
Fleming White Shropshire 202
Gus Shropshire 173
Harry Shropshire 135
George Simmons 20
Elizabeth Caldwell Sims 62
Grace A. Sims 20
Katherine Louise Sims 27
Mary P. Sinyard 168
Magdalena Skute 157
Battie Lee Smith 43, 47, 55, 56, 227
Nelle Smith 134
Smyrna Memorial Cemetery 165
Snow Lowther 42
Allen Sogan 195
Henry S. Sparks 198, 201
John Sparks 201
Margaret (or Mary) Jane Sparks 199, 201
Jack Stansell 32
Nancy Matilda Steward 127
Minnie D. Strickland 27
Subligna 34, 154, 171–174, 226, 228
Subligna Baptist Church 135, 171–172, 217
Subligna Cemetery 155, 165, 184
Subligna Methodist Church 171
Subligna School 35, 108, 172, 175, 230
Suttle family 139
Georgia Ann Suttle 140
James Thomas Suttle 139
John Byars Suttle 139, 140
Suttle's Mill 139
Ed Sweatman 33

T

Talley Cemetery 65, 69
R.E. Talley 135
Mrs. Earl Tate 172
Pinckney Tate 34
Jesse Hawkins Tatum 90
Jerel Teems 209
Susannah Trail 213, 215
Trans 58, 65, 69–71
Trans school 69, 71
Harvey Turner 94, 97

U

William Dunlap Underwood 32, 171

V

Varnell Cemetery 93
Marty Vess 33
Villanow 20–26, 31–35, 37, 41, 43, 62, 66, 73, 108, 222, 226
Villanow school 35, 71
Lany Visant 149
Francois Visinand 42
Guillaume Visinand 42
Philip Peter Visinand 42

W

Wahoo Baptist Church Cemetery 168
Absalom Ward 215–216
Alfred C. Ward 172, 215–218
Andrew Clement Ward 208, 213, 216, 222
Georgia Ward 173, 217, 222
James Ward 213, 216
John Anderson Ward 217
Julia Estella Ward 213, 215–216, 218, 224
Julius Ward 32
Nancy Elizabeth Ward 217
Nathan Ward 213, 215–216
James A. Wary 43–44
Andrew Watkins 136
D(?) Watkins 135
Homer Watkins 104
Sam Watkins 135
Winney Rene Watson 126–127
William Bowden Wells 20
West Armuchee school 71, 137, 139
Jennifer West 99
Westview Cemetery 167
Barbara Sarah Whisenant 37, 42
John Adam Whisenant 42
John Nicholas Whisenant 42
John Nicholas Whisenant [II] 42
Mrs. Aleta Baker White 172, 230
Ben White 33
Mrs. Eunice White 172
Jeff White 171
Lee White 171
Milton White 173
Tom White 171, 173
Will White 135, 171
Thomas Milburn Whitson 92
Henry Widener 199
Elizabeth Wiggins 99
John Wiggins 94, 97
John Wesley Wiggins 94, 97
Elizabeth Lancaster Wilbanks 213
T.B. Williams 222
Henry Wilson 202
Winton 90
Jeptha J. Wisner 195, 201
Samuel Woodall 201
Wood Cemetery 197, 201
Elias Jackson Wood 201
Wood family 139
Jefferson T. Wood 198–199, 201
John Henry Wood 193, 195, 198–199, 201
Joyce Wood 201
J.Y. Wood 32
William Alfred Wood 201
William D. Wood 199
Jane Worthy 20
Mary Wright 199, 201
William M. Wright 201

Y

Martha Yandell 227
Caroline Pracilla Young 191–197
Jackson Young 194
J.C. Young 137
Safrona Young 196
Wiley Young 196

www.ingramcontent.com/pod-product-compliance
Lightning Source LLC
Chambersburg PA
CBHW061118010526
44112CB00024B/2903